"Veteran, creative and well-known pastor Bill Bausch has written a truly terrific book on homilies. His text will comfort and challenge preachers. It incisively sketches the changed and diverse contemporary audiences before them, sympathetically describes the personal difficulties they face, practically details helpful ways of preparing effective sermons, and offers many of his own homilies as illustrations of those pastoral suggestions. A bishop, wishing to indicate the high priority he attaches to preaching, would do well to send a copy to each of his clergy and to others who proclaim the word of God."

Rev. Joseph M. Champlin
Rector, Syracuse's Cathedral of the Immaculate Conception
Co-author, *A Thoughtful Word, A Healing Touch*

"This is an uncommonly useful wedding of realistic recommendations and anecdotal homilies, a storehouse of stories woven into the liturgical readings and grafted onto the everyday experience of today's Christians. No Catholic preacher I know tells stories more often, more graphically, and more effectively than Fr. Bausch."

Walter J. Burghardt, S.J.
Woodstock Theological Center
Author, *Preaching the Just Word*

"Bill Bausch amazes me! He is a prolific writer and yet, everything he turns out is first class. This time, he turns to homily writing. He provides a solid theoretical base to a storytelling approach and remains real, honest, and practical.

"This is a book you will want to read and keep handy. It is a show and tell. He tells you how to write homilies, gives a number of samples, and even includes over one hundred usable stories."

Rev. Frank J. McNulty, pastor
Author, *Preaching Better*

"One of the truest marks of a good pastor—and a good homilist—is that he knows how to speak the truth with an honest perception of his real life environment. He can challenge his people with the power of Jesus and the gospel through the transparency of his own spiritual journey, his own human vulnerability, and yet be a compassionate communicator of hope.

"In his latest book, *Storytelling The Word: Homilies and How to Write Them*, Fr. Bill Bausch shows himself to be both compassionate pastor and challenging homilist. From the opening chapter's perceptive look at our 'preaching environment' to the wise and practical 'how-tos' in the later chapters, he invites preachers, particularly parish priests, to renew their passion for preaching, their purpose for going regularly before their people, and their pursuit of life and ministry habits that guarantee time for prayer, quite reflection, and various methods of preparation.

"This is not a theory book. It is the wise and practical reflection of a skilled and beloved pastor and preacher. The book is a joy to read, because it is so obvious that Bill Bausch has 'wrestled with the angel' and needs to share the fire of his convictions and the warmth of his compassionate care for God's people!"

Rev. Nick Rice
President, National Federation of Priests' Councils

"Fr. Bausch's new book is enjoyable and informative. He writes as a good storyteller does: engages the imagination while teaching. His knowledge of the discipline of preaching and its literature is comprehensive and up-to-date. His analysis of those to whom we preach will be especially appreciated.

"*Storytelling the Word* will become a useful reference on any shelf of preaching resources. It's well designed to be easily accessible. As Fr. Bausch says, 'We're all colleagues in preaching the Word of God, and getting the Word out is what counts. And it's far better to borrow and preach a captivating idea or story than to put forth indifferent, uninspiring original ones.'

"All who preach will be grateful to Fr. Bausch for sharing his knowledge of homiletics and storytelling. As preachers adapt his ideas and stories, the church will be the richer for that implementation."

Rev. Thomas Condon, O.P.
Aquinas Institute of Theology

STORY TELLING
The Word

Homilies & How to Write Them

William J. Bausch

XXIII
TWENTY-THIRD PUBLICATIONS
Mystic, Connecticut 06355

Twenty-Third Publications
185 Willow Street
P.O. Box 180
Mystic, CT 06355
(860) 536-2611
800-321-0411

ISBN 0-89622-687-5
Library of Congress Catalog Card Number 95-62067
Printed in the U.S.A.

DEDICATION

For *"That Old Gang of Mine"*

Fran, Lou, George, Mary, Mary & Tread, Jean & Jerry

Contents

STORYTELLING
The Word

INTRODUCTION

Preaching today and for the next century is challenging. Think on this: Fifty years ago, 80 percent of all Christians were in Europe and North America. Today, 80 percent of all Christians are in South America, Asia, and Africa. Christians in Europe and America are in the minority. Fewer than 30 percent of American Catholics attend church regularly on Sunday. According to CARA (The Center for Applied Research in the Apostolate). Masses of immigrants to our shores are not Catholic or Christian (e. g., the Chinese). Even those who are, for example, the Hispanics, are being won over to Protestant Evangelical churches. This is sobering. According to Gallup, only 53 percent of teenagers of Hispanic origin now say they are Catholics by preference. Mosques and temples are rapidly vying with churches and synagogues. Christianity is quickly becoming a religious option. Practical evidence of this can be seen in the loss of the monopoly Gideon used to have of placing its Bibles in the hotel and motel rooms of America. Nowadays such places are likely to include the Koran, the Talmud, the Book of Mormon, and a Kwanzaa Keepsake.

On the cultural front, science has taken the wonder out of the stars, psychology has explained away the supernatural, and secularism has eaten away at the spiritual. Religious symbols have been dismantled in the name of no establishment. Religious vocabulary has all but disappeared. Biblical lore, which once united the country with its stories and metaphors, has been depleted. Multicultural tolerance has rendered all things relative. People live out their lives in segments. They go to school, go to college, buy a car, meet a girl or boy, establish a career, get married, move, buy a house, raise some kids, move again, divorce, plan for retirement, etc.

In a capitalist society, all citizens are treated and programmed as marketable consuming units whose buying habits from infancy are unstintingly stimulated by advertising and whose zip codes reveal how deep are their pocketbooks and who gets what catalogues. After all, every student in Advertising 101 knows that children and young adults spend an estimated $102 billion annually and influence their families to spend an additional $130 billion. Every birth presents, not a boy or a girl, but a consumer.

Indeed, from the moment they are on the planet, people are treated as commodified, interchangeable atoms—even before birth since babies' genetic parts can be purchased at a sperm bank, their gestation put out for hire, and their birth bought. There is no overarching meaning to life, only episodes, and therefore meaninglessness has become the primal sickness of society. There is no sense of community among a people so physically and socially mobile and therefore loneliness has become the primal symptom of society. We see it all in the faces of our youth: the clueless clothes, the casual violence at younger and younger ages, the frail, disposable relationships, the lack of conscience. A compulsive media, consumerism, and drugs act as a narcotic for such nihilism.

What all this is saying is this: preachers should know—deeply, profoundly, and spiritually—as they stand at the dawn of another millennium, that they are in the same position as Gregory's monks whom he pulled out of their monasteries in the sixth century to evangelize barbarian Europe. They are preaching to a de-Christianized people for whom sin, redemption, and glory are no longer viable terms. Preachers should know too the task. Since Christians are by definition a people of meaning, they are preaching to those who have none, but wish they did. Being by definition a people of a hope grounded in the promises of Christ, they are preaching to those who have given up, but don't want to. As columnist William Raspberry writes in *The Washington Post* concerning youth:

> One of the remarkable phenomena of our time is the persistence of the belief among those in power that we can coerce people into decent behavior if we only make punishment tough enough. We keep imagining that the problem is that young people aren't frightened enough, so we keep toughening criminal sanctions to the point where our national incarceration rate is the highest in the Western world. The real problem is that our young people aren't hopeful enough.

Nor are our older people. So, we are the new twenty-first century missionaries. We must preach hope to the new civilized barbarians who, between episodes, are desperately looking for meaning and an escape from loneliness. We are preaching to indoctrinated individualists who are beginning to intuit the deep truth that they are never saved in isolation but no longer know how to discover and maintain community. We are casting the word of life to a people truly hungry for it, even if they can't name it. It's an enviable position.

To preach to such in the new millennium, we preachers, of course, will instinctively turn to the Bible. But here's the rub. We misuse the Holy Book. We dip into its pages to pick out a golden age and we tell the people this is how it was. But the biblical folk never saw it that way. They never got stuck in the past. Their cry was always what the Almighty could do for them in the future. The psalms sang out for a deliverance to come. A new dawn was always arriving. A woman intoned that some day, in the future, all generations would call her blessed. The reign of God was always at hand. The last word in the Bible says it all: *Maranatha,* Come, Lord Jesus! In other words, the people of the Bible were quintessentially a people of hope. They were an eschatological people.

We never preach eschatology. We have forgotten that revelation occurs in the midst of a future expectation of God. We rather focus on the personal present. As a result, what do we preach? We preach individual pietism for here and now. Or, to put it more directly, forsaking the heady promises of the Kingdom, we shamelessly preach the therapeutic. We offer the nostrums of the currently 15-minute-famed guru, adopt the jargon of psychology, and offer self-improvement techniques for feeling good about oneself. But no more. This is no longer adequate (not that it ever has been). Rather, using the Bible must inspire us to inspire them with those promises that eye has not yet seen, ear heard, nor hearts grasped by those who love God. In any case, what I want to say is that, today, in an increasingly secular society, preaching is a missionary enterprise, an evangelization challenge, and we should know that in our bones.

Now, for this generation and the one to come, there are many approaches to meet this challenge, many theories of preaching. In this book I take the approach of storytelling. I think it is an effective way to preach, but I immediately hasten to undermine my case, at least to hedge it a bit. One thing: even though in the main text I will note, rightly so, that in many ways, the Bible is a book of stories, it also has large stretches that are not: laws, proverbs, lists, poems, and so forth. Furthermore, it should be declared that, while this book focuses on the story as "a natural speech-form for the gospel" (Amos Wilder), it is open to the faults that often go with such an approach; for example, the tendency to reduce too narrowly the biblical story, which is then illustrated by a story, or to reduce the biblical message to a mere decoration or lead-in to the story so that the story is fondly remembered but not the demanding biblical truth behind it. (For a good critique see Richard L. Eslinger's *A New Hearing*, Abingdon, 1987.) Besides, not everyone can tell a story and draw good theology from it. Maybe, as David Buttrick wryly observes, Graham Greene or John Updike can and, even then, it takes them a whole novel to do it. Life, after all, is more than stories.

There *are* other effective ways of preaching, from the expository to the exhortatory, from the deeply scriptural to the meditative, from the inductive to the phenomenological. Still, this book focuses on just one approach—which, naturally, is not mutually exclusive of any of the others—and, I believe, for all of its possible misuses, the way of the story is a satisfying way both for the homilist and the listener, the listener of today and of the next millennium. I would even venture to say that storytelling the word has a better chance of bringing the Bible back to its appreciation of first being a many-centuries oral tradition. That's something we forget, and in one way it's the preacher's job to pull the text off the page and restore it to the mouth—and the heart. And even those extensive "non-story" sections such as the laws and proverbs and the psalms can be placed in the context of narrative and story. As Walter Bruggemann remarks *(Theology Today,* "Preaching as Reimagination," October 1995, p. 326):

> To be sure, there are many texts in the "script" of the Bible available to the preacher that are not narrative. Given my presuppositions, these are the most difficult to preach. It is my impression, nonetheless, that every text in any genre has behind it something of a narrative that generates it and through which the texts in other genres are to be understood. Thus, for example, the Psalms are notoriously difficult preaching material. I suspect that the preacher characteristically either presents a narrative situation that is critically recoverable (as in Psalm 137) or imagines such a narrative construal. And in the letters of Paul, a critically recoverable or homiletically imagined narrative context serves the preaching of the letters.

I say all this because, basically and observedly, a good story is a delight and that's that. Right off, it catches us whether we want to be or not. Sometimes, for example, when I give workshops, I will start by saying I was almost late in getting here. Did you see that old man outside with the wheelbarrow blocking traffic and singing "Onward, Christian Soldiers"? I stopped a minute to talk to him and . . . I might go on for a while until, by coming to a slow halt, I get my audience to suddenly notice that they and the others are mesmerized—at least mildly so—with this fictitious setup. They *do* want to know who is out there and what he's doing. They're caught by the story. And that's my point. A good story invites people to enter into another's experience and make it their own. And experience has shown that one good point in a homily reinforced with a story can be more effective than ten deep but abstract ideas.

Hence, again, this book on storytelling. A futile effort to some degree since, as I shall honestly mention several times, good preachers are more born than made. Still, to justify this book, they *can* be made, or can be made better than they are. Or, at the very least, they can be made more interesting through the use of storytelling.

I follow the lectionary readings in this book and there is a helpful appendix at the end to help you follow homiletically the liturgical year and all three years of the cycle. Most times the lectionary choices are good; other times you wonder what the authors had in mind. Why did they chop that passage off? Why did they edit out some verses smack in the middle? How does the second reading fit in with the others? How do you relate all three passages? Answer: you don't. And, in fact, such a relationship, a wholistic theme, was never really intended anyway. So I do what most (Catholic) preachers do: stick with the gospel. And that's what you'll find in these pages.

This book is divided into two sections. Part I continues the tradition of St. Augustine who gave us the first Christian treatise on homiletics in his fourth book, *On Christian Doctrine* (although earlier St. John Chrysostom, the golden-mouth preacher, gave us a chapter on the office of preaching in his book *On the Priesthood*).

This part consists of eight chapters exploring the dynamics of preaching which range from the make-up of the audience to the preparation of a story-homily. True to the title of this book, throughout these chapters I've interspersed stories that illustrate what I'm talking about. I've marked them with a square (□). Part 2 is an offering of 42 (45 if you count the three in Part 1) new homilies that illustrate the principles in Part 1. It too (I hope not) may here and there continue *another* early tradition: the lousy homily. We have an early gospel example of that in the instance of the parable of the sower that some preacher inserted in Chapter 4 of Mark's gospel, as Joseph Lienhard reminds us (*The Bible, the Church and Authority*, The Liturgical Press, 1995, p. 53):

> The tendency to allegorize the Scriptures is evident in early Christianity; we find it in the New Testament itself. The most striking example is found in the fourth chapter of Mark's Gospel: Jesus narrates the parable of the sower, and then is said to provide an explanation. The explanation is complicated, even incoherent, and anything but natural. It is probably the work of an early Christian preacher, and may stand as the first bad homily, but hardly the last.

All right. Having written all these solemn things, it is now time for me, at this point, to shift gears and declare my very human prejudices before I proceed.

I write from a biased stance of a parish priest who must come up with a creative homily *every* week—never repeating myself—for every month for every year for over 20 years, *not* as a speaker who has a couple of finely honed, audience approved, super talks that he carries with him from fresh place to fresh place.

I write as one confined to 7-13 minutes to address an audience with its own agendas, crying babies, and sirens going off outside—ever mindful of the sage advice: "In a homily, if after 7 minutes of digging for oil you come up dry, stop boring!"

I write for all preachers who have to face a mediaized congregation who are unconsciously comparing us to Donahue, Oprah, Dan Rather or, God forbid, Geraldo.

I write as one who, when I thought I had just delivered the homily of the century, no one said anything, and when I thought I had laid the bomb of the century, everyone praised me.

I write as one who has to resist the urge to kick the usher in the shins (or worse) who sends you out of the sacristy with the stage-whisper advice, "Keep it short, Padre."

I write as one who, alas, too often is like "the third brother." That is, like anything else in life, I ebb and flow with good, bad, and indifferent homilies.

❏The "third brother" reference comes from the story of the woman preparing to go to church. She told her husband that there was going to be a guest preacher, one of two brothers, both priests. "Who are they?" the husband asked. "I don't know their names," the wife replied, "but I did hear someone refer to one of the brothers as 'the good preacher' and the other as 'the good-looking one.'" Later, when the wife returned, the husband asked, "Well, which one was it? Was it the good-looking one or the good-preacher one?" She replied, "There must be a third brother."❏

I write as one who, unconsciously, like most of you seasoned veterans, has developed a style—one that some of you will not necessarily like or relate to, so you're in for an excruciating read.

I write as one who is conscious that inspiration is an important ingredient in the creative process—and that some are more sensitive to inspiration than others—and that all of us try to "catch" it by various means from study, prayer, to a walk by the shore.

I write as one who every weekend of my priestly life preaches at several masses—at least always three—and have discovered that a homily, a pun, or a story that captivates and enthralls one church full of Mass-goers, leaves others cold and indifferent, and you can hardly get a response from them; that different Masses have a different clientele and different corporate personalities; but that also, having bombed at one Mass, you have the time to do a rework and wow them at the following Mass.

I write as one who, very frequently, has to change tones or, to use today's jargon, change channels, within 24 hours: a Saturday funeral at 10:00 followed by a nuptial Mass at 3:00 followed by the Children's Mass at 5:00 followed by the regular Mass on

Sunday: four or five different homilies on one weekend!

I write as one who has learned that often the congregation is preoccupied with *its* agenda, not mine. Their kids are sick. Who has them this weekend? Did I turn the iron off before I came? My in-laws are coming for dinner. I have learned that, like the sower in the gospel, the ground varies to receive the seed.

I write as one who has my own approach—some, for instance, dialogue with small groups to plumb the Scriptures, others copy canned homily services talks; some write them out, some outline them; some listen to other preachers and attend Masses in disguise and learn from them; others methodically scan the Scriptures, underline captivating words, and pray over them assiduously.

I write as one who has secretly judged other priests as giving what I thought to be a rather indifferent homily, only to hear people say how much they enjoyed his homily. The reason? Because he himself was his own best words, his own best message. He himself had a presence, a prayerfulness, sincerity, and pastoral style that *was* the homily, and people sensed that and he touched their lives and made me ashamed that, if I had better words, I also had a poorer spirit.

I write as one who, on each and every occasion, without fail, when I bend over the altar to pray the prayer before the gospel, I never, never neglect to add my pleading with the Lord, these heartfelt words, "For their sakes, O Lord, for their sakes!" In short, don't let my shortcomings shortchange them. They deserve better than I am. And on occasion when the Lord delivers, I simply shrug my shoulders and say that if he wants to horse around like that, it's O.K. by me.

Still, when I do connect, I must admit that I too often fail in faith. Someone was actually touched by my words and wants to become a saint. What do I do? I go into reverse and try to tone them down. "Let's not take me too literally," I protest. Well, I tell you this. I was glad to discover I'm not the only one who reacts this way. Consider the example Barbara Brown Taylor writes about ("The Unfettered Word," *Reflections*, Summer-Fall 1993):

I remembered the response to a sermon of my own. Who knows what it was about? All I remember is the man who came out afterwards—a sensible, well-heeled fellow, looking slightly stunned—who told me that God had spoken to him during the sermon that morning. He was going to quit his job on Monday. He was going to sell his car. He was going to change his life, he said, to which I said, "Good grief! It was only a sermon! Sleep on it! Go get a cup of coffee! See how you feel in the morning!"

I write as one with trepidation asking myself what in the world I'm doing writing for my peers and homiletic betters who can teach me a thing or two and who therefore are an unwelcomed prod to my humility which I don't need more of.

Finally, I write as a parish priest for parish priests and assume their contexts, but clearly and willfully beyond that, it is my intent to write for all who preach: Catholics and Protestants, pastors and deacons, catechists and lay administrators, clergy and laity who, more and more, are ascending the pulpit.

PART 1

PRINCIPLES TO FOLLOW

1.

SLINGS, ARROWS, AND JIBES

We might as well get it over with. I mean all the slings, arrows, and jibes we preachers have to put up with.

☐We preach too long, they say (whoever "they" are). George Burns: "A good sermon should have a good beginning and a good ending, and they should be as close together as possible." Or there's the pastor who announced that if the congregation reached their fund-raising goal, he would allow a clock to be installed in the pulpit. If they exceeded the goal, he would allow it to be plugged in. If the offerings exceeded the goal by $4000, he promised he'd look at it.☐

Do we really have to suffer this poem?

I cannot praise the reverend's eyes;

I never saw his glance divine;
He always shuts them when he prays,
And when he preaches, he shuts mine.

☐And who passes around stories like this: A paramedic was asked on a local TV show talk program, "What was your most challenging 911 call?" "Recently we got a call from St. Al's church at 11th and Walnut," the paramedic said. "A frantic usher was very concerned that during the homily an elderly man passed out in a pew and appeared to be dead. The usher could find no pulse and there was no noticeable breathing." "What's unusual and demanding about this particular call?" the interviewer asked. "Well," the paramedic said, "we carried out four guys before we found the one who was dead!"☐

And who's the smart aleck who thought up the Eutychus Club? That's from the Acts of the Apostles which relates that St. Paul may have been the first Christian preacher who had to revive from the dead a victim of one of his homilies. Yes, you guessed it, the man's name was Eutychus.

Tell me, who defined a preacher as a person who talks in other people's sleep? And why do they ("they" again) keeping sending me that quote from the masterful and celebrated novelist Anthony Trollope who in *Barchester Towers* (Everyman's Library, pp. 151-52) wrote these unwelcomed words:

There is perhaps, no greater hardship at present inflicted on mankind in civilized and free countries than listening to sermons. No one but a preaching clergyman has, in these realms, the power of compelling an audience to sit silently and be tormented. No one but a preaching clergyman can revel in platitudes, truisms and untruisms and yet receive, as his undisputed privilege, the same respectful demeanor as though words of impassioned eloquence, or persuasive logic fell from his lips. . . .No one can rid himself of the preaching clergyman. He is the bore of the age, the old man whom we Sinbads cannot shake off, the nightmare that disturbs our Sunday rest, the incubus that overloads our religion and makes God's service distasteful. We are not forced into church! No, but we desire more than that. We desire, nay, we are resolute, to enjoy the comfort of public worship, but we desire also that we may do so without an amount of tedium which ordinary human nature cannot endure with patience; that we may be able to leave the house of God without that anxious longing for escape, which is the common consequence of common sermons.

Great parallelisms and rhythms, to be sure, but do we need it? And, yes, to be sure, we sometimes come out with an occasional blooper such as the priest who read the gospel with a couple of transposed words: "At that time, Jesus came from Nazareth in Galilee and was baptized by Jordan in the John." But, hey, let those critics stand up there Sunday after Sunday and preach and let's see how they do. Let them be compared with the likes of Dan Rather and Diane Sawyer and with those great hairdos of the TV evangelists. We're in the communication business every time we stand up there in the pulpit and everyone knows communication is never easy.

☐Cartoonist Rube Goldberg tells the story about the time he traveled to Europe on an ocean liner. He was assigned to a table with another single passenger. His companion was a Frenchman who spoke no English. Goldberg spoke no French. Each night the Frenchman would come to the table, click his heels, bow, and say "Bon Appetit." Goldberg says, "I would get up and reply, 'Goldberg,' and shake his hand and sit down." This routine went on for three or four nights. Then one day, Goldberg happened to mention this to an acquaintance. "You know, it's the strangest thing. I'm sitting with a Frenchman in the dining room and at each meal he tells me his name is Bon Appetit and I have to tell him who I am." "No, no," said the other. "That's not his name. That's a French phrase for good appetite." Oh," said Goldberg. "I feel so stupid. Well, I'm going to have to correct that." That night, Goldberg came to the table late and the Frenchman was already seated. Goldberg bowed, clicked his heels and said "Bon Appetit." The Frenchman stood up and said, "Goldberg."☐

Well, it's time to get serious (not that I wasn't) and admit we preachers are in trouble. You know it when a sound publication like *Commonweal* (4/7/95) not only prints an article entitled "Why Priests Can't Preach," but gets lots of replies with answers! The main point of the article is that Catholic preaching is poor because we preachers simply don't spend enough time in preparing. And this is the devil we struggle with in the painful context of the priest shortage. Pastors who used to have three or four associates are down to one or two. Standard issues and problems remain— funerals, weddings, hospital and nursing home visitations—and so many new ones added—AIDS, commonplace divorce, teenage pregnancies, violence, dwindling finances, drugs, ethnic waves of immigrants—that most priests are stretched, a stretching aggravated by aging. Of course, this is a clarion call for much more shared and collaborative ministry with the laity, but, even so, enough time to prepare a homily is not always quite there.

Besides, the Sunday homily is only one of many prepared and impromptu speeches we have to make all the time. During the week, we may have a funeral, a baptism, and a wedding, all within one weekend, and you're not allowed to bring the feelings from the previous talk to the next one. (Think of that: coming from the terrible trauma of a child's funeral to a wedding.) Then there's the talk at school, novena, the catechumenate (RCIA), First Communions, the Rotary Club, the ecumenical panel, and Lord knows what else. And we're expected to be good at all of them. And still, remember, we have to come up with a homily *every week*.

And, then, too, we're up against people who, as we shall see in the following chapter, are not really an audio people. They're immersed in visuals: TV, movies, videocassettes, computers, Internet, computer games, talk shows, and so on. Even their audio time is loud rock and blaring ads. In other words, today's audience is not congenial to listening to workshops, lectures, or homilies. All this is not an excuse for poor preaching, but it does help us appreciate a context in which we work to prepare.

Still, the question nags: why are we considered so inept in the pulpit? There are as many reasons as pundits. Walter Burghardt gives four reasons: "fear of the Scripture; ignorance of contemporary theology; unawareness of liturgical prayer (i.e., homily equals liturgy equals prayer); lack of preparation." I can only add some of my own, five of them.

1. *We are not convinced—nor are our bishops—that preaching is our main priority.* I will mention in the body of the book texts from Vatican II and the United States bishops saying that indeed it is so, that in fact, preaching is more of our identity than celebrating the Eucharist. True. Nevertheless, the unspoken mandate from any bishop is that we get out there and administrate. There are things to be taken care of and we must pay those assessments. Of course. But nowhere is there a similar urgency that we should preach well. Whoever was made a monsignor because of his preaching? But we have scores of priests were made monsignors because of chancery jobs, having a high school, or paying off a debt. That shows what is valued. Then, too, we know for sure that no bishop would ever ordain anyone who had absolute stage fright when he stood behind the altar or dissolved in nervousness in the presence of more than ten people. But he *will* ordain a candidate who is a poor preacher. My thought is that, for all the rhetoric, all the moaning, preaching is not a practical priority, and until it is, we won't be convinced and therefore we won't improve.

2. *There are no officially sponsored mechanisms to monitor our preaching*—which in itself would send a strong signal as to the importance of preaching. I will mention in this book the efforts of Bishop Ken Untener who meets with his clergy to listen to tapes of their homilies. He's the exception. And I must add, too, that Bishop Anthony Pilla of Cleveland, in September 1995, established the Institute for the Ministry of the Word in his diocese offering the opportunity "to participate in a proven method of homily preparation" or to renew skills through workshops and courses. Still, it remains the fact that there are no people appointed to check on us, no feedback to help us, and few workshops to show us. Again, all this gives silent consent to poor preaching.

3. *We ourselves are not always convinced of preaching's potency.* I like what the late Yves Congar said and wish it could be embla-

zoned over every chancery and rectory door: "I could quote a whole series of ancient texts all saying more or less the same thing, that if in one country Mass was celebrated for thirty years without preaching and in another there was preaching without the Mass, people would be more Christian in the country where there was preaching."

4. *We're not convinced that good preaching is a real need.* People are hungry for spirituality as we shall discuss. For all the electronic distractions, there's an emptiness out there, a cry of the heart. Why else would people be making bestsellers out of all those pseudo-New Age books?

5. *When all is said and done, good preaching is a charism.* No doubt we can all improve—else why would I be writing this book?—but the fact is there: some are gifted in this area, others are not. If in fact a priest does not have that charism and really does not or cannot improve, why not let those who do have it preach? This means laity. I introduced that in my parish several years ago, having lay people preach at one Mass a month on a rotating basis; that is, one month at one Mass, the following month at the next scheduled Mass and so on. Many laity today are articulate and theologically savvy. In 1988, the U.S. bishops issued *Guidelines for Lay Preaching* which did forbid laity to give the homily but did allow them to preach at retreats, revivals, missions, spiritual exercises, and any large gathering of the faithful. They have, in effect, recognized the gifts and experiences of the people. Canon Law itself (canon 225) recognizes the obligation of the laity to spread the gospel, especially, as it says, "in those circumstances in which people can hear the gospel and know Christ only through lay persons." I wonder if such a condition exists where you have a foreign priest who understandably cannot speak English well or clearly? I wonder if such a condition exists where you have a home-grown priest who is a congenitally poor preacher? Baldly, it comes down to this: week after week, which would you prefer, a priest who preaches poorly or a layperson who preaches well? The bishop who makes this decision is the bishop who says preaching is indeed important. And we'll improve.

So these are some of the reasons "why priests can't preach."

You can add your own. In any case, we can all learn to be better. At the very least, we can tell better stories.

❑Shall we end with one of them (a wretched one at that)? Once there was a parish in which a special committee was appointed to carry out a single duty. It was the committee members' responsibility to patrol the church aisles every Sunday to see if anyone was asleep during the homily. If anyone was found sleeping, one of the committee members would go to the pulpit and wake up the preacher!❑

2.

Who's Out There?

We should begin with who's sitting out there (or not). Some might suggest that sitting out there is a congregation and thus resent the title of this chapter. But this is a book on preaching through stories and on the receiving end of that preaching are listeners: people in an audio mode, as they say, and therefore very much an audience. That's why the audio system should be superb, the preacher clear, and the message compelling. In any case, we basically have an audience made up of two polarities: the Boomers and the Aged. There is a third group, the youth, of course, but they are absent. Absent and indifferent—and this is the great tragedy, because *we* have promoted this indifference. Since we have, allow me a few pastoral comments on the youth before we turn to the others.

There's a fine article in Jan./Feb. 1995 issue of *Praying* called "They Want Life" by Robert Ludwig, who remarks on the general indifference of youth concerning organized religion, offering several reasons for it. First, they have simply not been socialized into organized religion—especially into the *experience* of religion, even at Catholic schools. Prayers, devotions, lives of the saints are missing from their lives. Second, they are raised on the criticisms of their elders: the pope is obstinate, the hierarchy out of touch, priests are predators, women are subjugated, etc., etc. They are so dunned with the arguments and the discontents of their elders that they simply have no chance at the experience of religion or compelling exposure to the spiritual dimension of the Catholic faith. As Ludwig writes: "What we have shared is that the church excludes women, that it doesn't understand human sexuality, that it's recalcitrant in reforming its structure. We clamor for greater participation and a role in decision-making, *but what about the deeper values and beliefs?*"

Third, young people can no longer rely on the parish, the school, the neighborhood, and so they are left with the mass media culture to form their minds and ethics. A media that tells them to use condoms, while bombarding them with explicit sexual images all day long, whose talk shows (of which they are rabid watchers) blur the line between normalcy and pathology. They memorize rap lyrics, not catechisms. Add to this any disruptive personal social elements such as widespread divorce and you have a youth too troubled and distracted to be effectively evangelized, much less to be present in church. They may be part of the 24 percent of American children living without fathers or children of unwed mothers, which rose 54 percent from 1980 to 1992, with the out-of-wedlock birth rate for white women surging 94 percent since 1980.

Which is not to say that they do not have deep spiritual hungers. Perhaps, for the reasons we mentioned, even more so. They seek transcendence, personal integrity, a need for contact with the deeper mysteries of life—for God. They want to know that their lives mean something, that they are connected, that they are loved, how to relieve suffering. Even their use of drugs, Ludwig suggests, is a disguised search for deeper experience, the need to peel off the surface and seek out a numinous dimension to life. The trouble is that the youth get no serious religious dimension from their elders who are preoccupied with careers, jobs, materialism. Not even from their parishes nor the occasional homilies they hear at weddings and funerals. Preachers need to retrieve that religious experience and stop parading their gripes or favorite discontents. As Ludwig says, "Teachers wind up teaching their anger. Parents share their cynicism." And we preachers: what about us?

Anyway, enough said about the youth. For those of you who specialize in youth I suggest Ludwig's articles. And, as a balance, tap into the many highly effective and successful reach-outs to youths such as the noted Life Teen Conference centered in Mesa, Arizona, under the direction of Fr. Dale Fushek, founder of Life Teen (1730 W. Guadalupe Road, Mesa AZ 85202). For our purpose here, we'll focus on the elderly and the Boomers.

Both groups have common interests and therefore, common ground for the preacher. As for the aged, the statistics tell us—experience and observation tell us—that Americans are aging, *fast*. By the turn of the century, the most prominent population in a church will be senior citizens. In fact, the "People Patterns" section of the *Wall Street Journal* (12/2/94) reports that "Churchgoing declines among all age groups except the elderly." Look at your congregations now. See all the gray heads? Look at ourselves. See all the gray heads?

On the other hand, the Princeton Research Center, Martin Marty, Robert Wuthnow, as well as a George Gallup poll, contradicting the People Patterns estimate that churchgoing is down, reported that church attendance is *up* two percent over the previous year. The Hartford Seminary Center for Social and Religious Research reports, "The overall picture is that people are returning to religion in greater numbers" (*Wall Street Journal* 12/9/94). And this includes the Baby Boomers who pretty much stopped their active religious observance when they left their parents' homes, but, nevertheless, as Professor Roof found, show a substantial religious interest, even among defectors.

The Boomers are the 76 million people born between 1946 and 1964, the most educated and most affluent group in the United States—60 percent attended college. They are products of the fabled 1960s (e.g., Clinton, Gore) or products of the experimental 1970s. They are the heirs of Woodstock, the drug culture, the sexual revolution, feminism, and mostly, the breakdown of authority and widespread divorce. They themselves are statistically children of divorce and devotees of anti-institutionalism, which includes organized religion. Born into affluence and technology, choice is their creed. Plus freedom. Dogmas and popes are out. So let me share eight characteristics of the Boomers and in fact our "audience" in general, and then some suggested topics for preachers:

1. *They are eclectic.* Dogma is not a strong point as they (and indeed clergy) slide from one denomination to another. As Victoria Rebeck, writing in the Nov./Dec. 1994 issue of *Christian Ministry,* says:

> The established religions face a lot of competition these days. This summer at a retreat I attended . . . several people revealed their affinity for alternate spiritualities. One participant had brought along incense-like brushes she identified as "smudge sticks which certain Indian tribes use for spiritual purposes." . . . Another person said she believed herself to be the reincarnation of a witch burned at Salem: "I didn't want to burst her cosmic bubble," another participant told me, "but witches weren't burned at Salem; they were hanged or crushed by rocks." I have friends who attend "churches" that borrow heavily from vaguely understood Eastern traditions and New Age fashions but neglect Christianity.

2. *They are oppressed by time*—never enough!—and know they are drowning in consumerism. They are selective consumers of institutional religion and are cautious about becoming active in church because this would limit their personal options. They are very leery of demands on their time and resources, as evidenced

in the difficulty in getting them to meetings and retreats and missions. This story—The Wristwatch—is made for them.

❑A man in an airport was quite worried about missing his plane and didn't have a wristwatch and he could not locate a clock, so he hurried up to a total stranger and said, "Excuse me. Could you give me the time, please?" The man smiled and said, "Sure." He set down two large, heavy suitcases he was carrying and he looked at this wristwatch. He said, "It's exactly 5:09, the temperature outside is 73 degrees, and it's supposed to rain tonight. In London, the sky is clear and the temperature is 38 degrees celsius. The barometer reading there is 29.14 and falling. And, let's see, in Singapore, the sun is shining brightly and, by the way, the moon should be full tonight here in Los Angeles, and . . ." The man interrupted him and said, "Your watch tells you all that?" "Oh, yes," said the man, "and much more. You see, I invented this watch and I can assure you there is no other timepiece like it in the entire world." The man exclaimed, "I want to buy that watch! I'll pay you two thousand dollars for it right now." The man said, "No, it's not for sale," and he reached down to pick up his suitcases. "Now, wait," said the other man. "I'll pay you four thousand dollars." And he reached for his wallet. The man said, "No, I can't sell you this. You see, I planned to give it to my son for his twenty-first birthday. I invented it for him to enjoy." "Well, OK," the man said. "Listen, I'll give you ten thousand dollars. I've got the money right here." "Ummmm," the stranger paused. "Ten thousand bucks? OK, it's a deal. It's yours for ten thousand dollars even." The man was absolutely elated. He paid the stranger, took the watch, snapped it on his wrist with glee and said "Thanks" as he turned to leave. "Wait a minute," the stranger said, as he handed the two heavy suitcases to the man. "Don't forget the batteries!"❑

That's a funny story and a delightful allegory on the moral and spiritual cost of consumerism and materialism—a story made for Boomers. (See Homily 15, "Our Three Temptations," for a similar theme.)

3. *Our audience is—like us all—incessantly shaped by the media* in every way and therefore are a highly visual generation. Video

games, computers, the ever-present and ever-watched television, books shape their perceptions. Therefore, they are a tough audience because they already have been brainwashed with sophisticated, glossy, secular images—and brainwashed 24 hours a day:

- In the U.S. there are 1220 TV stations, 9871 radio stations, 482 newspapers, and 11,328 magazines.
- Americans watch 1550 hours of TV a year
- listen to 1160 hours of radio on one of the 530 million sets
- view 38,822 commercials a year—or over 100 a day
- spend 180 hours reading 94 pounds of newspapers and 110 hours reading magazines with the opportunity to read any one of the 30,000 books published each year
- receive 216 pieces of direct mail advertising
- are subjected to 50 telemarketing calls to each person or 7 million altogether
- have their children subjected to commercials in school with the likes of 7Up ads and Burger King logos on their school buses, Reebok commercials on Channel One television, and Coca-Cola on Star Broadcasting radio, which is piped into schools.

As Phyllis Zagano, a professor of communications at Boston University, writes in *America* (3/5/94):

> There are a billion Catholics in the world, about 59 million resident in the United States, where 92 million homes count 193 million television sets and nearly 67 million VCRs. These Catholics, a large portion of them between the ages of 12 and 34, are not reached by preachers, teachers, catechists or catechisms nearly so effectively as they are reached by MTV and its legions of imitators. . . .

(And this provokes, if I may insert a pastoral note, a dumbfounded exasperation as to why the National Council of Catholic Bishops does not sponsor a prime-time Catholic speaker, a la Fulton Sheen. My candidates would be Michael Himes, Jack Shea, or Richard Rohr, a proven and gifted speaker, who, I have no doubt, would draw a national audience of spiritually hungry people.)

Anyway, all this means that more than half of their—and our—waking hours are spent under the (passive) spell of the mass media. This tells us four things. First, they, the people—your audience—are used to polished performances. The news anchors are picked for their smooth, attractive deliveries. We should know with whom we are competing and therefore practice our homiletic style. Megan McKenna, a theologian who tells fabulous stories, makes a far-out suggestion. Take off all your clothes, stand in front of a full-length mirror, and keep on delivering your homily till you are no longer conscious of your reflected body and can let the words take over and flow. (Be sure to lock the door. We have enough trouble). Second, they are not used to listening, not much tuned in to lectures, debates, and homilies. They want action. Teachers all over the land lament the shorter and shorter attention span of children and the need to constantly entertain them. Thus, we must make the most of our short time with them. Third, they—and we—are consequently highly susceptible to "visual" stories, image stories. They are a visual, not audio, people. For example:

☐In one seat of the bus, a wispy old man sat holding a bunch of fresh flowers. Across the aisle was a young girl whose eyes came back again and again to the man's flowers. The time came for the old man to get off. Impulsively he thrust the flowers into the girl's lap. "I can see you love the flowers," he explained, "and I think my wife would like for you to have them. I'll tell her I gave them to you." The girl accepted the flowers, then watched the old man get off the bus and walk through the gate of a small cemetery. ☐

A lovely story, a visual story, easy to imagine in one's mind, and easy to be touched by it.

And fourth, as Thomas H. Troeger, a preacher, puts it (*Imagining a Sermon*, Abingdon, 1990, p. 19), their values and behavior are shaped by the mass media:

My eyes travel back to the tube, where a news story on starvation is followed by a commercial for a luxury car, which drives off toward a beautiful mountain, which gives way to a woman in a sweatsuit telling a middle-aged man why he needs a high-fiber cereal before we hear the weather report. A blast of cold arctic air is shown on the national map as a cartoon cloud with billowing cheeks. The cheerful advice of the meteorologist to "bundle up when you go out" gives no indication that many people are already out there on the sidewalks and in cardboard cartons in the back alleys, where they have been all night.

Television is filled with classy, smart, selective images and international corporate myths that infiltrate the human mind and moral sensitivities. These myths, all hostile to the teaching of the gospel, are, according to Peter Horsfield (*Religious Television: The American Experience*, Longmans, 1984, pp. 47-48):

• The fittest survive.
• Happiness consists of limitless material acquisition.
• Consumption is inherently good.
• Property, wealth, and power are more important than people.
• Progress is an inherent good.

The point is that we have to counter with our own "Christian myths," images, and image-stories that challenge the current myths and that, above all, linger. For example, in Part 2, pay attention when you come to them, to the Tony Campolo story in Homily 10, the soldier's story in Homily 17, the Franny and Zooey story in Homily 21, the Old Governor Campbell story in Homily 24, and the Bob Smith story in Homily 26. They are all "visual" stories, attentive to human life, laden with counter-images and values. As such, they effectively "storytell the word" to a media generation.

4. *Those in our audience are what Dean Hoge et al. call "lay liberals,"* which means they have a high tolerance toward people of differ-

ing opinions and beliefs. Tolerance, in fact, is *the* Boomer virtue. Absolutes are not in their mentality; different moral and religious strokes for different folks is their creed. This is how they cope in a highly pluralistic society. For them, particular religious traditions are seen as spiritual resources, not as ultimate authorities by which they should guide their lives. Which is why unbending or unnuanced orthodox positions turn them off. To them, truth comes in many guises and it is arrogant to think, for example, that Jesus Christ or the Catholic church are the only routes to salvation. In fact, to them, Christian teachings are but one resource among many. Which is why these well read, articulate lay liberals are very reluctant to engage in any kind of evangelism. It smacks of colonialism.

5. *They are not quite sure they need salvation*, in the sense of salvation from what? Flannery O'Connor, as usual, catches it nicely. Crazy, God-obsessed Hazel Motes retorts in the short story "Wise Blood" when someone mentions something about redemption, "Any man with a good car don't need redemption." That's hilarious and right on. Anyone with a good Toyota, a good heart rate, low blood pressure, job security, and a pension plan doesn't need redemption. We'll redeem ourselves, thank you. Alas, as Elizabeth Achtemeier observes, our task is to preach salvation to those who don't believe they need it.

6. *Our congregation of Boomers and others are totally saturated with the modern mindset which is technical, computer oriented, and so-called scientific.* This, says Walter Brugglemann (*Finally Comes the Poet*, p. 2), "reduces mystery to problem, transforms assurances with certainty, revises quality into quantity, and so takes the categories of biblical faith and represents them in manageable shapes."

7. *Our congregation no longer holds common values in a clear and unmistakable way.* Nor do they, children of a confused religious education era, any longer share a common vocabulary. As Robert N. Bellah points out in *Habits of the Heart*, "Relatively few middle-class urbanites described themselves as 'children of God,' created in his image and likeness, bound by his commandments, and inspired by his love."

8. Finally, since we are them too, *we tend to preach the gospel tai-*

lored to this technological mindset which long ago dismissed the Good News as news at all, since they've heard it a thousand times before. Instead, we tend to preach to their feel-good reductionism. "Smile. God loves you!" we say, thus making God a conspirator in a cover-up. Would God indeed meet me with a smile or a deep cry for a life run amiss?

So, that's their profile. They, of course, are not without problems. It seems the Boomers have do indeed have them, five main ones in fact:

1. *Authority*. Authority, they have been taught, is a synonym for oppression. For it has been aligned with power, with patriarchal, hierarchic, monologic power. And, philosophically, exterior authority, dismantled by the Enlightment, has found itself situated in an intolerable vacuum with no place to go except the interior, to within oneself—ultimately a scary thing. The current feel-good, self-esteem New Age pop psychologies feed this anxiety and are current manifestations of it. As Walter Brueggemann wrote in *Theology Today* (October 1995, p. 317):

It is difficult to take in the radical shift of assumptions in "world making" that occured at the beginning of the seventeenth century. The collapse of the hegemony of medieval Christianity, hastened by the Reformation, the Thirty Years War, and the rise of science, produced, as Susan Bordo has made clear [*The Flight to Objectivity: Essays on Cartesianism and Culture*, SUNY Press, 1987], a profound anxiety about certitude. It was clear that certitude would no longer be found in "the truth of Christ," for confessional divisions had broken that truth. Believers henceforth could appeal only to reason guided by the spirit, or the spirit measured by reason, clearly a circular mode of truth. Indeed, Descartes introduced his massive program of doubt as an attempt to link the new truth to the claims of Christianity. What emerged was the individual knower as the decontextualized adjudicator of truth.

Modern culture feeds off that fact and capitalizes on it. That is why, after sex, defying authority is the chief lure that advertising uses, as in: "Just do it" (Nike), "Sometimes, you gotta break the rules" (Burger King), "When you have a passion for living, nothing is merely accepted. Nothing is taboo . . . Break all the rules" (Don Q rum), [Our shoe] "conforms to your foot so you don't have to conform to anything" (Easy Spirit Shoes), "Relax. No rules here" (Neiman Marcus), "Peel off inhibitions. Find your own road" (Saab), "Your world should know no boundaries" (Merrill Lynch).

So chants the cultural mantra. External authority is out—except that, ironically, the young are beholden to it more than ever in a world of constant knowledge explosion. Let the medical field, for example, give its warning of the week, say, that oat bran is good for you, and all the yuppies with "Question Authority" emblazoned on their T-shirts rush out to buy all they can. Let Bill Gates brandish Windows 95 and the stampede is on. Otherwise, the sad thing about an understanding of authority as oppression and its corollary, that therefore no one's opinion is better than anyone else's, is that the Boomers and Generation X forfeit the strength of their own convictions. As Joseph Leinhard observes:

> A generation of college students has been so anesthetized by relativism that they cannot say that Shakespeare was the greatest master of the English language for fear of offending someone who thinks that Danielle Steel is. But if they can never say, "You are wrong," they can never say, "I am right," either. Or, to put it in the words of the popular slogan, "If you stand for nothing, you'll fall for anything."

And so it is in the field of religion. Authority used to mean the pope, the church—but no more. Both, for one reason or another (suppression? pedophiles?), have lost their credibility. They are children of their age: anti-institutional in mindset from government to corporations to universities to church. Authority also used to be the Bible but biblical criticism has shown them (via the popular press) that it is rather a book riddled with errors. It certainly does not contain the verbatim words and happenings of Jesus. Scripture scholar John Meier notes that many scholars recognize some gospel content as "the work of catechesis and reflection in the early church and not simply a verbatim report of what Jesus said." And they've read enough of the popular press report on the Jesus Seminar which declares that of all the words in the Lord's Prayer, Jesus probably only said "Father."

So, how do Boomers use a book, read as a secular collection of myths, put together by a lot of unknown hands with point of view to push, to judge right and wrong? Where do they go? What is the ultimate basis for truth? Lacking any other guides, they fall back on personal experience. In short, they become extremely privatized and relativistic. Absolute affirmations about salvation or anything are non-existent.

2. *Death.* There is one area where personal experience is obviously limited, and that is death, and consequently questions about the afterlife perplex many aging Boomers and they make bestsellers out of books that give answers. In *America* (10/22/94) editor Jim Martin tells of finding himself at Barnes & Noble where 200 young, well-dressed people were gathered. He asked himself what they were there for: Tom Clancy? Anne Rice? John Grisham? No, they were there listening to bestselling author Mary T. Browne speaking about her bestselling book, *Mary T. Reflects on the Other Side.* He mused, ruefully, that any Catholic parish would give its right arm to have a group of 200 young adults discuss the afterlife. Martin then read *Embraced by the Light* and *Saved by the Light,* two other very popular books. He comments:

It is obvious why *Saved by the Light* and *Embraced by the Light* are so popular—they present comforting visions of the afterlife and answers to life's big mysteries. Yes, the answers are often ridiculously simplistic and much of what they say is outlandish. So it is tempting to snicker at their audiences and dismiss them. . . .But it would be foolish to do so. For beyond their simplistic worldview, I suspect their attraction for some intelligent people is that they treat religious experience in a way that mainstream religious leaders often avoid.

He adds a postscript, "When I bought the two books, I told the goateed salesman at Barnes and Noble that I wanted to find out what made them so popular. As he wrapped up the books he said, 'Hope you like them. And, hey, you wanna read something else? Try angels. They're huge.'"

3. *Evil.* And what about evil: AIDS, divorce, broken relationships, addictions, drinking? Boomers' vaunted individualism is beginning to slip a bit. They found success at the expense of relationships. Some are now asking, "How can I build lasting friendships (marriages) and where can I find trustworthy friends?" Their search takes them to malls, bars, fitness clubs, self-help groups—and some to the churches they deserted. Many are seeking a religious experience that can heal their broken lives.

4. *Transcendence with caution.* They want to know, is there something more? Yes, they believe so, hope so. As we just mentioned, they devour New Age books about angels and after-death experiences which offer a kind of spirituality without religion or demands. (See *Theology Today*, October 1994, for a penetrating look into the meaning behind it all.) In fact, books on religion and spiritual topics are flourishing. We should note, for example, that M. Scott Peck's *The Road Less Traveled* has been on national best-seller lists for eleven years. Christian bookstores have done some $3 billion in sales in 1995. There's something afoot. Jubilant publishers offer their theories, from the desire for moral and spiritual guidance in a world where the old rules have broken down to disillusionment with a computer-driven and increasingly violent society, to seeking some kind of meaning for frazzled lives that are treadmill busy but unfulfilled. National magazines have taken notice: *Time* with a cover story on miracles (not to mention Pope John Paul II being 1994 Man of the Year), *Life* with a cover story on prayer, and *Newsweek* with its cover story on "The Search for the Sacred."

5. *Their children and values.* As the *New York Times* (12/26/94) article the day after Christmas put it: the Boomers are

... torn between guilt, reluctance and nostalgia, between the sense that religion would be good for their children and their own lack of belief in some spiritual doctrines, as well as their discomfort with the way many religious institutions are run. In a society that seems more and more frightening and amoral than ever, many parents say they yearn for a moral safety net, a place that will reinforce the values they hope to teach at home. Others feel they should at least expose children to religion, as a possible source of comfort and faith. Still others conclude that religion is not the answer.

Nevertheless, Boomers, so uncertain in their own lives, are highly supportive (96 percent) of Christian education and will *insist* on sending their kids to some form of it. But, of course, if they want their children "exposed" to the historic tenets of the Christian faith, they certainly don't want them "indoctrinated" with any absolutes. But their children are a linchpin and their search for support is acute and their need for some kind of enduring values for their children is very strong. As Martha Fay, author of *Do Children Need Religion?* (Pantheon, 1993), observes, "I'm struck by how difficult it is to find support for one's convictions anywhere. We're all out there jumping from ice floe to ice floe."

So this, for the most part, is our audience. One conclusion about them is that, if there is one thing that characterizes them, at least the younger people present or absent, is that they are turned off by organized or institutional religion, but very much turned on by spirituality, spirituality being defined as, where is God in my life? Never mind, as Ken Woodward sagely points out (*Commonweal* 9/9/94):

One often hears among educated Catholics the phrase, the institutional church, used as a term of derision. How very American—and, sociologically, how naive—to suppose that anything of value can survive without institutions. The early Christians would never have begotten a second-generation church if the charismatic first generation did not develop institutions, chains of command, and eventually a hierarchy. But no society can survive without institutions, which are not just buildings and chains of command, but also patterns of behavior. It is only through institutions that traditions are passed on, the young brought up, the undisciplined disciplined and society sustained—including the society we call church. I have done my share of institutional criticism. There isn't a religious group, I suppose, I haven't offended. But what offends me is the romantic notion that all the ills of the church reside with the institution—so that if only we could reform it, we ourselves would be better Christians. The truth quite often is the other way around.

Still, for all these wise words, "institutional church" is a negative term. But as we said, spirituality is another thing. The phenomenon of bestseller books on spiritual topics, as we have seen, the multiplying of small groups from AA to Bible studies (4 out of every 10 Americans belong to one of the 3 million groups in this country), the loss of millions of Catholics to fundamental evangelicals, the huge appeal of spiritual rallies—all testify to the search. One striking example: the 50,000 young all-male audiences that jam the stadiums (at $55 apiece) to attend a "Promise Keepers" rally where speakers tell them to love Jesus and their wives and children, to go church on Sunday, form friendships with other men with whom they can pray and confide in. Something's happening. People are looking for something, but not always in church.

All that we have written so far about our audience is leading somewhere; namely, in the preaching business, what shall we preach? What shall we not? Some conclusions and suggestions:

1. *Do preach spirituality.* By that I mean, take them where they are and try to help them decipher where God is to be found. They—we—have problems: forced retirement, loss of a job, a harsh economy, sickness, broken relationships, drugs, AIDS, children or grandchildren who have broken Boomers' hearts because they no longer go to church or are living pagan lifestyles. You name it. They want not a dissertation on the Trinity (but see Homily 4), but how in the world to discern God—if God's there

at all—in all this mess. They want to make some spiritual sense out of it all. They want, most of all, to know that *God* knows about them, notices, and cares.

If you want to know what to preach on, I suggest you take a look at the first 25 bestselling titles of those Care Notes. Most of us are familiar with these highly popular pamphlets in our bookracks (put out by Abbey Press in St. Meinrad, Indiana). Notice the ones that move quickly: Climbing Up From Depression, When Your Son or Daughter Gives Up on the Church, Learning to Live Alone, When Your Son or Daughter Divorces, Finding Your Way After the Death of a Spouse, Keeping Your Spirits Up While in the Hospital, When You Need a Hug, When Cancer Strikes, Finding God in Pain and Illness, Losing Someone Close, Easing the Burden of Stress, Giving Your Worries to God, Making Sense Out of Suffering, Coping With Anxiety, Squeezing Prayer into a Busy Life, Helping a Child to Grieve, When You Can't Pray, Feeling Depressed at Christmas Time, Learning to Live With Chronic Illness, etc. This is where they are. This is the gamut of human life. These are the topics that fly off the shelves. The preacher must seize them and weave them into his preaching. The preacher must take the ancient Scripture and make it live in their lives today, here and now.

Of course, we must go beyond these self-interest topics to an authentic sense of discipleship and mission. All this is saying is, begin where they are.

2. *Preach absolutes but not absolutely.* Absolutes in a highly relativistic society, where tolerance equals all-is-the-same, are not palatable. The trick is not to forgo preaching absolutes, but the way we do it. "I see you are a very religious people," said St. Paul in observing their many gods. "Well and good, but let me tell you about Jesus." That sort of thing: the manner of persuasion, the presentation of truth, but in a way that does not shove it down their throats. Never outright condemn a bad teaching, such as the really abominable and naive "theology" of all those after-death and angel books, but build on them. Lead them elsewhere.

3. *Preach social justice second, not first.* And immediately I must explain this remark by pointing our the failure of liberation theology and the option for the poor in South America. These should

have revitalized the church. Instead, by the year 2000, it is estimated, the evangelical churches there expect to have 100 million converts—all former Catholics. What happened was that the emphasis and the preaching focused so much on poverty and social injustice that religious practices were neglected, such as processions, devotions to the saints, especially Mary, and even Sunday Mass became a rally to deal with social issues rather than worship. As one observer, Fr. Orien Key, S.J., wrote in *The Priest* (January 1992): "In the Catholic Church they found only the Social Gospel which was set before them as the way of Christ. This gospel left them spiritually empty. In the Evangelical churches, as some of these converted Catholics themselves said, they found Christ." In this context, it's appropriate to quote Scripture scholar Raymond Brown (*The Churches the Apostles Left Behind*, p. 97):

> That Christ willed or founded the Church may be an adequate theology for some; but an abstraction, focused on the past, will not be enough to keep others loyal to a Church unless they encounter Jesus there. They will join some small group where they find an encounter with Jesus, even if these are tangential to or separated from the church.

Please understand me. Social justice is indeed constitutive to the gospel and we must preach it, but in context and with the prior foundation of why it counts at all. Which is to say, social justice is an outgrowth and expression of a deep and abiding spirituality. It has been wisely observed that those who did most for earth were those whose eyes were fixed on heaven. Master homilist Walter Burghardt is working hard to help us all "Preach the Just Word" by grounding that just word in sound theology and spirituality. Begin with spirituality and move to social justice, not the other way around.

4. *Preach Jesus, not the church.* I mean this in two ways, one diplomatically and the other theologically. As to the first, when I say "preach Jesus not the church," I do not mean to denigrate the latter. Far from it. It's just that church equals institution, equals

rules, equals oppression, or whatever hangups people have. The church continues Jesus' mission and message, true enough; but, as a matter of diplomacy, it is better to open the Scriptures directly, to speak of the spirit of Jesus rather than to say always, "the church says" or "the church teaches," and to convey that the church is us, living and witnessing the Spirit of Jesus in the world.

As to the second, it is worth remembering our discussion on authority, how the dismantling of any external authority has thrown people back on themselves. Where else can they go? This position is what basically drives the ubiquitous self-esteem movement and its aggressive self-regard, where people get fascinated about how they feel and with how they feel about how they feel. It produces a culture where, as *Newsweek* ("Hey, I'm Terrific!" 2/17/92) pointed out, schoolchildren outrank Asian school children not in math ability, but in self-confidence about their ability, where, in the words of Cornelius Plantinga, Jr. *(Not the Way It's Supposed to Be: A Breviary of Sin*, Eerdmans, 1995, p. 83):

> . . .trendy preachers imply that the main problem with savings and loans embezzlers is that they do not love themselves unconditionally. After all, didn't Jesus and Paul talk a good deal about self-love? "I can see it now," says John Alexander, "Jesus gently saying, 'Woe to you poor scribes and Pharisees! Nice guys—but your self-esteem is low'" (Mt 23:13–36). Or Paul writing the Judaizers, "Neither circumcision accounts for anything nor uncircumcision, but feeling good about yourselves" (1 Cor 7:19).

All this self-serving navel gazing reaches its ultimate religious idolatry in Carol Christ's much-quoted cry of triumph, "I found God in myself, and I loved her fiercely."

For the preacher, the task is obvious. It's to move such self-esteem people to seek salvation, not in more therapy or truth by feeling, but in Another, in Jesus Christ. It's to help them turn outward and resonate with St. Paul: ". . . I see in my members another law at war with the law of my mind, making me captive to the law of sin that dwells in my members. Wretched man that I am!

Who will rescue me from this body of death? Thanks be to God through Jesus Christ our Lord!" (Rom 7:22–25).

5. *Keep it simple.* People are used to one, repetitive commercial message with the company's logo or phone number being repeated endless times. Complicated messages in a short 10- or 12-minute homily for a people raised on mini-second sound bytes are lost. One message, turned around two or three times (the famous three points), does it.

6. *Preach what evokes experience.* Remember, people today are hostile to authority, past as well as present. For them, all of the systems of the past have been found wanting in this new, post-modern age. This includes the church we have known for the past 1600 years whose traditional configuration is quickly fading. Its paradigms show cracks. Its master narrative is being replaced or at least is increasingly being greeted with suspicion and even incredulity. Rationalistic doctrines, wrapped in Thomistic arguments, no longer have an appeal. In a word, the old givens religiously and philosophically have collapsed, leaving people grasping for something and, by default, causing them to fall back on experience. The skeptic Ian Malcolm, in Michael Crichton's popular *Jurassic Park* who rejects the park's creator's rational certainty that all will be controlled, is the perfect Boomer postmodernist pew sitter. All will *not* be well. All is *not* predictable. All is *not* as it was in the past. We can no longer count on the signposts of old. That's why logic and propositions will not convince. Didactic, propositional homilies will not register. Three-point argumentation will leave people cold. What, then, is left? The imagination. Only the imaginative that taps and evokes experience will persuade. In short, only the affective will get through. Hence the primary power of the story and the importance of awakening an experience through the story.

To take a timeless example: what makes the scriptural Infancy stories so powerful and appealing—even though all scholars, from conservative to liberal, acknowledge that they are not literally true in any detail or fact, not historical—is that they resonate precisely on the experiential, feeling level. In and through this story the fundamental hopes and fears of all parents are played

out, because, when you come right down to it, it is the story of a
special child (aren't they all?) and an imperiled child, imperiled
from wicked kings and senseless slaughter—and aren't all children? The instinct to protect a helpless infant is common to all
humans and so all are immediately pulled into the drama as their
worst fears are elicited and inflated. As Jack Miles writes, "The
story's clash of sublime promise against heart-stopping danger
has its anguished analogues everywhere from Bosnia to the South
Bronx." People resonate with such a story because deep down it
is theirs. That's why they have always been attracted to the
Christmas story on its own literary merits, on its own capacity to
excite the imagination and touch the common human experiences
of hope and fear, deliverance and love. That's why I say that we
should preach experience through stories because an affecting
experience, provoked by the narrative, is where the postmodern
person is, what he or she thinks is the one thing they can rely on.

□Once there was a singularly unattractive little girl in an
orphanage. The people in charge didn't like her and dearly hoped
that someday some long lost relative would come and claim her.
One day one of the staff spotted the little girl writing a note and
leaving it tucked in a branch in a tree near the gate and reported
it to the authorities. They were delighted. Could she at last be
communicating with a friend, perhaps even a relative? Hopes
soared. As soon as she was out of sight, they went to the tree,
fished out the wrinkled note, opened it, and there in a child's
scrawl were the words, "Whoever find this, I love you."□

Who among us has not had the experience of rejection, loneliness, the need to be held? This is what I mean when I say we
should preach what evokes experience.

7. *Tap our own riches.* We have a tremendous tradition, but, alas,
so seldom used. The communion of saints (see Homily 1) is such
an antidote to the endemic loneliness that plagues America.
Surely they had teenage pregnancies in the Middle Ages. What
do our mystics have to say? How do we make sense of tragedy?
What do the lives of the saints tell us? How did orphans (Mungo)
and widows (Elizabeth Ann Seton) and hotheads (Francis de
Sales) and people with faith problems (the Little Flower) and for-

mer communists and out-of-wedlock mothers (Dorothy Day) cope? How can we live the faith in a hostile society? What are people doing quietly and heroically now? (That will be the point, as we shall see, of telling stories). What is the tradition—not just a recent one, but long ago, deep down—on death and heaven and angels that so preoccupies people today?

Listen to two preachers being interviewed *(Leadership,* Fall 1995, p. 20), the renowned black preacher, Gardner Taylor, and former atheist, now preacher, Lee Strobel, who was converted by a sermon by Bill Hybels of the famous Willow Creek church (yes, words do touch!):

> What changes in preaching have you observed during your ministry?
>
> **Taylor:** There was much more a sense of the transcendence of God in the preaching of the forties and fifties.
>
> There was also a much greater confidence in America—what it was and where it was going. I think we are in the midst of a great disillusionment about the land and about its future and about our future. So the emphasis has changed. Now one needs to preach about an authentic hope.
>
> **Strobel:** We're seeing a difference in the kind of person that comes to our seeker service today compared to the person who came five years ago. Five years ago, people were more cynical; they arrived with arms folded, saying, "I dare you to communicate something to me that matters."
>
> Now they're saying, "I'm in my third marriage, and it's failing. I've got my second BMW, which hasn't brought satisfaction. I've risen to the top of my company, but it doesn't fulfill me the way I thought it would." They see the moral fabric of America coming unraveled, and they're scared.

That's the audience out there. True, not too many of them on Sunday since we Catholics are down to 25–28 percent attendance (a stunning decline!). But if word gets around that the message is for them, for their lives, more will return. They're spiritually hungry for the word, but it must mean something to them. Arthur

Miller once was asked to describe the difference between an ordinary play and a great drama. "In any successful play," he said, "there must be something which makes the audience say to themselves, 'Good Lord, that's me! That's me!'"

In any successful preaching, the standard is the same.

3.

Being There

What was it Woody Allen said? Eighty percent of life is just showing up? I said in the last chapter that our weekend attendees are down and I tried to give a sociological and psychological profile of who they are. But when all is said and done, who is there are human beings, people who, for one reason or another, have come. And they are a mixed audio-group. Carl S. Dudley claims to pick out the Learners who sit forward to catch the message before it reaches anyone else, the Fortress people with folded arms daring you to breach their minds with humor or a new idea, the Next Pointers who seem ready to finish your sentence and move you rapidly to the next one, the Scratchers jotting notes on a piece of paper they took from their wallets or purses (you'd like to think they're taking notes on the homily but in your heart you know it's the dinner menu items), the Drifters who stare into space, and the Sleepers who have slipped out of gear altogether.

But they're there, and they're there as a Christian congregation who remind us that the ultimate measure of a homily's success is not what happens in the pulpit but what happens in the lives of these people. And there's our challenge: how to move them from individuals to a community of saints. In former days, you already had community. People lived in the same towns for generations and acted and reacted together in many daily social circumstances. Many would have had strong social or blood ties to one another before they ever came to church. Many of their best friends would also be members of the church. Today, in our great physically (lots of moving from one state to another) and socially (divorce) mobile society, the local church is but one of many stops along a busy highway. In these days of legitimate parish hopping, many come from 20 and 30 miles away, especially if you have one of those "magnet" parishes with a reputation.

But, again, they're there. And if you have been at a parish a long time (as I was for 22 years as pastor), you develop a deep and abiding respect for who's there. More, an admiration and a genuine love of them as family. You know their secrets. You know their burdens. You know their struggles. You've seen their triumphs and failures. Nothing less than a profound humility descends on you as you stand in that pulpit and wonder if, with some of their burdens, *you* would be there. (Homily 13, "Abbot Macarius," reflects such feelings.) The mother who has a son with AIDS, the closet alcoholic and pillar of the community, the wounded divorced, the embarrassed who have a child who joined another religion, the forced early retiree—all are there. And so are we. Certainly a critical issue in preaching is the pastoral presence of the pastor. *How well we have pastored the people is as valid a question for a successful homily as how well we have prepared it.* They go hand in hand. You can't really divorce the preacher from ministry to the people—and their ministering to him or her. As one priest wrote (Jim Vahle in *Upturn*, Nov.-Dec. 1994):

I remember hearing a new preacher and thinking that his technique wasn't very good, only to overhear parishioners saying how much they enjoyed his homily. I was perplexed until I saw that he stayed in church to pray, visited with parishioners and seemed interested in what was important to them. I realized my mistake: I listened to his words, they listened to him speaking. Perhaps it was then that I first formulated the idea that preaching is a part of pastoral care.

How true. It calls to mind one of the old Brother Juniper stories:

❑Brother Juniper once asked St. Francis, "Teach me to preach as eloquently as you. I am not good with words."

"I will teach you to preach more eloquently than I," said Francis. "Meet me tomorrow and I shall teach you to preach."

Brother Juniper dutifully met Francis early the next morning. To Juniper's surprise, they began walking. They walked through the marketplace, smiling at the laborers, the merchants, the children. They helped an old woman carry her wash up a set of stairs. They walked. Finally, an exasperated Brother Juniper asked, "Francis, when shall you teach me to preach?"

Replied the saint, "Why, we are preaching."❑

The fact is that sooner or later you get to read people's faces and hearts, become familiar with the religiously skittish, the chronically late, the early leavers. You know them well enough so that they worry you to death and send you back over your notes when they laugh at places they're not supposed to and not at all where they should, when they're too pensive (am I getting across?), frowning (did I say something to offend them?), or bored (I wanted so badly to feed them, but my fare is poor). But they're hungry, all of them, for something, something to give affirmation to their lives. I try to respond with homilies such as "The Saintly Chorus" (Homily 1), "God Notices" (6), "Beloved" (12), and the like.

And, more timidly, I must admit, I try occasionally to challenge them. I appreciate great preachers like William Willimon of Duke University who knows the temptations of us preachers: to pander to the congregation and their consumer mentality, to avoid the controversial, to cater to the current feel-good philosophy, to suc-

cumb to cynicism about people's ability to accept challenges—
and, we must add, to want people to like us. He consistently confronts such postures, for he knows as well as we do that the word
should make a difference in their lives and ours, and he continually prods us to try to make that difference. As a pew-sitter and
mother of four, Tina Beattie, puts it ("The Challenge of Catholic
Preaching Today," *Priests & People*, April 1995):

> . . . I think few Christians today leave Mass with their hearts
> on fire. Encumbered as priests are by the pastoral problems
> of lives disintegrating under complex social pressures,
> many see the Sunday Mass as a place of respite and retreat
> for their beleaguered congregations. They hesitate to intro-
> duce controversy or to risk alienating parishioners. . .
> Catholic homilies do little more than comfort the comfort-
> able, and many good people who are profoundly uncom-
> fortable with the present state of society and the world stay
> away because the Church fails to address their need to
> engage with the political and social issues of our age.

Dan Berrigan sums it up when he says, "If you want to be a
good preacher, you better look good on wood."

Let me share here three homilies from previous collections.
Inspired by Willimon, they were my attempts to challenge the
congregation. One is entitled "Christmas Passion" (Homily 25
from *More Telling Stories, Compelling Stories*). The second is from
the same volume, "The Visit" (24), and the third is "Easter" (32),
from *Telling Stories, Compelling Stories*. In this volume, Homily 35,
"Christ the King," has a confronting message.

Christmas Passion
Luke 2:1–14

Have you ever done what your better judgment said you
should not? Most of us have at one time or another. Well, let me

play the "Grinch" tonight and confess that what we did at the
opening of our Mass this evening and will do at all the Christmas
Masses—namely, having sweet little shepherds install the baby
doll Jesus into the manger—was against my better judgment. It
was against my better judgment because, touching as it is, it gives
the wrong message. The wrong message is to focus on the sentimentality of the little baby. And who of us did not nudge our
neighbor and whisper, "Isn't that darling? Isn't that cute?" even
though, as a matter of record, the Baby Jesus has no role in the
gospel narrative.

So you say, "Well, what is the right message?" The right message, I repeat, is not a soft, darling baby. The right message is a
fierce and a passionate God. The Christmas message and the
Christmas celebration is God's great zeal for us, a commitment
not to leave us abandoned. It comes down to that. Not to leave us
in the darkness of political, social, or personal tyrannies. The message of Christmas is summed up in the communication the angel
made to Mary at the Annunciation when he made a play on
words. He said, you shall call his name Jesus and he shall be nick-
named Emmanuel, which translates "God with us." What you
have, then, in the Christmas story is a terrible desire on God's
part to "be with us," to be a part of the human condition: our losses, our recessions, our disappointed and fractured relationships;
the deaths we've had in the past year; the difficulties, the addictions, the alcohol, the drugs, sex; things that turn us upside down
a great bit. In all of our entire human condition, the Christmas
message is that God doesn't want to leave us alone but wants to
reach out and be with us. God, the most passionate of Lovers,
wants to be Emmanuel.

Let me restate this by sharing a true story with you. The story
mentions a baby because it's told by a woman, the baby's mother, but the point of the story lies far beyond the baby. It tells of
God's passion for us. Here is this mother's story:

☐It was Sunday, Christmas. Our family had spent a holiday in San Francisco with my husband's parents, but in
order for us to be back at work on Monday, we found our-

selves driving the 400 miles back home to Los Angeles on Christmas Day. We stopped for lunch in King City. The restaurant was nearly empty. We were the only family and ours were the only children. I heard Erik, my one-year-old, squeal with glee. "Hithere," the two words he always thought were one. "Hithere," and he pounded his fat baby hands—whack, whack, whack—on the metal high chair. His face was alive with excitement, his eyes were wide, gums bared in a toothless grin. He wriggled and giggled, and then I saw the source of his merriment. And my eyes could not take it in all at once.

A tattered rag of a coat, obviously bought by someone else eons ago, dirty, greasy and worn; baggy pants; spindly body; toes that poked out of would-be shoes; a shirt that had ring-around-the-collar all over; and a face like none other—gums as bare as Erik's.

"Hi there, baby, hi there, big boy. I see ya, Buster." My husband and I exchanged a look that was a cross between "What do we do?" and "Poor devil."

Our meal came and the banging and the noise continued. Now the old bum was shouting across the room, "Do you know patty cake? Atta boy. Do you know peek-a-boo? Hey, look! He knows peek-a boo!" Erik continued to laugh and answer, "Hithere." Every call was echoed. Nobody thought it was cute. The guy was a drunk and a disturbance. I was embarrassed. My husband, Dennis, was humiliated. Even our six-year-old said, "Why is that old man talking so loud?"

Dennis went to pay the check, imploring me to get Erik and meet him in the parking lot. "Lord, just let me get out of here before he speaks to me or Erik," and I bolted for the door. It soon was obvious that both the Lord and Erik had other plans. As I drew closer to the man, I turned my back, walking to sidestep him and any air that he might be breathing. As I did so, Erik, all the while with his eyes riveted to his best friend, leaned over my arm, reaching with both arms to a baby's pick-me-up position. In a split-second of balancing my baby and turning to counter his weight, I came eye-to-eye with the old man.

Erik was lunging for him, arms spread wide. The bum's eyes both asked and implored, "Would you let me hold your baby?" There was no need for me to answer, since Erik propelled himself from my arms to the man's. Suddenly a very old man and a very young baby consummated their love relationship. Erik laid his tiny head upon the man's ragged shoulder. The man's eyes closed and I saw tears hover beneath the lashes. His aged hands, full of grime and pain and hard labor, gently, so gently, cradled my baby's bottom and stroked his back. I stood awestruck. The old man rocked and cradled Erik in his arms for moment, and then his eyes opened and set squarely on mine. He said in a firm, commanding voice, "You take care of this baby." And somehow I managed "I will" from a throat that contained a stone.

He pried Erik from his chest, unwillingly, longingly, as though he was in pain. I held my arms open to receive my baby, and again the gentleman addressed me: "God bless you, Ma'am. You've given me my Christmas gift." I said nothing more than a muttered "Thanks." With Erik in my arms, I ran for the car. Dennis wondered why I was crying and holding Erik so tightly. And why I was saying, "My God, forgive me. Forgive me."□

I would like to suggest that the meaning of Christmas is Erik. Erik is God. Erik is Christmas. Erik is God's arms, zeal, and passion for us, tattered bums with our tattered lives, our tattered hurts, our tattered relationships, and our tattered sins. Erik is two arms determined to break into our lives.

Erik is a fierce little baby who makes no distinctions, but would embrace the least likely. And that's what Christmas is about. It's an enormously unrelenting kind of a feast. It is not sentimentality. It is not soft. It is as hot and hard as any romance. It is God's fulfilled desire to be with us. And that's why we celebrate.

If God is not with us and if God has not embraced our tattered lives, woe is us. There is no hope. And there is no light, only darkness and despair. And we are here tonight out of fruitless hope, pressured routine, or empty sentimentality.

But if we are here because of love and here like rag-tag shepherds to kneel and rejoice, then we have caught Christmas's meaning: Emmanuel, the passionate God, has had his way and has hugged us fiercely.

That's a terrific story, isn't it? It held the people spellbound. Its analogy, which desentimentalizes Christmas, is strong and it takes a certain amount of boldness to call people away from the feel-good, littlest-angel cuteness to the powerful, fundamental implications of this feast. The same kind of strength is found in the following homily.

The Visit
Luke 1:39–55

I always feel a certain love-hate relationship with this particular gospel. This gospel has been enshrined in Catholic tradition in what we know as the Visitation. Most of us could probably conjure up pictures of drawings and famous paintings of the meeting of these two women, Mary and Elizabeth. And included in the mental imagery that we have of the Visitation is this: that Mary, the perfect flower of God's creation, entertains an angel, learns that she is full of grace, is to become the mother of the Messiah, and in her superb charity, runs to her aged cousin Elizabeth to selflessly help her in her pregnancy. And so our concept of the Visitation is complete and we have another tableau in the life of Mary.

But the fact is that this is simply piety gone astray, and if we believe that, then we lose the whole impact of today's gospel which absolutely must be seen in the context of the Annunciation. And when we go back to the Annunciation in the gospels, we see that this gospel today is not a celebration of an angelic visit to a queen who was kneeling at prayer, but rather the unexpected breaking into the life of a peasant who very likely had just taken out the garbage. It's the story of a shrewd and witty native woman who wanted to check her facts.

After all, remember the message of the Annunciation was that both she and Elizabeth would become pregnant. Mary believes, but still she is a hard-nosed, common-sense peasant woman and she would like to have a second opinion. And so what does she do? She puts on her shawl and she runs over to her cousin Elizabeth and before she can ask the delicate question, Elizabeth greets her with, "Blessed are you among women and blessed is the fruit—the baby—of your womb, and how is it that the mother of my Lord should come a-calling?" And Mary laughs because she heard what she had come to hear, namely, "Yes, dearie, we're both pregnant!" And Mary knows it's true and the peasant girl breaks out in song.

And what does she sing about? You heard what she sang about. She sings about God's subversion. She sings about how God reverses all plans and designs. He chooses the little instead of the big. He chooses the weak instead of the strong. He lifts up the lowly. He puts down the mighty. And he makes fruitful both a young virgin and an elderly woman. How Mary and Elizabeth must have laughed and cried and hugged each other and had a good time. Mary knew! She knew that she was chosen not because of her purity and goodness—later generations would get sidetracked into that—but because she was a nothing. She was a nobody. And still God broke into her life.

We sing about Mary's maternity because she deserves it. Mary sings about it because she doesn't deserve it. You see the point of the gospel? As long as we project Mary as the perfect woman of queenly stature, then we know it's absolutely right that she should be the mother of the Messiah, that the break-in of God's word into her life was completely fitting and totally to be expected. She is a quality person. She is holy. She is a great saint. And what else would a great saintly woman do but forget herself and run and take care of her elderly cousin? And the result of that understanding is that we applaud Mary and then we go about our business because we certainly are not made of the same stuff as Mary and therefore can expect no breaking-in of God's word into our lives. And Mary weeps over that.

She weeps because we have it all wrong. She did not sing about herself. She sang about God and how God turns everything upside down—for her, for you, and for me. The episode that we call the Visitation says that if God could break into the life of an ignorant, small town peasant girl, God could and would do it to all lonely, lowly, broken, and insignificant people such as you and me. That's what Mary sang about. She was sounding the note of the mission of Jesus himself. After all, he was born in stable rather than in the local Holiday Inn. He came and lived in Nazareth, not the capital city of Jerusalem. When he grew up, he hob-nobbed with the poor, the destitute, those outside the law. What Mary is singing about is simply that same motif, about how much God has preference for those who are nobody like herself. What did she call herself? "Behold, look at the handmaid, the servant, the slave-girl of the Lord—and the one who is mighty has done great things for the likes of me!"

The gospel, then, is not the story of the visitation of two reigning queens. It is the story of the meeting between two bewildered peasant women who are drunk on God's breaking into their insignificant lives. And when we understand that, we open our lives to God as well. Otherwise, if we project too much on Mary, saying she was so great and queenly that it was only right that God would enter her life . . . but since I am neither great nor queenly nor kingly, I cannot expect that. Remember, that's not what the gospel says. The gospel speaks consistently of the little people being broken into by God's word. And therefore it does not permit us to put God off because we are not qualified. That's what I find wrong with our concept of the Visitation as we understand it.

☐ A good number of years ago, you may recall, the great, black contralto Marian Anderson—magnificent woman, magnificent voice—about whom the Broadway impresario Sol Hurok liked to say that she had not simply grown great, but rather she had grown great simply—well, this same Sol Hurok recalls that one day, at the height of her career, reporters asked Marian Anderson to name the greatest moment of her life. Hurok recounts:

I was in that dressing room when the reporters came in and I was curious to hear the answer. After all, I knew that she had many, many great moments to choose from. There was the night, for example, that Toscanini told Marian Anderson that she had the greatest voice of the century. There was the private concert that she gave at the White House for the Roosevelts and the King and Queen of England. There was the time that she got the famous ten thousand dollar Bach award from her hometown of Philadelphia. Then, of course, to top it all, there was that famous Easter Sunday in Washington when she stood beneath the statue of Abraham Lincoln and sang for seventy-five thousand people, including members of the Supreme Court, the cabinet members, and most members of Congress.

Which of these big moments did she choose? Sol Hurok says she choose none of them. Miss Anderson told the reporters that the greatest moment of her life was the day she went home and told her mother she wouldn't have to take in washing any more.□

And that, in a nutshell, is the gospel we heard today. Mary was a washerwoman, a minority figure in an occupied territory, living in the hick town of the time, for Nazareth was a wretched, backwater place. And as Marian Anderson came home one day and told her mom that she wouldn't have to take in washing any more, so God came into Mary's home one day and said she was to be the mother of the Messiah. Marian Anderson's mom and Mary are sisters under-the-skin. We are therefore celebrating in this gospel today what God did for her, what God can do for you and for me.

When we picture this tableau of the Visitation, we should always remember the song Mary sang about God and make it our song: "He has lifted up the lowly and put down the mighty. He has given the hungry good things to eat and has deprived the rich. He who is mighty has done great things for the likes of me and holy is his name."

This homily turns the traditional mythology on its head. It's strong and perceptive and far more meaningful and identifiable.

Finally, there's this challenging homily given to people on Easter, many of whom are there for the second time this year and want to hear about Easter bunnies and lilies and go home:

Easter
John 20:1–18

☐Stories about golfers' fanaticism are legendary. Here's one to add to your repertoire. A golfer named George finally got home. "George," his wife scolded him, "you promised you'd be home at four o'clock. Look, here it is eight o'clock." George protests, "But, honey, please listen to me. Poor old Fred is dead. He just dropped over right there on the eighth green." "Oh, that's terrible," his wife exclaimed. "It sure was," said George. "For the rest of the game it was hit the ball, drag Fred, hit the ball, drag Fred."☐

Well, the laugher is good for two reasons. One is reflected in the custom in some parts of Easter Catholicism to tell jokes on Easter Sunday to imitate God's last laugh on Satan, who thought he had won with the death of Jesus. The other reason is that it may be the last laugh you get from this homily because my message may prove disturbing and annoying to some. My message is that Easter, as we know it, is a fraud.

What do we associate with Easter? Easter bunnies, Easter eggs, crocuses blooming, hyacinths and tulips as gifts to Mom, springtime, the first robin, cocoons soon to bring forth butterflies. Ah, yes, the sweet resurrection of nature is all around us.

And we say that Jesus is like that, a variation of spring. We liken him to the lowly caterpillar who was wrapped in the cocoon of death on Calvary and on Easter emerged as a divine butterfly and went his way to sit at the right hand of God in heaven. A lovely springtime tableau but, of course, it's all pure parody, pure pagan drivel.

Easter is not bunnies and butterflies. Easter is about a body

that somehow got loose. It's about a dead Jesus, horribly crucified, who came back to harass us. And that scares the hell out of
us. Easter is about a Jesus who while alive was so radical, so
countercultural that the prevaling culture killed him. He was a
threat to the world as it was and is more of a threat now that he's
footloose after the resurrection. Bunnies and butterflies we can
handle, but a risen Christ, just as radical as he ever was, is too
much. Maybe that's why we settle for spiritual Disneyland.
But the plain fact is that Jesus is not Disneyland. He is a way of
life. He is not Dear Abby or Leo Buscaglia or, God forbid, Dr. Ruth
dispensing advice and warm fuzzies and what we want to hear.
He is demand. He is not flow, he is counterflow, counterculture,
because the culture is wrong and selfish and sinful as it is. If you
don't believe me, remember this is the culture that gave us
Hiroshima, Dachau, and Auschwitz; racism, discrimination,
poverty in the midst of plenty, drugs that crossfire young lives
into oblivion, and a savings and loan scandal so riddled with
fraud that every American will pay for decades to come. To see
just how much Jesus is opposite to these things, how countercultural Jesus and the Christianity he founded is, look at life from the
bottom up, from the other side.

Take a sensitive issue. Jesus speaks of no divorce and would
not be swayed by jargon about "an exciting new option for personal freedom." Looked at from the bottom up, divorce is a
painful tragedy; it is parents abandoning their children. Period.
And that brutal fact hurts and continues to hurt as every study
ever produced shows.

A very recent survey in *Seventeen* magazine shows that 24 percent of 15-year-olds have had sex. By age 18 that figures climbs to
60 percent. From the bottom up view, the annual one and a half
million babies being aborted are the most unfree in a free-sex culture. All over America parents who already have raised *their* families are newly bound in raising the second families of their
teenage children. And those slowly dying of AIDS would like to
take a second look, if they had the time, at the promises of the sexual revolution.

Don Mattingly of the New York Yankees just signed for 19 million dollars—nineteen million dollars!—to play baseball while the poor in squalid Brazilian barrios or the homeless of New Jersey haven't even 19 dollars or 19 cents. Jesus weeps over that. The self-centered 25-year-old adolescents who, as the newscasts show us, pay $7000 to have hyped-up stereos in their cars, who have that kind of disposable income to disturb neighborhoods and spend on themselves and their empty lives without a thought to the needy, they are very much a part of a culture that should find Jesus Christ disturbing—because he would find *them* disturbing.

The glitter and glitz of Atlantic City's multimillion dollar casinos stand in mock contrast to the squalor and poverty just a few streets away. The minority and elderly poor of that city are still waiting for some trickle of the millions spent each day in their city. Would Jesus go to Atlantic City? Not on your life. Unless it were to sit in the middle of the road with a half-fed child between his knees, midway between the casinos and squalor in silent witness until they carted him away for disturbing the peace. Unless it were to show Donald Trump a better way or to remind him and Ivana that they have three children who have a far more desperate need for parents than for publicity.

At this point you say: Hold it! Let's go back to some more golfers' jokes. A little lightness, please. At least bring in some bunnies and butterflies. After all, it's Easter and I have my parents and children here and we want to hear something nice. It's part of the holiday.

But I tell you, I would like to say something soft and innocuous about Easter—but the fact is, it's not there. What *is* there is a Jesus who said that it's easier for a camel to pass through the eye of a needle than for a rich person to enter the Kingdom. He said it; I didn't. He said to seek first the Kingdom of God, which he described as feeding the hungry and giving drink to the thirsty. In short, being concerned about others. He told those disturbing stories about the rich man and Lazarus at the gate; about the man who built bigger and bigger barns—security annuities—only to die that night without having kissed his children.

He spoke about forgiving one's enemies as a condition for

being forgiven ourselves, for being whole. He said that; I didn't. He said that we do not live by bread alone. He asked: What does it profit us if we gain the whole world and lose our very souls? He spoke of treating women with respect and not even lusting after them in one's heart. He said nothing about safe sex. He spoke of compassion and he gave everyone he met a second chance. He said that we were to absolutely and without equivocation believe in God and God's wild, wild, love for us and that we count far more than the sparrow that falls to the ground.

And what's more—and this is the clincher for which he was killed by the culture—he actually *did* those things! He fed the poor and healed the sick and took time with friends and prayer and threw out money-changers, hugged children, and he had little patience with hypocrites, religious or otherwise. Oh, he was countercultural all right. His choices. His values. You can see that in the long run his culture could do nothing but pin him to a cross. And so they did.

But what a revoltin' development occurred, as television's Chester A. Riley used to say. Jesus' Abba— the "daddy" he spoke so much of—turns right around and sets him free and he's at his mischief again! What are we to do? We've run out of crosses to nail him to, so we go one better. We make him over into our image so we can go on living our lives and being very much a part of our culture so that no one knows we're Christian. As for Jesus, we drag him out for baptism and first communions—so sweet—and Christmas, Easter, and funerals. For the rest of our lives, it's hit the ball, drag Jesus, hit the ball, drag Jesus.

But that's not what he's all about. He's about happiness and a way of life. He's about the decisions we make at business and school. He's about honesty, caring and concern for others. He's about whistle-blowing and ethics. He's about chastity and fidelity. He's about truth. He's about making relationships work. He's about keeping one's word. He's about life—life here and hereafter for those who listen to him. He is about real joy and fulfillment. He is about a thirtyfold and a sixtyfold and a hundredfold abundance for those who are true disciples.

Jesus is radical, countercultural—and risen! He's a body got loose. *That's* the Easter message. He has nothing against caterpillar, eggs, and butterflies. They belong to Hallmark. He's looking for fellow radicals. They belong to him.

Whew! The people were sitting on the edge of their chairs. That was socking it to them. It was an attempt at an antidote to the jolly-smiling, do-as-you-like-because-Jesus-loves-you-anyway approach. Many were enthusiastic in their comments afterwards. But, of course, I didn't hear the dissenters.

We can never turn into scolds, but more often than we think we can challenge a people to move from being Christian to being disciples.

4.

GUIDELINES

In this chapter, I want to continue where I left off in Chapter 2 and share some basic guidelines for good preaching.

1. *Proclaim the word.* Don't preach your pet peeves. As we said earlier, people are hungry for the numinous. It's time to call a moratorium on all the wrongs in the Church and tap into our spiritual heritage. Leave your personal agenda behind.

2. *Preach about the signs of God in their lives,* the revelations, spirituality, and challenges of everyday experiences. I mentioned this in the last chapter. Allow me to expand. Listen to preacher Robert McAfee Brown's words in *The Christian Century* (7/27/83):

> By looking into people's faces I discovered that I'm not faithful to the gospel if I preach only judgment and social concern week after week. Not only do members of any con-

gregation need to be roused out of complacency; most of
them are hurting and need support and comfort, not an
unwavering diet of chastisement. . . .A rousing denunciation
of the Gulf war isn't necessarily what a couple needs when
they've just learned that their daughter has cancer. Every
week some worshippers are hurting and some are exultant;
some have lost their jobs and some are aflame with the need
for justice in the workplace.

In his introduction to *The Novels of Charles Williams* (Oxford
University Press, 1963), Thomas Howard gives a more poetic and
dramatic emphasis:

> The noblest poetic imaginations have persisted in seeing the
> commonplace routines of human experience against an
> immense backdrop. Eliot spoke of "the fear in a handful of
> dust," referring to the enormous and alarming significance
> lying just under the surface of even the most ordinary
> things. . . .Prophets see another aspect of it when they tell us
> that modest items like casual oaths and cutting remarks and
> icy silences will damn us to hell. Poets see yet another
> aspect of it when they see the whole Fall of Man in a field
> mouse scampering away from a farmer's plough, or a work
> of hypocrisy in the fur trim on a monk's cuffs.
>
> The ordinary stuff of our experience seems both to cloak
> and to reveal more than itself. Everything nudges our
> elbow. Heaven and hell seem to lurk under every bush. The
> sarcastic lift of an eyebrow carries the seeds of murder since
> it bespeaks my wish to diminish someone else's existence.
> To open a door for a man carrying luggage recalls the Cross
> since it is a small case in point of putting the other person
> first. We live in the middle of all of this but it is so routine
> that it is hard to stay alive to it. The prophets and poets have
> to pluck our sleeves or knock us on the head now and again,
> not to tell us anything new, but simply to hail us with what
> has been there all along.

Or, in the words of the U.S. bishops' 1982 document on preaching, "Fulfilled in Your Hearing": "Ultimately, that's not what preaching is all about, not lofty theological speculation, not painstaking biblical exegesis, not oratorical flamboyance. The preacher is a person speaking to people about life and faith." Or, finally, as the old Sufi tale puts it, Jesus is the one who stands by the Jordan selling river water. That is, he is showing them for the first time what they see all the time.

What they're all saying is that preaching should be nourished by the Scriptures, but not in the sense that Scripture is applied to life but rather life is interpreted in the light of Scripture. Which is why, by the way (to jump ahead a bit), stories were remembered, because they told people about their lives and at the same time told them that there was something more.

3. *The homilist should never be the focus of the homily.* Professor Mary Jo Weaver writes a telling letter in *America* (11/19/94):

I was glad to read the Rev. Robert P. Wasznak's article, "The Catechism and the Sunday Homily" (10/22/94). I agree that the new catechism and some clear slippage in doctrinal understanding tend to draw many priests toward instructional sermons rather than scriptural homilies. But I believe there is a larger issue here. Most of the homilies I have heard in the past few years are neither about Scripture nor about doctrine. They are usually about the homilist, about his past week, his feelings, his love for nature, his vacation, his insecurities, his hopes or anxieties. A good homilist must read carefully and reflect prayerfully on the texts, but in these days of priest shortage and chronic burn-out, who has time and space for spiritual interaction with the word of God?

I cannot image better homilies until we begin to discern a gift for preaching within the congregation. Many of those listening to the latest personal escapades of the priest *do* have time and space for reflection; they *do* have a developed spiritual life; they *do* have the means "to teach, to delight, and to persuade" as Augustine defined preaching. I am all for scriptural homilies, but trying to find them in the hearts of overworked priests seems to me to be hoping for miracles on a weekly basis.

Besides, to talk about one's self and one's experiences all the time is to be basically out of communal context; that is, your personal story hasn't as yet gone through the community's judgment and reflection. There's usually a transition needed between your story and the others' stories until yours becomes universal and therefore validated by the tradition.

4. *Avoid personal references* because they set up the preacher as the norm for the community's experience of faith. (This is different from the preceding where the homilist is the whole focus of the message. He *is* the message.) Unconsciously, people will begin to measure their faith against yours which, to them, has an official seal on it. "After I had spent the day in prayer, the Lord told me . . ." intones the sacred preacher. For someone who spent the day with her head in the oven and who has never heard the Lord speak to her in her life, this can only incite guilt or anger or, if she's intelligent, disdain. Not that you cannot and should not make comments on your own experience and feelings, nor indicate that you too are a fellow pilgrim, but it should not be a habit. In fact, some authors say never to talk about yourself. That's a little too broad. Perhaps they're reacting to letters like Mary Jo Weaver's. It's all right to make personal references if they really intersect with the listeners' experience, but it should be sparing.

5. *Be specific,* which is only another way of saying: avoid platitudes and generalizations because they fall flat. "Love your neighbor" is much too broad. "Do good and avoid evil" is sound, but boring. "Let us all resolve to be better people" makes you wonder what other options you might be urging.

☐However, even as I write that, I think of the priest who was the envy of all the clergy. Whenever he spoke publicly, the people were enthralled. Whenever he spoke one on one, people were touched. One time a well-known housekeeper's husband died. All the clergy went to the wake. One after one they spoke to Mary, the widow. She just nodded sadly to each one. This priest came in, went up to Mary and spoke to her, and she lit up and looked so grateful. One priest couldn't stand it any longer. After everyone left, he went up to her and said, "Mary, you looked so relieved and comforted when Father so-and-so spoke to you. Tell me, just what did he say?" "Oh, Father, "Mary said, "he was wonderful. He just took my hands, looked me in the eyes and said, 'Mary, these things happen'"! That's just one notch above the priest who, learning that a long-time hardened sinner had returned to the faith because of one of his sermons, asked the man what it was he said that touched him. The man replied, "When you said, 'We must turn over a new leaf'"! Sometimes, you just can't win.□

6. *Avoid mixed metaphors.* "She charged into my office like a bull and fired off one rocket of criticism after another!" "He spoke like a well-mannered gentleman who spat out machine gun fire words that ricocheted around the canyons of the mind." And avoid distracting your audience with incorrect language. That is, if you have a rather well-educated audience, language poorly used or bad grammar interferes with their receptivity.

7. *Avoid negative associations.* "The Devil prowls the streets like Mother Teresa looking for the weak and dying" leaves something to be desired. And avoid negative messages. One priest I heard of preached on asking St. Michael to "smite" the United Nations Council on Population. Another told his audience that their loved ones were writhing in agony in purgatory because they weren't praying for them and, besides, no matter how good we thought they were, they all had flaws and had landed in purgatory where they're suffering. Then there's the priest who felt compelled to remind mothers that their unbaptized infants are not suffering, but they will never, never, never see God. How's that for Good News?

8. *The opening line or lines are important.* Which translates as meaning they should be credible to your audience as well as ear-catching: To the Rosary Altar, "Today I would like to talk to you about the false philosophies we find all around us. The pragmatic concept of a materialistic world . . . etc." At the Communion Breakfast of the Amalgamated Garbage Haulers Union: "My dear friends, in even the most cursory exegesis of this morning's

gospel. . ." These opening lines just don't cut it any more than St. Augustine's did when he explained at length, as was his wont, neo-Platonism to farmers and stevedores. Nor should the opening lines begin with a long poem or *anything* long for that matter. It's too long of a wind-up and the people won't be mentally there for the pitch. "Fourscore and seven years ago" is catchier than "Eighty-seven years ago." How about this one: several blind people were begging on a street corner but one seemed to be getting more than the others. That's because all the others simply had "blind" written on their signs. But this man's sign said, "It's April and I'm blind."

We might remember the opening (and closing) lines in Jack Lemmon's homily in the movie, *Mass Appeal.* He was playing an older priest who had been more interested in pleasing his people than God, but had a conversion. So this Sunday he stands up and begins:

My homily this morning will be exactly 30 seconds long. [Great opening line!] That's the shortest homily that I've ever preached in my life, but it's also the most important homily I've ever preached. I want to make just three points. First, millions of people in the world are hungry and homeless. Second, most people in the world don't give a damn about that. Third, many of you are more disturbed by the fact that I just said *damn* in the pulpit than by the fact that I said that there are millions of hungry and homeless people in the world.

With that, he made the sign of the cross and sat down.

9. *Unity, coherence, and emphasis* form an old triad that is a sensible and solid guide for preparing a homily. Again, we take our cue from the media and advertising. They mention the product and phone number to call over and over again to distraction. They have but one message that doesn't get muddied with ten others. That's the principle of Unity. Have a point, one point. Or have those famous three points as long as they serve the overall theme. What do you want to say? We've all heard homilies that

had some wonderful points but there were so many of them that there wasn't a unifying message to take home. Some preachers do that. They've got some real gems and they think they must spill the whole darn works. They jump from here to there, put in side remarks (entertaining as they may be), add asides so that, by the time they're through, you don't what in the world the point was or which of the 33 points you're supposed to remember. Too many ideas are introduced and left hanging; too many images left undeveloped. The best thing is to put a title, a theme, to the homily. Ask yourself what you want to say, what your main point is, and write it down. What do you want the people to remember? Unity equals one message with two or three points. As veteran church-watcher and pew-sitter Robert Burns sums it up:

> I firmly believe that a homily that develops, usually with brevity, a single idea will be greatly more effective than one with even a short laundry list of thoughts. A conscientious homilist, knowing that he has only one crack at his congregation, will undoubtedly be tempted to cover more ground. But "Keep it simple" is invariably good advice.

I use the acronym KISS: Keep It Simple, Stupid!

Again, let me repeat (for this, I find, is the most serious problem of preachers): have a point, an objective, a message—one message for the TV generation who are raised on a single message repeated over and over again. Know where you're going, what you want to say, and when you're done preparing, check it out to see if there is one message there. Avoid side trips or issues that subvert or intercept the basic message. As Clyde Fant in *Preaching for Today* advises, "A three-point sermon, each with three sub-points is a nine-point topic. All that a preacher can do with a sermon like that is talk himself to death trying to explain so many ideas." Here is a place to jump ahead again with reference to stories. Sometimes a preacher has such a good and captivating story—or even a joke—that he can't discipline himself and simply must tell it because it's so good. But if it's not germane, save it for another time. Else people get caught in the distracting delight of the story and can't move on to the topic of your homily.

Coherence means that it must all hang together. When we say someone is incoherent we mean that he or she jumps all over the place or can't be understood. The preacher may have some wonderful points but it's not clicking overall. They're not connected. They don't relate to one another. There's no center.

Emphasis deals not only with voice inflection, but the way we place sentences and words. "Great is the goddess Diana!" is decidedly more emphatic that "The goddess Diana is great." A staccato sentence after a long sentence can be effective. Leaving a line hanging in the air can be effective (see Homily 17, "What I Have Failed to Do," or Homily 20, "Doctor Life").

10. *Keep within the unspoken or spoken time limit.* Is this a holy hour? a novena? a mission? a Sunday homily given within the context of a parking lot that has to be emptied? To mention again someone's advice: "In a homily, if after seven minutes of digging for oil you come up dry, stop boring!" Seven minutes? Four minutes? Twelve minutes? It's hard to say what the ideal homily length is, although twelve to thirteen minutes would seem to be the limit. I guess the answer about time is, whenever the message is finished. Actually, the real issue of time is to cut out the extraneous. If eight minutes does it, then don't go to nine minutes. And you have to—and should—work hard to get your homily tight and effective and not waste people's time with extra flourishes. It's worth remembering, after all, that one of the finest orations or "homilies" of all time lasted two minutes, 262 words at moderate speed: The Gettysburg Address. The old axiom is true: the less prepared you are, the longer you talk.

11. *Keep religious language alive in your homilies.* This is a severe dilemma. As a nation, as I pointed out in the introduction, we have lost biblical and religious language. Our culture is no longer scripturally literate. Scriptural allusions, stories, images, and proverbs no longer gain recognition. As a result, the most fundamental questions of life get trivialized or at least difficult to pose. Furthermore, as Craig Dykstra points out in *The Living Light* (27, 1990): "The same is true for personal life. A deep, rich, complex,

nuanced language of spirituality seems long forgotten as the church itself chases the pop-gnosticisms like 'co-dependency' and 'twelve-step recovery' as a proxy diction for telling the tale of redemption." The dilemma comes in because we want to relate to the audience and they know the language of pop culture. Yet, the more we speak only and exclusively in those terms, the more we continue to devalue any common religious language. The more we offer shallow and secular nostrums—those purveyed by Mary T. Browne, Leo Buscaglia, John Bradshaw, Shirley MacLaine, or Dr. Ruth—the more we present redemption without Christ, without the Spirit. The more we mimic pop culture, the more we subvert the gospel. And, I might add, the more we do mimic the culture in our homilies, the more we may need to examine our own spirituality and theology.

People really do yearn for a first-hand encounter with the church's accumulated wisdom. The people, says Dykstra, "do not want this in summarized or diluted form. They do not want it second-, third-, fourth-, or fifth-hand. They want it as directly as possible. And they want to know it, handle it, interpret it themselves." In any case, the homilist's skill is to tap into the world—and yes, even the language—of the culture, but to lead the people elsewhere, to the deeper mysteries of faith, to the tradition and the religious language of redemption through Jesus Christ.

(For pertinent reflections on these issues, I suggest George Lindbeck's essay, "The Church's Mission to a Post-Modern Culture" in *Postmodern Theology: Christian Faith in a Pluralist World*, [Ed., F.B. Burnham, Harper & Row, 1989] and Wendy Kraminer's penetrating article, "Chances Are You're Co-dependent Too" in the *New York Times Book Review* [2/11/90]).

12. *Tape your homilies live.* For years before I knew it, a woman was sneaking into the sacristy and plugging into the PA system and taping my homilies. When I found out, I didn't object for they were a revelation to me, I could hear where I was indistinct, too rapid, garbled. And it gave me a chance to check the content and that trio: was there a unity, a clear point to what I was saying? Did it hang together? Was there proper emphasis at the proper points? I think any serious homilist must have his homilies taped. Who

knows, people may begin to ask for copies if they know that. On the other hand, if they know that and nobody asks for copies except your mother, you're in homiletic trouble. Of course, there are always some that you don't want on record:

❑One Sunday morning the preacher went into the pulpit and began to read an Old Testament passage from an old falling apart Bible which had recently been repaired. He was unaware that the page he was reading from and the next page were stuck together from the glue that had seeped in between them. "When men began to multiply on earth," he began, "and daughters were born to them, the sons of heaven saw how beautiful the daughters of man were, and so they took for their wives as many of them as were"—and here the preacher turned the stuck page—"three hundred cubits long, fifty cubits wide, thirty cubits high, made of gopher wood and covered with pitch." After his initial shock, the still puzzled preacher recovered well enough to say, "I must admit that the passage I have read is unfamiliar to me. However, I can see that it affirms a more familiar passage which says that we are 'fearfully and wonderfully made.'"❑

5.

AND THEN SOME

Let's continue with our guidelines.

13. *Improve your homily skills communally.* This, of all the suggestions, along with the next one, is the most practical and effective. Here we take a page from Bishop Ken Untener, Bishop of Saginaw. After talking it over with his presbyteral council for two years, he finally took the plunge and sent a letter to his clergy. In part it read: "What about our preaching? It's a critical part of our ministry. We do our best but rarely, if ever, get hands-on or on-site help to improve or to catch bad habits that creep in unnoticed....There's no single right way to preach, but each of us could benefit from stepping back with someone and taking a look at our preaching now and then." He proposed to gather about four or five priests at a time each week to work together to improve their preaching. Each of them would make an audiotape of the Sunday's homily

and then come together for a two-hour session to give and receive feedback and coach each other. They would meet and do this four times. The program has been a huge success and preaching in that diocese has noticeably improved. Worth trying. By the way, the bishop's thinking of videotaping as well to check the overall impact of the liturgy.

The other communal dimension is to listen to the voices of the people. Fred Craddock has proposed that, since the Bible is the community's book, preaching should speak both to and for the congregation (*Preaching*, Abingdon, 1985). These days, when there are so many faith-sharing groups in the average parish, the preacher can be a part of one, sit in and listen and get direct input. I remember attending one such session just before the weekend on which Father's Day occurred. One of the ladies, recently from another parish, told this story—which in turn I told that weekend:

❑A lovely couple had gotten married and desperately wanted to start a family but could not. However, after many years, they had two daughters. They were thrilled. Then, about a half dozen years later, the wife became pregnant again. They were ecstatic. This time the other two girls were old enough to be helpful to their mother and to go to the hospital with her when her time came. The baby was born—another girl. But shortly after the birth the baby had an aneurism and died. They were all devastated. The doctor wanted to dispose of the day-old infant, but the family wanted a burial. Usually the church really does not have a ritual for such a newborn child, but the parish priest acceded to their wishes and they had a funeral. There was even a tiny white coffin, the size of a bread box. When the time came for the funeral, the father took the coffin and waited to walk up the aisle with it and put it place. The parish priest thought that was too much for him. He said, "Bob, you don't have to do that. It might be too hard on you. The funeral director will bring it up." "No, Father," said the father. "I'll take it up. I made a promise that I would walk all my girls down the aisle."❑

14. *Get feedback.* This is difficult. When people come out of church and say your homily was "interesting" or "nice," you

know in your heart you got two thumbs down. One preacher always knew he had bombed whenever a very senior parishioner would remark, "Father, you've been very busy this week, haven't you?" Or, how about this one: "I loved your homily, Father. Each week your homilies are better than the next." (Think that one over.) One way, for the brave, is to ask a small committee to hand a brief questionnaire to random parishioners and have them fill it out on the spot anonymously—out of sight and range of the preacher. Actually, people are pleased to be asked. Likewise they gain a new sensitivity to the preacher, attending to gestures, voice, mannerisms, etc. One fine preacher, Minister Ross Bartlett, made up a one-page feedback form that covered five brief areas: Organization (introduction, structure, climax), Content (appropriate, convincing, appealing), Style (grammar, language), Delivery (interested in you, effective), General Effectiveness (understandable, meeting a need).

We all have quirks we're unconscious of, bad habits we no longer are aware of. Someone has to monitor us. Fr. Tony Phippot writes in *Priests & People*:

The other day a parishioner asked me whether I was signing for the hard-of-hearing as I spoke. "Not at all," I said. "What gave you that notion?" "The gestures you make, Father," she said. "I was sure it was a language, and I was trying to read it." Heavens, if I am doing that to people, what else am I doing to them? Clearly it is time for the readership of *Priests & People* to set up a branch of Twitchers Anonymous, to rescue priests and deacons from their idiosyncrasies. I for one would welcome it.

A caution: if you don't get feedback voluntarily, someone will do it for you. It's already happened in England. Someone's started a new journal there called *Pulpit* in which its editors promise go around anonymously (and fairly, they claim) and sit in the pews to evaluate homilies being given by the clergy in their land—and *publish* their reviews! So there you are. How long before it happens here? Don't say I didn't warn you.

15. *Use homily helps.* I'll list some of them in the bibliography. They're uneven in quality but very helpful. They can provide insights and stories. Their authors never intend that we use them verbatim (give a canned homily), but they are there as aids. And good aids they are.

16. *Remote preparation.* Whenever you come across an insight or story, clip it out, photocopy it, hole-punch it, and put it in a three-ring binder. Soon you'll have a repertoire of good source material. Likewise, some preachers spend a good amount of time mulling all week over the coming Sunday's text and even the whole month's readings. This way you can subconsciously be on the lookout for those stories. Others underline words or phrases that stick out for them.

17. *Proximate preparation.* Here your own level of comfort will have to dictate what you do. Some preachers write out their homilies. I'm one of those who do—at least a good outline that I can follow with the stories in the right sequence. I'm also one of those who brings the text with me and plops it right on the lectern. What I do is photocopy the gospel and put it and my homily in a three-ring binder and carry that to the pulpit with me. The lector has learned to remove the lectionary to its holder so I have room to do this. I guess for me it's a security blanket. Everything's in one place. I find this especially helpful at funerals and weddings. I have photocopied everything from the gospel to the homily to the liturgical texts and canons and put them all in one binder so I don't have to juggle four or five books. Anyway, some write out their homilies, others make outlines so they can be more spontaneous. If you write it out and bring it with you, it doesn't mean you have to read it. It's just there as a guide and security. Some find it helpful to dictate their homily to a tape recorder so they can hear how they'll sound to the congregation.

18. *Never repeat.* In the same parish never repeat a homily or a story. People will remember. Even if you move elsewhere, it's good to resist the temptation—except occasionally—to repeat past successes. Otherwise, you'll grow lazy and will succumb to just reaching into the file. It won't be long before you'll become stale. And don't bring living examples from another parish. One

of my favorite cartoons, entitled "Worst Moments in Ministry," shows a couple sitting there with arms folded and frowned faces as the caption reads, "Midway through his sermon illustration about 'a couple from my last church,' Pastor Fillbert realizes they came for a surprise visit" (*Leadership*, Winter/94).

19. *Remember your audience.* Remember, as we have reminded you before, that they are a TV image generation, that the mass media has shaped their imaginative world. Therefore homilies that depend exclusively on the old verbal rhetorical devices are not as effective anymore: repetition, biblical allusions—people no longer, alas, resonate to Abraham and Sarah, David and Goliath, Aaron and Marion, Ruth and Boaz—a rousing exhortation. People, we repeat, are a visual people. The question for the homilist therefore becomes, "How can I telecast the scriptural word?" That is, how can I call up the images that will make their mark? How I can make the words live in a story that will catch the imagination?

For example, suppose you're preaching on Memorial Day weekend. In the course of your homily you might say something like this:

We do well today to remember those who have gone before us, who laid down their lives that we might be free. Were it not for their noble sacrifices, we would not be here today, free to worship, free to assemble, free to be who we are. It would be a dishonor to their memories to take for granted our freedoms, an insult to their deaths to waste our lives, a desecration to their graves to barter away our souls to materialism, pollution and the slavery of addiction. Let us prove our gratitude by lives lived in the freedom of God's children.

That's quite good, I think. It has nice parallelisms and a good rhythmic message. But try this:

❏There was once an ancient temple bell famous for its beautiful tone. It had been commissioned by a king as a way of showing the people's devotion to Buddha; for the king's advisors had told him that making a huge temple bell in honor of the Buddha would secure the nation from foreign invasion. So the king approached the greatest bell maker in the realm. This man worked hard and produced many bells, but none that was extraordinary, none that had a special tone. Finally, he went to the king and told him that the only way to get the kind of bell he wanted was to sacrifice a young maiden. So soldiers were sent to find and fetch a young girl. Coming upon a poor mother in a farm village with her small daughter, they took the child away, while she cried out piteously, *"Emille! Emille!"*—"Mother, O Mother!" When the molten lead and iron were prepared, the little girl was thrown in. At last the bell maker succeeded. The bell, called the Emille Bell, made a sound more beautiful than any other.

When it rang, most people praised the art that had produced such a beautiful sound. But whenever the mother whose child had been sacrificed heard it, her heart broke anew. Her neighbors, who knew of her sacrifice and pain, could not hear the beautiful tone without pain either.

Only those who understand the sacrifice can feel the pain. Others just enjoy the sound.□

+   +   +

Both versions tell the same truth. The first version is fine. It's good rhetoric and gets a nod of the head. But the second version—the story version—is good imagination, a good verbal visual, and gets a response of the heart. And it ruminates and lingers longer.

(The story is from Lee Oo Chung in "One Woman's Confession of Faith" in *New Eyes for Reading: Biblical & Theological Reflections by Women from the Third World*, eds., Pobee and von Wartenberg-Potter, Geneva, 1986, pp. 19-20).

20. *Go, sit at the feet of the Master.* By this, I don't mean do the Martha/Mary contemplative thing, with Mary "choosing the better part." I mean that in every area within 50–100 miles of you there are outstanding preachers, Catholic or Protestant. Go sit in the pew and listen to them. Learn from them. Get out of your

books, your rectory, your classroom, and go and sit at the feet of a Master of any denomination.

21. *Finally, be humble.* It's good to remember that, like all human enterprises, our preaching does ebb and flow. Week after week, month after month, year after year—we're bound to go through some cycles. Hang in there. God's grace comes in through other cracks, as we hear from Flannery O'Connor *(The Habit of Being,* p. 348):

> Madison Jones stopped by here a few Saturdays ago and sat a good while. . . .It seems that his wife and four children are Catholics. He said he guessed he was intellectually convinced but just didn't have the faith. My cousin's husband who also teaches at Auburn came into the Church last week. He had been going to Mass with them but never showed any interest. We asked how he got interested and his answer was that the sermons were so horrible, he knew there must be something else there to make the people come.

When all is said and done, when all these principles have been carefully followed, sometimes reality operates differently. Sometimes an indifferent homily can work well because somehow the whole liturgy clicked and suddenly there was a synergy that made everything satisfying, even a terrible homily. On the other hand, a stunning homily that left people in ecstasy in Cinncinati leaves them throwing missalettes at you in Walla Walla. Not even a slight guffaw at your time-proven joke! What's wrong with these unregenerate people? As our priest friend says, "These things happen."

6.

SCRIPTURE AND STORY

In 1943 Pius XII gave the world the encyclical, *Divino Afflante Spiritu*, that opened up the study of Scripture for the Catholic world. And Vatican II, which ran from 1962 to 1965, furthered and expanded that encyclical by its document, *Verbum Dei*, issued in 1965, which led us to become very much a far more biblical church than we had been in the past hundreds of years. We were told to study Scripture and that our preaching was to be fundamentally nourished and ruled by it. In fact, which may surprise some clergy, the 1965 decree on the *Ministry and Life* of priests stated that celebrating the sacraments is *not* the main and primary duty of the clergy. It is preaching! "Priests as co-workers with their bishops, have as their *primary* duty the proclamation of the gospel of God to all" (Chapter II, article 4, emphasis mine). Perhaps we should not put too fine a point on this, for although

Vatican II's decree on priestly life does indeed say in article 4 that priests "have as their primary duty the proclamation of the Gospel of God to all," article 13 says, "Priests fulfill their chief duty in the mystery of the Eucharistic sacrifice."

In any case, the U.S. Bishops' Committee on Priestly Life, in its fine document called *Fulfilled in Your Hearing* (1982), wrote:

> These clear and straightforward words of the Second Vatican Council may still come as a surprise to us. We might more spontaneously think the primary duty of priests is the celebration of the church's sacraments, or pastoral care of the People of God. Yet, the words of the document are clear: the proclamation of the Gospel is primary. The other duties of the priests are to be considered properly presbyteral to the degree they support the proclamation of the gospel. . . .A key moment in the proclamation of the Gospel is preaching, preaching which is characterized by "proclamation of God's wonderful works in the history of salvation." . . . We also recognize that for the vast majority of Catholics, the Sunday homily is the normal and frequently the formal way in which they hear the word of God proclaimed. For these Catholics the Sunday homily may well be the most decisive factor in determining the depth of their faith and strengthening the level of their commitment to the church.

So, preaching is our primary duty and preaching the Scriptures, the word of God at that. Which means realizing that the Scriptures are pretty foreign to most folks. Agricultural motifs, kings, angels, demons, animal sacrifice, a strange pre-scientific cosmology, a lack of secondary causes—all these things are not compatible to the modern, scientific mindset. And yet, we have not only to know and study such Scriptures but to bring them into the twenty-first century. Fortunately, in the last 35 years there have been such tremendous developments in Scripture. A little intimidating, perhaps, but there. In fact, as Scripture scholar Wilfrid Harrington reminds us, there are five such developments.

First, there has been an explosion of resources for the study and reading and preaching of Scripture. There are new books, improved Greek texts, scholarly tools, concordances, dictionaries, and new translations from the cooperative efforts of Jews and Christians. It's quite overwhelming, but we have to keep up with some of it through reading, study, and current magazines and computer disks. That's all I want to mention here: there's lot out there.

Second, we have a more accurate history. We know so much more today about the biblical world and how New Testament Judaism was in fact very much a part of the Graeco-Roman world. If 30 years ago scholars focused on how different Jesus was from his contemporaries, today they focus on how much he fit into first-century Judaism. The point is that, through the journals such as *The Bible Today* or *Biblical Archaeological Review*, we should be in touch with that world and so make Scripture and our preaching more relevant, more colorful.

Third, interdisciplinary studies have also enlarged our knowledge of Jesus' times. Archaeology, which neither proves nor disproves anything, simply and powerfully reveals the times which in turn can illumine the biblical texts by making clear the situation presupposed by the text, by bringing to life what a metaphor might be referring to. Social history sees history from the ground up and highlights the differences between the biblical people and ourselves. In a word, the more we are in touch with the biblical world and its worldview and setting, the more alive the text becomes.

Fourth, there is the development of new hermeneutics or ways of interpretation. This places emphasis on the reader and his or her predispositions. Who and where I am has an effect on a text (e.g. feminists who remind us that important biblical characters have been overlooked by males). Liberation theologians help us to see the word from the point of view of the disenfranchised. Globalists look at texts as Asians, Africans, and Americans. All this has led to a new respect for the rabbis' and Church Fathers' interpretations.

Finally, there has been, in all this explosion and research, a great emphasis by the scholars on Scripture as literature—and here we begin to touch more closely on our topic of storytelling. Here the point is to focus on plot, structure, images, and underlying narratives. We are challenged to see the Bible as narrative, as story, *and* (as we shall see shortly) be aware of the reader's response or involvement in the text. For the Bible, as we are well aware, is a compendium of stories, laws, hymns, proverbs, poems, letters, and visions that are timely and unforgettable. Tom Winton, a prize-winning author and one of Australia's most popular, when asked about his Protestant church and what grabbed his imagination, answered (*Image*, Summer 1995, p. 50):

> When I look back I see two things. One is the complete lack of any intellectual life in that church community. I see a complete aridity of the physical and sensual life of the church. But I do remember the richness of the life of story that came out of that. The *storyness* of Scripture, its narrative nature, appealed to me instantly.

From the Catholic side, Andrew Greeley maintains that story— the biblical stories and their spinoffs—is the reason why Catholics stay in the church. It's the poetic, metaphorical, and ritual dimensions of our faith, he says (*New York Times Magazine*, 7/10/94) that are so captivating and possessing:

> Because we are reflective creatures we must also reflect on our religious experiences and stories; it is in the (lifelong) interlude of reflection that propositional religion and religious authority become important, indeed indispensable. But then the religiously mature person returns to the imagery, having criticized it, analyzed it, questioned it, to commit the self once more in sophisticated and reflective maturity to the story. . . .if you want to understand Catholics—and if Catholics want to understand themselves—the starting point is to comprehend the enormous appeal of that [religious] sensibility. It's the stories.

The biblical stories are captivating. They do work and they

ultimately give us a countercultural view of life and values. In other words, preaching the Bible story keeps our memories intact, our identity, our heritage. If you want a little schema, it would go like this: The current culture stresses individualism, the biblical revelation stresses community. The current culture stresses a voluntary social contract, the biblical revelation stresses a prior contract by God. The current culture stresses secularization, the biblical revelation stresses the vision of God as the Holy One.

In any case, Scripture is a literary communication, and thus we treat the Bible as literature as we do any other book. Thomas Long (*Preaching and the Literary Forms of the Bible*, Fortress, 1989, p. 66) expresses it this way:

> The . . . odd thing about biblical stories is that there are so many of them. There are battle stories, betrayal stories, stories about seduction and treachery in the royal court, stories about farmers and fools, healing stories, violent stories, funny stories and sad ones, stories of death, and stories of resurrection . . . the claim that the Bible is a "story book" is not far off the mark.

Therefore, simple literary analysis is the most basic starting point for reading and preaching the Bible. This requires no special training or sophistication in order to be aware of images, characters, plot, form, and theme, and so we can share these things easily and relate and translate them within the context of everyday life. This is what is called biblical conversion, that is, framing the common experiences of the congregation within the scriptural message. In other words, we are not so much explaining Scripture with a view to applying it to life as we are interpreting life in the light of Scripture. The biblical message is the same but it is allowed to contexualize current terminology and social situations. In a word, to approach Scripture as literature can activate our imaginations.

The easiest example I can think of is to take the Martha/Mary story to a group of church folk and ask them if they see themselves as Martha or Mary—and listen to the anger of the Marthas! Or, less threateningly, take the example of Jesus sleeping in the boat. "Don't you care that the waves are threatening?" can be converted into "Don't you care that children are homeless? people are dying? marriages are falling apart?" (The people can name their own lament.) The boat image of this famous gospel becomes contemporary and we can consider our place in its context.

Another example. Here's the introduction to a homily that uses biblical conversion. It's about the Bartimaeus story (Mk 10:46–52, from my book, *Telling Stories, Compelling Stories*):

❑If we are not blind, it is most difficult for us to imagine what it must mean to be that way day after day, year after year. We can get some inkling from Sheila Hock. She is a British housewife who for thirty long years had not been able to see. Then she was operated on. She was in the hospital when the bandages came off. She had never seen before and suddenly she saw. She explained later, "It was like an electric shock, as if something hit me." She had gotten a plate full of food, the first meal she ever saw, and she said, "I thought it would be easy to eat because I could see what I was doing. I would aim my fork for a piece of tomato and miss it." She had to close her eyes to be able to eat that first meal.

She went into the street to go home and said, "I looked at the pavement and it was moving and the lampposts and the trees were moving so fast that I wanted to shout stop!" Then she added, "I never knew the world was so beautiful. I had a picture in my mind of what I thought my husband looked like because I had felt his features, but he was a lot better looking than I thought and I was pleased about it."❑

Things like that, I imagine, must have happened to that man Bartimaeus at the moment he saw.

To be able to see suddenly must be a terrific experience. Very many people, even today, have that kind of experience in a spiritual way. I mean, they suddenly "see." They see all. They can't stop talking about it. They say that they see Jesus as their personal Savior, that they are born again and they write books and pamphlets with titles like "Suddenly I saw," meaning that they accepted the Lord Jesus Christ.

Your response to all of this might be: Good for them. Good for Sheila Hock. Good for Bartimaeus. I envy them. But me? Me, to tell the truth, I have a different experience. I feel like I'm still sitting in the dark crying out:

"Jesus, Son of David, have pity on me. I begin to clean the house and before I'm half finished, the dust is beginning to settle again. What's the use? I prepare a meal and while I'm doing it, I'm thinking of a menu for the next meal. And the cycle continues and no one cares. I was considered important when I was raising the children, but they're on their own now. Oh, I know they love me, but the fact is they have gone and they don't call or visit me that much. I work and my husband works, but we don't seem to get anywhere. I feel useless and I don't see anything down the road. I'm a blind beggar."

"Jesus, Son of David, have pity on me. I go to work and live with a company that does things I don't like. I disagree with the dog-eat-dog attitude and the ruthless methods that are used, but I feel stuck, powerless. My opinions don't seem to count. My job is not really secure. I'm too old to start anywhere else again and too young to retire. I have to protect my pension and my family's security. I take my paycheck and go and sit at the side of the road and don't see anything down it. I'm a blind beggar."

"Jesus, Son of David, have pity on me. I spend most of my time in a senior citizen's apartment. The children don't call very often. I'm no longer able to work or get around much. I feel useless and don't see anything down the road. I'm a blind beggar."

"Jesus, Son of David, have pity on me. Our marriage is falling apart. He won't go for counseling. We don't believe in divorce and the children need us. But it's a dead end. I dread the years ahead of just coping, arguing. I don't see any solution down the road. I'm a blind beggar."

+   +   +

See how powerful that can be. This is a Scripture that people can identify with as soon as they enter into the gospel story and change places with Bartimaeus.

I often use such conversion at a funeral homily (see my book, *More Telling Stories, Compelling Stories*, Homily 28) when the deceased had been suffering from cancer a long time. Using the traditional gospel of Lazarus (Jn 11:32–45) I make note of the four main characters in the gospel: Lazarus, Martha and Mary, Jesus, and the crowd. Lazarus has been wrapped round and round with the linen burial strips. So too the deceased; she has been wrapped slowly but surely round and round with illness, the hospital, medication, machines, the sickbed, and finally, death. Each week when people would visit they would see another strip. Martha and Mary are the family and relatives and friends who minister, weep, and pray. Jesus, the third character, comes as a friend, a grieving friend. The crowd are well wishers, co-workers, neighbors, those present at the funeral. It is all worked into an effective homily which has high identity with everyone.

Let me take this from another angle. L. Patrick Carroll, a Jesuit from Tacoma, Washington, told his congregation when he first got to his parish that he was determined to tell the Jesus story, and tell it, as he says, "over and over again until I got it right—until we got it right." He was in fact repeating Fr. Jack Shea's workshop theme: "I wasn't there; I didn't see him. I never witnessed a miracle, never heard a sermon he preached, never rejoiced in his presence. I wasn't there. I didn't see him, didn't hear him; didn't touch him. But some other people did, and they told their friends, who passed it on to other friends, who shared it with their children through generation after generation, one telling the other until, thank God, someone told me. I'm telling you so that you will never forget. It's the story of Jesus."

So Pat Carroll, who sat in many a pew, was dismayed to find out how few preachers preached Jesus—his life and message—and the connection to our lives today. To many people, he realized, it mattered little that Jesus walked on the water 2000 years ago, and that Peter walked with him. What matters to them, he knew, is whether, when they are sinking, Jesus—in whom they put their faith—will lift them up. What matters is whether they can muster the courage to step out of the boat into the storm. What matters is that there is a connection between the biblical story and theirs, whether they fit into the plot and relate to the character.

Pat says that you can take three stances to any gospel story. First, you can be the *Bystander*, watching the scene, letting it occur in the life of someone else and therefore be in awe of "the wonderful works of God." Second, you can be the *Object* of the words of ministry of Jesus, letting him speak to you or act upon you. Third, you can be the *Subject*, one of the agents getting Jesus to act in and through us as he did with his disciples. You can be the power and the presence of Jesus. Consider, for example, the healing of the paralytic man in Mark 2 who was let down through the roof. As a bystander you can be there in wonder and hope, helping the man get on the mat. To this degree, maybe the congregation has someone in mind they would place on the mat, someone in need, in want, they would bring to Jesus. As the Object, people can imagine themselves on the mat knowing that in fact *they* are paralyzed, unable to walk, love, forgive, be free. As the Subject, the people could be urged to *be* the presence of Jesus. They can be the encouragers, "Get up, take up your mat and walk!" They can be the reconcilers. "Your sins are forgiven!"

Bystander, Object, Subject—each category lends itself to being a character in the biblical story. We can enter into the scene, become part of the plot, take part in the dialogue, witness saving power, and so feel that same power in our lives.

Try this homily which I gave years ago (forgetting now its source) using Matthew 25.

"Come, you have my father's blessing. Inherit the kingdom prepared for you from the creation of the world. For I was hungry and you gave me food."

And Ida Bennett of Lexington, surprised to be there, will speak up and ask, "When did I ever see you hungry and feed *you*?" And Jesus will answer, "As long as you did it for Cecilia Bender, you did it for me." And Cecilia Bender, hearing her name, will step forward to speak. "I was born, as you say, mentally retarded. And as I grew to be a child I had less and less place in the normal world: no friends, no job, no family. I was left a vegetable. And so I would have remained if Ida Bennett here had not started Ida's

Deli. It was more than a place to eat. It was a place where people like me could find work. I found there a sense of my own worth. I was the sandwich maker there, and I was able to buy my own car and to learn to drive to work each day. Thanks, Ida."

"Come, you have my Father's blessing. For I was thirsty and you gave me to drink."

And Father Bob from Arizona will ask, "When did I see *you* thirsty?"

And Jesus will answer, "As long as you did it for Arlene Williams, you did it for me." And a woman with a bright smile on her face will step forward. "For years I was a secret and compulsive drinker," she will say. "One Sunday morning at church we had a young visiting priest who began his homily with the words, 'I am Father Bob, and I am an alcoholic.' He told how he had come to depend on alcohol. After Mass I went home—and got as drunk as I had ever been. Later I came back and talked to Father Bob. He offered me a drink—coffee, and he offered me the understanding support I needed to begin the difficult journey to sobriety. It saved my marriage, certainly."

"Come. For I was a stranger and you welcomed me."

And Gary Flannagan of Seattle will ask, "But when did I welcome you, a stranger?"

And Jesus will answer, "When you did it for Steve Carroll, it was for me." And Steve will be there to tell his story. "On July 16, 1986, I was at the Raritan Bridge looking down into the dark, swirling water 180 feet below. Despondent over business losses I was about to jump—when a police office came along. He talked me down gently and promised me help. In time and with professional counseling, I learned to handle my tensions and stresses better. That office who saved my life was Gary Flannagan here. In his years with the police department he has talked hundreds of persons out of suicide. For my life, thanks, Gary."

"I was naked and you clothed me."

And Dorothy Groll from Scarborough, Maine, will ask, "But when . . . ?"

And Al Donado will move beside her and take her hand. "I suffered from cerebral palsy," he will say. "I walked like a drunken man and slurred my speech. My parents had always been very protective. But after they died I was very much alone and afraid; yet I wanted some freedom. I found a job and moved into my own apartment, one designed for the handicapped. Dorothy Groll was 73 and then a widow. She lived across the hall. Every day she came in and would cook for me and do my laundry and shave me and, yes, dress me. Without her help it would have taken me two hours to put on my clothes. Thanks. Dot." And he will kiss Dorothy standing there at his side.

"I was ill and you comforted me."

Dr. Charles Hayne of Denver, Colorado will respond, "But I never treated *you."*

And Jesus will answer, "Never?" And Bill Perdoni will speak up. "I lost my sight in a machine shop accident. For 23 years I saw nothing. When I was 65, Dr. Hayne told me he thought a corneal transplant would restore me vision partially. He operated and when I opened my eyes, I could see again. It was a more wonderful and beautiful world than I had remembered—the rivers, the trees, the snow. Thanks, Doc."

"Come. For I was in prison and you visited me."

And this group will be very few in number. But Pat Reynolds will be standing next to Bob Irwin whom we had simply referred to as N 130539 at the state prison in Trenton, New Jersey, where he was serving a sentence for first degree murder. "Over the years," Bob would say, "Pat must have corresponded with hundreds of prisoners. These letters forged real friendships that helped to combat the loneliness which in prison can turn sanity into insanity. She helped me to see myself as a name, not a number. A person, not a reject. Thank you, dear friend."

Then the king will say to those on his left, "Out of my sight, you condemned . . . for I was hungry and you gave me no food . . ."

And those on the left will be heard muttering as they depart, "It's not fair. All I needed was one more day. I had already made plans to help out at the soup kitchen—tomorrow."

+ + +

You leave that hanging in the air and go sit down. It's a strong homily that does its biblical conversion thing and places our lives squarely within the gospel's challenge. And so it goes. There is fertile ground here in seeing Scripture not only as God's word but also as God's *literary* word, replete with images and stories waiting to be claimed by today's listeners. The preacher is one who truly brings new things from old.

7.

THE STORY IN OUR BONES

It is always salutary to remember that Jesus wasn't a lecturer. He was a storyteller. As Anthony de Mello, S.J., said—in true story form (*One Minute Wisdom*, Doubleday, 1986, p. 23):

> The Master gave his teaching in parables and stories, which his disciples listened to with pleasure—and occasional frustration, for they longed for something deeper. The master was unmoved. To all their objections he would say, "You have yet to understand that the shortest distance between a human being and Truth is a story."

The reason for this is that storytelling doesn't give the answers to life, but reveals life's meaning. The human experience is inherently narrative in form and our lives are played out in stories—as you can readily affirm at a funeral. What does the family instinctively do? They sit around the table and tell Mom or Pop stories. Jesus told stories or parables to a people who did not need or require literacy or complex reasoning, only life experience and imagination. As Barry Lopez puts it, "The stories people tell have a way of taking care of them. If stories come to you, care for them. And learn to give them away where they are needed. Sometimes a person needs a story more than food to stay alive. That is why we put these stories in each other's memory. This is how people care for themselves."

Stories arose around the campfire where people spoke and exchanged experiences. For life always takes place in the particular, always in a story. That's why many contemporary theologians have taken an interest in story, not as the key to life's ultimate questions, but as the way in which life's meaning is revealed. In short, we don't tell stories to prove a point or hammer out a lesson, but to disclose a way of looking at life, a way of seeing. If you remember, for example, Harper Lee's novel or the film, *To Kill a Mockingbird*, you get an artistic narrative of the way people see blacks and whites, justice and injustice; a way of seeing issues. W. H. Auden was right in saying, "You cannot tell people what to do; you can only tell them parables." Stories also stand in contrast to "propositional" sermons, the old deductive method: a thesis plus three points to prove it; or, as we used to say, "tell them what you're going to say, say it, and then tell them what you have said." And that's why a story moves like a narrative rather then like a syllogism—like life itself. Moreover, not every element of a story has to fit, not every element has to make sense or be reduced to a comparison. It's the overall impact that counts. And impact us it does, which is why stories are so appealing.

We are in fact natural storytellers. "Wait till I tell so and so that . . ." easily springs from our lips. Writers simply capitalize on this universal impulse. "Once upon a time" settles us all down and makes us receptive. That's because all stories replay humankind's oldest metaphor: that of the journey. We all have a beginning, middle, and end. Stories recount that always. Stories are us. A good story invites us to enter into other people's experiences and make them our own. Moreover, stories basically are valuable as "variations on a sacred theme"; or, more exactly, as we have seen, reinterpretations or biblical conversions of the scriptural story. They are extensions, expansions, and carry the message forward. They have innate, natural appeal for they hit the right brain. They give healing. Note, as we said above, the first impulse at a wake: stories that re-connect, re-member. They are redemptive, especially the lives of the saints, heroes, heroines, the liturgy. So, stories touch us and give us both a personal and imaginative way of knowing truth. Even if we don't always catch the point of a good story, it comes back to haunt us. People remember stories long after the moralizing has died down, which is why we use them in homilies. Stories are evocative. Or, as they say, "Stories begin when the teller stops talking."

I like what Eugene Lowry says (*Doing Time in the Pulpit*, Abingdon, 1985, p. 91):

Anytime you tell a story, you open the door for metaphor to operate. When, for example, you describe the apprehension a child experiences in moving to a new school, you have done more than describe moving to a new school. You have produced a metaphor that touches images of apprehension throughout the congregation. You may not have intended to address that person who is about to retire from the railroad ... and that person may not be able to identify just what the connection was, but impact—however undefined propositionally—happened.

On a grander scale—if you want to wax philosophical for a moment—stories form our national and religious landscape. As Marina Warner says, "Stories held in common make and remake the world we inhabit." The stories we tell shape our thinking and our actions. Which is why, worrisome to many, are the mass media stories that shape the spiritual and moral consciousness of people, especially television. Warner speaks, for instance, of the warrior myths that dominate television:

Slaying monsters, controlling women, still offers a warrant for the emerging hero's heroic character; this feeds the definition of him as a man. But this narrative . . . has come away from the studs that held it to the inner stuff of experience: warrior fantasies today offer a quick rush of compensatory power but pass on no survival skills—either for a working or a family life.

She speaks of the stories, now unfortunately seldom told, about poor boys and little foxes who, without weapons, but with intelligence and high spirits outwit the monsters and the bullies. In a word, stories that say might doesn't make right and the possibility of change and growth is always there *(Six Myths of Our Time*, Vintage Books, 1995).

Piggy-backing on this, Kathleen O'Connell Chesto reminds us that by the ages of 2 to 4, a child's morality is already formed. She writes:

> Children have developed whatever sense of storytelling they will probably ever have. If parents don't tell the story of their experience through the eyes of faith, then children will not find God in their own experiences. . . .The only people who are telling stories to our children right now are on television. And the problem isn't just the kind of stories they're telling; it's the reasons they're telling them. We tell our children stories so they'll grow in wisdom and courage and will know who they are. Television tells them stories to sell them.

Perhaps William Bennett's book, *The Book of Virtues*, is so popular because parents realize the need for stories alternate to the exploitation and violence of the TV stories. As Bennett says in his introduction, "Along with precept, habit and example, there is also the need for what is called moral literacy." All this may seem like a wide excursion from our main point, but we should really appreciate the power of stories on a personal, moral, and metaphysical scale.

As Barbara Myerhoff wrote about her grandmother who raised her: "Sofie knew and taught me that everyone had some story, every house held a life that could be penetrated and known, if one took the trouble. Stories told to oneself or others could transform the world. . ." (*Number Our Days*, E.P. Dutton, 1979).

To put it all in the memorable words of George Gerbner of the Annenberg School of Communications, "If you can control the storytelling of a nation, you don't have to worry about who makes the laws."

So, to summarize: stories are appealing because narrative is written into our nature. We *are* a narrative. They are appealing because we have an innate curiosity. We want to hear the ending. We want to know "whodunit." They are appealing because they have many layers of meaning and so they "rinse" through us long after we hear them. Think of a good movie that sticks with you for many days, perhaps years. That's testimony to the ruminating power of story: it often provokes silence. As Leslie Kane puts it so elegantly, in *The Language of Silence: On the Unspoken and the Unspeakable in Modern Drama* (London: Associated University Presses, 1984):

> The dumb silence of apathy, the sober silence of solemnity, *the fertile silence of awareness, the active silence of perception,* the baffled silence of confusion, the uneasy silence of impasse, the muzzled silence of outrage, the expectant silence of waiting, the reproachful silence of censure, *the tacit silence of approval,* the vituperative silence of accusation, *the eloquent silence of awe,* the unnerving silence of menace, *the peaceful silence of communion,* and the irrevocable silence of death illustrate by their unspoken response to speech that experiences exist for which we lack the word. (emphasis mine)

How often people would tell me gratefully that they thought that in my homily I was talking directly to them. But I knew in my heart that it was the stories that got to them. Again, stories are appealing because they touch our sensate side, our imaginations with smells and touches and images that last. They are appealing because, in a sense, every story is our story.

But now to the main question: how do we do it? How do we tell stories, specifically in a homily? How can we be creative and how does this creativity happen? For some, of course, creativity comes naturally. They're born with it. ("Curse you, Red Baron!") They have a natural "third eye," in the phrase of St. Bonaventure (the eye of the soul or contemplation). Such people help us see what's already there, as we said—selling river water by the Jordan. That's just a fact of life and we can't do much about it. For those less naturally gifted, we can nevertheless acquire some skills. And we can become good at it. It's just that we have to work at it. "Working at it" suggests basically that we begin by studying those who in fact have the "third eye" and learn from them. Fr. Frank McNulty, a wonderful preacher himself, suggests five such categories of people and let's end this chapter by taking a look at them.

1. *Study the artists.* Not just those with paint and a brush, but sculptors, playwrights, columnists, novelists, and movie directors. Reading or listening to Garrison Keillor's books or tapes, for example, can show you the art of narrative. I suppose Alan Paton could have flatly declared that apartheid is wrong, but his novel, his story, *Cry, the Beloved Country,* says it far more powerfully. Pasternak's *Doctor Zhivago* does the same with oppression in the Soviet Union.

We should also study the artists' works to stir our own homiletic imaginations. Take a good look at them. If we are attentive to those works, we can start describing them in language. After all, the artists themselves have been attentive as to how light plays on a surface (look at the master of light, Vermeer), how snow rests on a bough, how a mallard takes to the wind, how beads of dew glisten on a spider's web. They see attentively. The challenge for the storyteller's imagination is always, "What do you see?" As the interrogator in the movie *The Silence of the Lambs* asks, "Hannibal Cannibal, what do you see?" Yahweh asks, "Amos, what do you see?" (Amos 7:8) Jesus asks the blind man whose eyes have been rubbed with clay, "What do you see?" It is important to look at the works of the artists and try to see what they see and put it into words, into stories, so that our listeners may see.

2. *Study the poets.* John Mella writes in the *New York Times Book Review*:

It has seemed to me for a long time that the entire apparatus of poetry workshops, writing schools, etc. would be better off totally dismantled and replaced with what Robert Graves assures us was the ancient Welsh method of training poets: by having would-be poets memorize thousands of lines of poems and composing their own work (after this rigorous apprenticeship) strictly on classical models.

Joe Nolan comments that such memorization is good for the savoring of wisdom, a sowing of the seed, the love of the language, and the preaching of better sermons.

As Frederick Buechner, a wonderful and powerful author, wrote in his autobiography about his old English teacher, Mr. Martin:

I had always been a reader and lover of words for the tales they could tell and the knowledge they can impart and the world they can conjure up like Scarecrow's Oz and Claudius' Rome; but this teacher, Mr. Martin, was the first to give me a feeling for what words are, and can do, in themselves. Through him I started to sense that words, not only convey something, but *are* something; that words have color, depth, texture of their own, and the power to evoke vastly more than they mean; that words can be used, not merely to make things clear, make things vivid, make things interesting and whatever else, but make things happen inside the one who reads or hears them . . . .

The poets give us memorable images and word pictures. We have Shakespeare's word for it (*A Midsummer Night's Dream,* Theseus, Act V):

The poet's eye, in a fine frenzy rolling,
Doth glance from heaven to earth, from earth to heaven;
And as imagination bodies forth

The form of things unknown, the poet's pen
Turns them to shapes, and gives to airy nothing
A local habitation and a name.

He practices what he preaches. Read his *Winter*:

When icicles hang by the wall,
    And Dick the shepherd blows his nail,
And Tim bears logs into the hall,
    And milk come frozen home in pail,
When blood is nipp'd and ways be foul
Then nightly sings the staring owl,
    Tu-whit;
Tu-who, a merry note,
While greasy Joan doth keel the pot.

Then there's Christopher Marlowe's "face that launched a thousand ships/ And burnt the topless towers of Ilium"; and Joseph Mary Plunkett's

I see his blood upon the rose
And in the stars the glory of his eyes,
His body gleams amid eternal snows,
His tears fall from the skies.

or Emily Dickinson's lovely imagery:

I'll tell you how the sun rose,
A ribbon at a time.
The steeples swam in amethyst,
The news like squirrels ran.

What about Gerard Manley Hopkins's "The world is charged with the grandeur of God/ It will flame out, like shining from shook foil." Or his poem "Christ Speaks":

To him who ever thought with love of me
Or ever did for my sake some good deed
I will appear, looking such charity
And kind compassion, at his life's last need
That he will out of hand and heartily
Repent he sinned and all his sins be freed.

There are Poe's lines:

> Hear the sledges with the bells,
> Silver bells!
> What a world of merriment their melody foretells!
> How they tinkle, tinkle, tinkle,
> In the icy air of night!
> While the stars that oversprinkle
> All the heavens seem to twinkle
> With a crystalline delight;
> Keeping time time, time,
> In a sort of Runic rhyme . . .

T.S. Eliot's line is memorable: "When the evening is spread out against the sky/ Like a patient etherized upon a table . . ."

It might be helpful to take a literature course at a community college or listen to tapes such as Bishop Robert Morneau's *The Power of Narrative: Poetic Stories and Stories of Poets* (Alba House).

3. *Check out the saints.* Their lives are colorful and dramatic, to say the least. There's some wonderful writings these days on the saints from the old Thurston-Atwater *Butler's Lives of the Saints* to Joan Windham's delightful *Sixty Saints for Children* to Leonard Foley's *Saints of the Day* and Michael Walsh's *The Book of Saints.* The Desert Fathers, for example, thrill us with their eccentric lives which were meant to teach us that "man can derive his life either from God or from the earth, and one way in which the lives of the desert saints can convey to us how much they depended on God, is to show us how little they depended upon earth" (Anthony Bloom). The Desert Fathers are perfect examples of what Flannery

O'Connor said when asked about the absurd and bizarre characters in her short stories. She defended them by saying that in a deaf world you have to shout. The Desert Fathers were shouters. Long, long before modern environmental consciousness, they had an enormous sense of the sanctity of all things. All that was made by God was holy. The stars were sacred, and so were spider webs and grasses waving in the wind. They spoke to animals as the later Celtic saints would frolic with otters, use a docile deer's antlers on which to rest their psalm books while they sang, and turn back the waves. Still later, Francis would preach to the birds and sing of Brother Sun and Sister Moon—all powerful symbols of the wholeness of holiness. The Desert Fathers, moreover, had wonderful sayings, teachings, and stories that were a kind of combination of parables and folk wisdom.

How's this for detachment? An old monk lay dying. His brethren were standing around his bed putting the habit on him and weeping, but he opened his eyes and laughed; then he laughed a second and a third time. The brethren asked him, "Abba, tell us how it is that while we are weeping, you are laughing?" He said to them, "I laughed because you all fear death; I laughed a second time because you are not ready; and I laughed a third time because I am leaving labor for rest." And immediately the old monk fell asleep.

I always liked this one:

☐Abba Abraham was a holy man and a great ascetic. He had eaten nothing but herbs and roots for fifty years in the desert. He lived simply and austerely. One day his brother in the city died and left a niece. There was no one to care for her so Abba Abraham, out of charity, took her in and nourished and cherished her. She grew up to be beautiful both in body and spirit. One day, a wandering monk came to hear a word of wisdom from Abba Abraham and was smitten by the beauty of his niece. While taking advantage of the hospitality offered by Abba Abraham who was out taking care of a sick monk elsewhere, he was overcome with lust and raped the girl.

She was so humiliated and ashamed that she fled Abba Abraham's dwelling and ran to the city where, feeling so violated and disgraced, she became a prostitute. In vain, Abba Abraham looked for his niece until one day he heard about her, what she had become, and that she was plying her trade at a certain tavern. Abba Abraham disguised himself as a military man, went to the tavern, and loudly ordered bottles of red wine and rich meat. He ate to his heart's content, downed it all to the amazement of onlookers and, when he was finished, asked the innkeeper for that "wench named Mary." "I have come a long way for the love of Mary," he shouted. She was brought to him but did not recognize this hard eating, hard drinking soldier. He grabbed her around the waist and she said coquettishly, "What do you want?" And he stopped and looked into her eyes and said softly, very softly, "I have come for the love of Mary." She immediately recognized her uncle and she wept bitterly and returned home with him.

She became known as St. Mary the Harlot. But Abba Abraham, who not for 50 years ate meat, did that night "for the love of Mary."□

The lives and times of the saints, the myths and legends about them are a rich mine of storytelling.

4. *Check out the cartoonists and the comics.* We laugh at Hagar, Cathy, For Better or For Worse, B.C., Hi and Lois because they are modern-day parables and we see ourselves in them. The political cartoonists give us a sometimes sardonic look at life but they can reveal the nonsense, in a few strokes of the drawing pen, in overly solemn and pretentious issues. Other cartoonists often have a wonderfully insightful and sometimes delightful way of looking at things. Think of Bil Keane's "Family Circus." Some present us with a "theater of the absurd" that forces us to look at things from another point of view. Think of Gary Larson's hilarious and fantastical Far Side cartoons or *The New Yorker's* sophisticated ones. In one way or another, in an imaginative way, they are all commentaries of life and, as such, are material for the homilist's craft.

5. *Check out the storytellers.* Jonesborough,Tennessee, as you might know, hosts a storytelling festival each year. They produce great books and tapes (The National Storytelling Press, P.O. Box 309, Jonesborough, TN 37659). Robert Bela Wilhelm (Storyfest

Productions, 18934-A Rolling Road, Hagerstown, MD 21742) gives workshops, storyfests, and produces tapes. Read or listen to anything by Jack Shea and Megan McKenna. The homily services, as I mentioned before, all have stories to fit the homily. Reading or listening to stories will stimulate your own storytelling abilities and at least give you a resource for stories. And be sure to listen to both male and female artists, storytellers. Feminist theologian Elisabeth Schüssler Fiorenza reminds us:

I have patiently listened to diatribes against the desire for power, the lust after pride—sermons that may reflect male drives and sins but do not take into account the need of women to take control over their own lives or to be encouraged in their search for self-affirmation. I have have listened to sermon after sermon denouncing our consumerist attitudes and self-serving wealth, sermons addressing the upper middle class members of the congregation but not those who struggle for economic survival. A homilist who has just returned sun-tanned from a vacation in Florida or Arizona is ill-equipped to preach against the consumerism of a suburban housewife who has not had a vacation in years.

And in commenting on a previous address by Walter Burghardt she writes (*Preaching Better*, p. 58):

. . . in this context [of preaching about Advent, Burghardt] states that he pauses to read Shakespeare, Gerard Manley Hopkins, and Tennessee Williams, and to listen to Beethoven, Barber, Tschaikowsky and even a dash of country music. He listens to the poets and musicians of his culture in order to formulate the details of the homily and enflesh the topic. Yet I was surprised that he does not think of taking into account the experiences of pregnant women and their sense of self. I wonder whether the male poets and artists he mentions can give his sermon the detail, sensitivity, and insight that he would need for presenting the pregnant Mary of Nazareth as a paradigm of Christian Advent hope. Instead, listening to the experiences of women with pregnancy, their fears, hope, trouble, and anxieties, their various experiences in giving birth and their exhilaration in touching the newborn child might have illumined and concretized our understanding of advent waiting. . . .One might also listen to single mothers on welfare or to women at the checkout counter trying to feed and clothe their children. If the word has to become flesh in the homily, then it must become flesh in the particular experiences of those about whom the homily speaks.

So, that is some suggested background to nurture whatever creativity we have. In the following chapter, we will get more specific. Meanwhile, we end with a story. Why not? And you might be thinking, what Scripture could this story open up?

☐Once upon a time in a forest, three young trees were growing side by side. As they grew, they shared with one another their dreams of what they would become when they grew to be big trees. The first tree said, "My dream is to become a part of a luxurious home where many famous people come and go and admire the grain and color of my wood." The second tree said, "My dream is to become a tall mast of an elegant sailing vessel that journeys to the seven seas." And the third said, "My dream is to become a part of a great tower, so high that it will inspire people who look at it. People will come from all over the world to see it."

And so the young trees dreamed. Eventually the trees grew to maturity and were cut down. The first didn't become a part of a luxurious home, as it had dreamed, but instead some of its wood was fashioned into a simple manger, a wooden trough to hold the hay that animals ate. The second tree didn't became the tall mast of an elegant ship, as it had dreamed, but instead became the side of an ordinary fishing boat like many others on the Sea of Galilee. The third didn't become a part of a tall tower, as it had dreamed, but was fashioned into the beams of a cross and used for a crucifixion.

8.

BASICS

Martin Thielen is a Baptist minister. Listen to him ("Beyond Infosermon" in *Leadership*, Winter 1994):

In my early years of ministry, my preaching was strong on principles, ideas, information. I encouraged listeners to take notes. But as the years passed, I concluded that effective preaching is not ultimately about points, outlines and information as much as about helping people make contact with God . . .

I've been preaching for twenty years. I served as a youth speaker during high school, an associate pastor during college, a student pastor during seminary, and a senior pastor after seminary. For four years I served as editor of *Proclaim*, the Southern Baptist journal for biblical preaching. Now I'm back in the pastorate. And I'm convinced one of the best ways to impact people is to follow Jesus' example in preaching.

Jesus' primary style of preaching was storytelling. When Jesus wanted to teach people about the love and grace of God, he didn't say, "Let me share three principles about God's love." Instead he said, "There was a man who had two sons . . ."

During my early years of preaching, I used stories to illustrate my point; today stories often *are* my point. My favorite method of preaching is to take a biblical story, retell it as creatively as possible, develop one primary point from that story and reinforce it with several contemporary stories.

Several comments. Storytelling the word appeals to right-brain activity, the senses, the imagination. And this is the theme of this book. But we should not dismiss the left brain homily, the expository, the teaching. For solid theological content is needed and it's worth noting that the first Christian writings were not the stories of the gospel but the theological letters of St. Paul. I just want to stress both the importance of expository homilizing and the deliberately limited focus of this book.

Secondly, those "contemporary stories" he mentions must be at hand. As we mentioned before, either buy books that have stories in them for the preacher or cull and save your own from whatever sources you can. For example, Mark Link has volumes of stories that relate to the Sunday liturgies, *Illustrated Sunday Homilies* (Tabor Publications). Take the story that ended the last chapter, the story of the three trees. It could be used in many contexts: disappointment, shattered dreams, and so on. The Scripture could be the seed that must fall into the ground in order to live, the parable of the talents, or other texts that have a death-resurrection motif. The connection of life situations, story, and the Scripture is an art. You have to have an ear for it, but practice can help. You might practice by taking some of the stories you find in this volume or in others and see how they might match up to and unpack the Scripture. For a good illustration of this, see my *Storytelling: Faith and Imagination*, Chapter 9.

Here, for example, is a good story waiting to be wed to a Scripture passage:

❑There once were two men, both seriously ill, in the same small room in the hospital. In fact, the room was so small that there was only one small window in it looking out on to the world. One of the men could move somewhat and was allowed once a day to sit up in his bed next to the window. So, on those occasions he could look out. Which is why his bed was next to the window. But the other man had to spend all his time flat on his back. Which is why his bed was not near the window.

Every afternoon when the man next to the window was propped up for his hour of treatment, he would pass the time describing to his roommate what he could see outside. From what he described, the window apparently overlooked a park where there was a lake. There were ducks and swans in the lake and children came to throw them bread and to sail model boats. Young lovers walked hand in hand beneath the trees and there were flowers and stretches of grass and games of softball. And at the back, behind the ring of trees, was a fine view of the city skyline.

All this the man patiently described to his roommate to lift his spirits. He told him how a child nearly fell into the lake and how lovely the girls were in their summer dresses and all kinds of adventuresome things to pass the time away. His roommate could almost feel he was there in the park.

Then one afternoon a dark thought hit him. Why should the man next to the window have all the pleasure of seeing what was going on? Why shouldn't he get the chance? It wasn't fair. He tried to stifle such thoughts, but each day, like Saul's jealousy of David, they became stronger and soured his soul. Something had to change. Well, one night as he lay with his thoughts staring at the ceiling, the man suddenly woke up with a start. He coughed and choked and tried to grope for the button that would bring the nurse running. The man, watching all this silently, managed to push the button just out of reach. In the morning, the nurse found the other man dead and quietly took his body away.

As soon as it seemed decent, the man asked if he could be switched to the bed near the window. So they moved him, tucked him in and made him quite comfortable. The minute they left, he laboriously propped himself up on one elbow and looked out the window.

It faced a blank wall.☐

+   +   +

You have to be careful that you don't use a story for its own sake, just because it's good and will get attention. If it doesn't relate to anything, then it's just another good story and leaves people in it rather moving beyond it The same way, you can start a homily with a joke as I did in the Easter homily I used in chapter 5, but not too often. In that homily, the joke came back at the end as a challenge ("Hit the ball, drag Jesus, hit the ball, drag Jesus"). If you always open with a joke, then you have the people looking forward to the Joke of the Week—and then tune you out for the rest of the message.

Don't hesitate to recycle and reinterpret a story. You can adjust a story to fit your agenda. The evangelists did that all the time with Jesus' parables. So did the Fathers of the Church. Here's one from Gregory the Great in his famous *Dialogues* (full of fabulous stories). In Book Two, Gregory tells many fantastical stories about St. Benedict, one being:

☐A simple and sincere Goth was brought by one Maurus, a pious Roman nobleman, to Subiaco to become a monk under blessed Benedict. One day Benedict had the man take a large brush hook to clear the briars from a place near the edge of a lake where a garden was to be planted. While the Goth was hard at work cutting down the thick brush, the iron blade flew off the handle and plopped down in the deepest part of the lake, where there was no hope of recovering it. This poor man ran trembling to Maurus and, after describing the incident, told him how embarrassed and sorry he was to be so clumsy. Maurus in turn went and told Benedict the whole story. Benedict went down to the lake, took the handle from the Goth and thrust it into the water. Immediately the iron blade rose from the bottom of the lake and slipped back onto the handle. Then he handed the tool back to the Goth and told him, "Continue with your work now. There is no need to be upset."◻

Now if you were a conversant Bible reader, you would find that this story is recycled from 2 Kings 6:4–7. The point is, if a story is good one and makes a point it can be used in a flexible way, changing some details, coming in with a different punch line. That's valid. Stories are like that; they ask to be reworked. What could you do with this one?

◻In the first grade, Miss Grant said that my purple tepee wasn't realistic enough, that purple was no color at all for a tent, that purple was the color of people when they died, that my drawing wasn't good enough to hang with the others. I walked back to my seat, head bowed. With a black crayon, I brought nightfall to my purple tent in the middle of the afternoon.

In second grade, Mrs. Abate said, "Draw anything." She didn't care what. I left my paper blank and when she came around to my desk, my heart beat like a tom-tom while she touched my head with her small hand and in a soft voice said, "The snowfall. How clean and white and beautiful." (Obviously one who would not "crush the bruised reed nor snuff out the smoldering wick.")◻

I prefer the deductive method of using stories. That is, I open up with the text's main theme and then usually develop three points. For each point I have a story (as you will observe in the next section). One story for each point is hardly necessary and for some a bit much. In any case, the story must be apropros and short. Too long or too convoluted a story will lose people. Certainly, three such will. Sometimes, very rarely, the Scripture is so succinct (by lectionary design or your own), and the seasonal context is such, that a single long story will do. I did that in Homily 13, "Abbot Macarius." Notice that I did two things. One, I omitted the fuller lectionary version of Mark's gospel which went from verses 39–45. Those verses talked about a blind man leading a blind man and a good tree not producing bad fruit and a bad tree not producing good fruit and the plank in your brother's eye. There were three ideas here—never a sound notion for a seven- to ten-minute homily to sound byte people—and to that extent they were distracting from a good single message, the one I chose, hypocrisy. So I read only the short passage beginning with "Why look at the speck in your brother's eye when you miss the plank in your own?" and told the story.

Sometimes I do that when the chosen reading has too many thoughts or, on other occasions, stops too quickly. You will find one of those occasions, for example, in Homily 9, "Hope." I wanted to play on the verses of the Magnificat that strangely were omitted. So I added them in the reading.

Well now, when all is said and done, and you really can't get into storytelling the word as much as you like to, what do you do? Borrow! Borrow preachable stuff. Borrow stories and homilies. You stand in a long tradition if you do. Aristotle, Milton, Coleridge, Dickens, Byron, Shakespeare, Disraeli, Churchill, and Alex Haley were all charged with stealing material. As Raymond Bailey, writing in the *Concise Encyclopedia of Preaching* (John Knox, Westminster, 1995), observes:

> The clergy have not escaped the temptation to steal sermons and illustrations. King James found plagiarism so widespread in Elizabethan England that he issued a decree that every preacher should deliver at least one original sermon per month. Famous preachers such as Cotton Mather, Peter Marshall and Martin Luther King, Jr., have been publicly accused of borrowing freely from others without crediting them.

But remember, those of us who write homily books and homily services write them precisely so that others *can* have resources at hand, can copy them, use them, borrow from them. After all, we're all colleagues in preaching the word of God and getting the word out is what counts. And it's far better to borrow and preach a captivating idea or story than to put forth indifferent, uninspiring original ones.

Most of us, anyway, borrow what we preach. I rely on people like Joe Nolan, Walter Burghardt, William Willimon, and several homily services. After all, choirs and lectors are always giving forth other people's words! However, if you borrow substantially, it is proper to mention the source. If you use direct quotes, then you must give some brief attribution (as I just did above with the Raymond Bailey quote). In any case, if you borrow, you have to really identify with the story or the homily. You can't force yourself into someone else's thoughts and expressions if they're foreign to you. It will show. You have to personalize someone else's homily, adding your own touches. And, as I said above, while you should give some attribution for substantial borrowing, you do not have to announce directly and publicly, "The homily this morning is courtesy of Walter Burghardt." First of all, they won't know who he is. Second, it just muddies the water. But, third, on the other hand, don't lie. If someone compliments you on a good homily, tell him where you got it (especially if it's from Bill Bausch). Otherwise, you know what's going to happen? When visiting another parish on vacation, your complimentor will hear the same homily and become suspicious. Generally too, you should not tell someone else's story as if it happened to you. You can always use the third person. There may be rare exceptions when it's called for, but not often.

So much for the advice. Now we get ready to homilize. Part 2 contains over 40 homilies. They attempt to illustrate what I have written. I guess, when all is said and done, we just have to get out there and do our best. But, hopefully, these chapters will make it easier or at least give us encouragement to do our best by trying the way of the story. And take heart, contemplating the words of Garrison Keillor *(We Are Still Married,* Viking Penguin, 1990):

To know and to serve God, of course, is why we are here, a clear truth, that, like the nose on your face, is near at hand and easily discernible but can make you dizzy if you try to focus on it hard, but a little faith will see you through. What else will do *except* faith in such a cynical, corrupt time? When the country goes temporarily to the dogs, cats must learn to be circumspect, walk on fences, sleep in trees, and have faith that all this woofing is not the last word.

Gentleness is everywhere in daily life, a sign that faith

rules through ordinary things: cooking and small talk, through storytelling, making love, fishing, tending animals and sweet corn and flowers, through sports, music and books, raising kids—all the places where the gravy soaks in and grace shines through.

And then there's George Herbert, not to make us smug, but to comfort us:

Judge not the preacher, for He is thy judge;
If thou mislike him, thou conceiv'st Him not.
God calleth preaching folly; do not grudge
To pick out treasures from an earthen pot.
    The worst speak something good;
        if all want sense,
        God takes a text, and preacheth patience.

And, finally, this from Sean Caufield, an Idaho pastor (*America* 8/13/95):

Good preaching, however, is not determined by theology alone; it is a special sort of gift. Not every priest has that gift. Many informed and otherwise intelligent men lack imagination, an essential ingredient in any good homily. Imagination can make Scripture interesting and tedious theology attractive. It can make what is difficult understandable. Imagination cannot be taught, and a man should not be faulted for the lack of a gift God never gave him. One might console oneself with the thought that the preacher is sincere, at best, at worst a stand-up comedian—though a sense of the incongruous, a dry wit used sparingly is acceptable. It is conceivable that the poor homilist might be good with the sick or the repentant—unimaginative, perhaps, but compassionate. It is sufficient. Most priests have no more than one gift that they use well.

PART 2

HOMILIES TO GO

Before reading these homilies...

Here are a few things to keep in mind in this section of 42 homilies:

1. Do remember the title of this book, *Storytelling the Word,* and its intent to show how to weave stories into the homily in order to unpack the sacred text. This means that if you read them one after the other non-stop you're going to become nauseated. One steak is great. The second one is good. The third one is a bit much. The fourth one will make you throw up. In other words, back to back, a whole series of story homilies can get a bit cloying. Thus, it is helpful to keep in mind (a) that these homilies were given over a period of months and years, (b) that they are not necessarily the best: I'm not especially pleased with some of them; I've done better—but they are gathered here (c) to demonstrate the principles of Part 1 and, (d) if nothing else, to give you some material to work with. (By the way, to show you that I can give a homily without a story, Homilies 1, 16, 18, 40, and 42 are storyless.) Anyway, enjoy the homilies. Not all will appeal to everyone, of course, but I hope enough will be helpful and (the greatest flattery) worthy of plagiarism.

2. Remember, too, what you have here is the *written* word. These homilies were delivered with all the inflections and nuances of voice, the shift and roll of the eyes, the gesture of the hand, the rising volume based on the old premise of "shout here, argument weak." Sometimes it might be helpful to read them aloud or into a tape recorder and then listen to them.

3. It is obvious that the stories in these homilies can be interchanged and recycled to other themes. To demonstrate this, I have included a homily entitled "The Transfiguration" (32) with a notation at its beginning indicating the recycled material and its source in other homilies.

4. It's advantageous to check the notes at the end of the series. They give some insights and sources.

5. If you figure that there are often up to three stories in a homily, you get about a hundred stories in this book if you add the stories scattered in Part 1. After you have read a homily for its overall impact, you might go back and review how each story is used.

(Remember, I have placed a square [□] before and after each story.) But please do that *after* you have read the homily. You want its total sense and do not want to begin picking out parts until you've experienced the whole.

6. Each homily has a reference after its title indicating the Lectionary reading and the Sunday it is assigned to.

It's a good idea to go back and read the Scripture passage first, so you can get the force of its homiletic development, a sense of the theme.

7. I remind you of the Appendix which gives you over 130 homilies (from this book and from my three other homily books) listed according to the liturgical year with its Lectionary scriptural references.

1. THE SAINTLY CHORUS

(Rev 7:2–4, 9–14 All Saints Years A,B,C)

Today's feast of All Saints is one of my favorite feasts because it conjures up that great panoramic and majestic scene that was presented to us in the first reading. It conjures up those vast multitudes of 144,000 multiplied endlessly. It conjures up the fact that, with all this incredible, astronomical number of people whom we call holy, that this feast is, when you come right down to it, a paean to God's mercy, to God's all-inclusiveness; and when we sing *When the Saints Come Marching In*, indeed it provokes an inspiring and truly awesome feeling.

The feast of All Saints evokes many observations. Wise ones like this from Sidney Harris: "The saint loves people and uses things. The sinner loves things and uses people." Or the always quotable Oscar Wilde: "The only difference between a saint and a sinner is that every saint has a past and every sinner has a future." So this feast is a fascinating and colorful tableau to contemplate.

But this morning I would like to forgo the grandeur and the pageantry that the feast of trillions of saints evokes in our minds and I would like to offer a different focus and imagery of the saints, the saints of the past, the saints who are present among us. And the imagery I would like you to think about when you think of this feast of All Saints is that of a *chorus*. Get into the mood. Close your eyes for a moment, if you wish, and picture yourself standing in a chorus of an endless 144,000 people, singing a song of faith, singing aloud, if you will, the Creed. And I ask you to be aware of two things that will be operating as each of us belts out our song, and you must listen to this seriously and carefully to catch its meaning.

The first is this: No one believes it all. No one believes it all. Each of us in the chorus is gifted with only a partial understanding of the mystery of God among us; and so, in our large chorus, one sings with great intensity and assurance, another sings with little attention and conviction. Or perhaps today we're caught by the words and melody because we happen emotionally and spiritually to be in a good place. But, another time, in another mental or emotional place, we feel doubtful and alienated and we can hardly get the words out of our mouths. That's O.K. No one believes it all, but, together, we sing more than we can sing alone. Together we sing more than we can sing alone.

And so the saints, you see, the saints are a chorus, a communion, that sings what we cannot and believes those parts we cannot accept. They chant the song of faith with us when we can join them and they hum the song of faith when we cannot. Together, we, the saints of yesterday and today, sing more than we can sing alone for no one believes it all, but all believe.

The second thing that operates is this: if no one believes it all, so also no one believes all the time. Our journey of faith is seldom smooth and uninterrupted. At times it fluctuates between belief and unbelief. A few years ago a friend of mine lost her son in an automobile accident. She says that she can no longer believe in God, in a God who would let her son lose his life, especially since she and her family are faithful Catholics and good churchgoers. How could God do this to her? There are three responses to this woman.

The first is to say, "Well, if you can no longer believe, you are no longer a Catholic. You no longer belong." That's a harsh view. That's to deny the seriousness of her loss. A second response is to say to her, "You haven't really lost your faith. You're just temporarily depressed. Everything will be fine." Everything will *not* be fine. This is to deny her pain.

But the third response is to honor her losses, the loss of her son, the loss, or at least, the shock to her faith. The fact of the matter is that tragedy has indeed broken her trust in a loving, provident God. Meanwhile? Meanwhile, the community believes for her. The saintly chorus picks up her faltering verses. The collective faith of the saints sustains her though her period of unbelief; and as she slowly encounters these saints of yesterday and today, she will begin to see *their* scars and sense *their* resilience and they will help her believe once more, in the face of tragic absurdity, in a new and different way. They will help her sing with a different modulation. They will sing the louder the phrases that she can only sing softly if at all.

So, you see, no one here—you or I—believes it all. And no one here believes all the time. No one accepts every verse and no one can sing every note all the time. But the chorus does. The chorus, or the community of saints, sings when you and I are unwilling or unable to do so.

Peter sang for Doubting Thomas until he could believe again. Thomas sang for Denying Peter until he could embrace again. Monica sang for her son Augustine when he was in his period of sinfulness and unbelief until he could repent again. Clare sang for Francis when he was sad until he was glad again. We are a whole community. We are a chorus of saints. That's what we're celebrating today. We support each other and we become more than the sum total of our individual selves as the Communion of Saints.

You exhibit the gifts I don't have and I exhibit those you don't have. You cry the tears I cannot cry and I laugh the laughter you cannot laugh. You believe when I struggle with doubts. I believe when you struggle with doubts. You smile when I am in tragedy. I grieve when you are in joy. Our individual pieces are partial. Our faith, our hope, and our love are quite incomplete. But this feast of the saints, of *all* the saints—past, present, and future, those in heaven, earth, and purgatory—tells us something. This feast gives us support. It reminds us of our faith family, that we belong to a vast community of time and space. It becomes a revelation and a comfort. It tells us a mighty truth: together we sing more than we sing alone.

2. OUT OF WINE
(Jn 2:1–12 2nd Sunday in Ordinary Time [O.T.], Year C)

This is the kind of a gospel you can enter into. If you want to, you can use your imagination and you can place yourself at this wedding feast at Cana. All of a sudden a woman's voice speaks, a little too loudly, so that you can't help overhearing her. "They have no more wine," you hear her say. You turn around and, to your horror and your embarrassment, the woman is not, as you thought, pointing to the bride and groom. She is pointing to you!

She has been milling around among the guests and has paused near you. She has sensed something about you. She studies you. She reads your face. She reads your heart. She reads your life. About you, she remarks to her Son, "They have no more wine. Their wine has run out."

Perhaps the wine *has* run out in the wedding of your life. The sense of satisfaction or celebration has perhaps run out of your marriage, your job, your project, your career, your friendships—and maybe even your faith. It happens.

❑I remember reading a story by Arthur Gordon, something he had in *Reader's Digest* years ago. It was a story of himself and how his wine had run out. He says this, and I quote him: "Not long ago I came to one of those bleak periods that many of us encounter from time to time, a sudden drastic dip in the graph of living, when everything gets stale and flat, energy wanes, enthusiasm dies. The effect on my work was frightening. Every morning I would clench my teeth and mutter, 'Today life will take on some of its old meaning. You've got to break through this thing. You've got to.' But the barren days went by and the paralysis grew worse. The time came when I knew I had to have help."

Well, the article goes on to describe how he went to his family doctor, not a psychiatrist, but a general practitioner, a man much older than himself, who had savored and learned much of the wisdom of life. He continues his story. He tells the doctor, "I don't know what's wrong but I just seem to have come to a dead end.

Can you help me?"

"Where were you happiest as a child?" the doctor asked.

"As a child?" he echoed. "Why, at the beach, I suppose. We had a summer cottage there. We all loved it."

"All right," said the doctor, "here's what I want you to do." He told Arthur to drive to the beach the following morning, arriving no later than nine o'clock. He could take some lunch, but was not to read, listen to the radio, or talk to anyone. "In addition," the doctor said, "I'll give you a prescription to be taken every three hours." He tore off four prescription blanks, wrote a few words on each of them, folded them, numbered them, and handed them to Arthur. "Take these at nine, twelve, three, and six," he instructed. Arthur glanced at him asking, "Are you serious?" The doctor gave a short bark of a laugh and said, "You won't think I'm joking when you get my bill!"

The rest of the article is about his going to the beach, a day of silence, of recollection, of memory, of being ministered to and healed by the sights and the sounds of ocean and sky. The doctor's prescriptions, as he opened them, were brief. The first one he opened said, "Listen carefully." At noon, that one said, "Try reaching back." And so on. His story ends this way, in his own words: "The western sky was a blaze of crimson as I took out the last piece of paper, six words this time. I walked slowly on the beach. A few yards below high water mark, I stopped and I read the words again. 'Write your worries on the sand.' I let the paper blow away, reached down, picked up a fragment of a shell and, kneeling there under the vault of the sky, I wrote several words on the sand, one above the other. Then I walked away and did not look back. I had written my troubles on the sand, and the tide was coming in."☐

At times we all feel the wine is running out. I see and hear it all the time. When I go shopping at the supermarket, at the checkout line, I see the tabloid headlines: Is Your Marriage Flavorless? Does Your Marriage Seem Like So Much Work? Cleaning the House, Taking Care of the Kids, Fixing the Leaking Roof, Having the Car Serviced? Is Your Job at a Dead End? Is Your Career on Hold? And so it goes.

I hear it in the voices of people whose wine has run out. "Why should I vote? It really doesn't matter who wins." "After all these years, I'm not gonna change. I was born this way." An old man sighs, "It doesn't matter. My life's almost over anyway." A young girl complains, "Same old thing. This place is boring." A Catholic laments, "Rome isn't going to change. I might as well give up." The husband or wife admits, "I guess we're just stuck in a rut."

So, at times we all feel like the wine has run out. The lady in the gospel story was right. She was perceptive. And she was right to point at us. But remember, she was speaking to someone else, another Guest, the Son, who could do something about it. And what did he do? In the story, he took ordinary things—water— and invested them with something. He took the common stuff of life and he made them gifts. And there's the key. And that may be the answer: to see life as a gift and grace in the ordinary.

But to let Christ perform this miracle, three things are needed, three things that the story of Arthur Gordon suggests, three ordinary things over which Christ can work his miracle.

First, you noticed that when this man went to the seashore, he listened. He listened to the sights and the sounds. He listened for the voice of God in the ordinary. And he also listened to the voice of God in the tragedies, discontents, and discomforts of his life because often there's where God speaks to us.

Some of you may remember Lee Atwater who was President Bush's campaign manager. According to his own admission, Atwater was an extremely ruthless man. He would find an opponent's weakness and attack without mercy. He was a difficult, ornery, unregenerate man. But he got brain cancer. In his sickness, in an interview with *Life* magazine, shortly before he died, he confessed that he had once told President Bush that his "kinder, gentler" theme was nice, but no vote-getter. But facing death, he spoke in a different voice, the voice of the Golden Rule. He found himself in a hospital with time on his hands and eventually listening: to God, to others. Suddenly he was doing something he had never done before: reaching out to the other patients, ruing the cruel things he had said about his opponents, attempting to mend his fractured and broken relationships. Because he listened in his sickness, he blossomed into something he never was before. He said,"My illness helped me to see what was missing in society, what was missing in me: a little heart, and a lot of brotherhood."

We have to listen or, as the mystics would put it, we have to ask, "What is the weeping asking of me? What is the sickness, the brokenness, the off-centeredness asking of me?" We have to listen. Listening has a name. It is called prayer. That's the first condition for Jesus to perform his miracle.

The second condition is to create space. Arthur Gordon went apart from his job, his house, and he went to the solitude of the seashore so that he could listen and pray. I suggest that for this year you do the same; that is, that you make a retreat. Surely, in these twelve months you can get away for three or four days to listen, to say to Jesus, "Look, your mother was right. The wine of my life has ebbed out. I feel flat and unprofitable. I've got to step aside and listen to your voice." In short, we must go on a little pilgrimage, not as a tourist, but as a seeker. So we must create space as the second condition for Jesus to perform his miracle.

Finally, we must observe Mary's last recorded words, "Do whatever he tells you." Do whatever he tells you. That would include reading the Scriptures, spiritual reading and, like Lee Atwater, doing works of charity because when we confront the living word and reach out to others in the ordinary kindnesses of life, then the ordinary begins to take on a different hue.

So, there we are: members of the wedding. Present at Cana. Confronted by a truth from a savvy woman who, standing beside her Son and looking at us remarked, "They have no more wine." Acknowledging that truth, we must listen. We must create space. We must act. Jesus is here to change drab water into intoxicating wine. He is here to touch the ordinary in our lives and make it sparkle. But, of course, there's one catch. It's up to you to invite him to do so because, after all, it all began, you recall, with an invitation: to a wedding feast, to your life. And that invitation is now in your hands.

3. TODAY
(Lk 1:1–4; 4:4–21 3rd Sunday in O.T. Year C)

Garrison Keillor, in his marvelous tales of Lake Woebegon, has a series entitled "Leaving Home," stories about what it means to go home, but not being able to call it home any more. He begins the series with these lines: "I can't stay, you know. I left so long ago. I'm just a stranger with memories of people that I knew here."

And this is the kind of introduction that Luke gives us in this gospel this morning. Here is someone who has been gone from his hometown for a while, but who is now returning for a visit. There are some there, of course, who remember him as a little boy; some who knew his mother and father; those curious to see what he turned out to look like or to be. In any case, he was not just any hometown boy coming home, for his reputation had preceded him because he had been speaking in various synagogues around the area and so he was something of a curiosity, if not a minor celebrity.

And so Jesus goes to his hometown synagogue where he sat as a boy and, in keeping with the custom of showing courtesy to a visiting rabbi, they hand him the scroll of Isaiah. He opens up the scroll and comes to these famous lines: "The spirit of the Lord is upon me. He has sent me to bring good tidings to the poor, to proclaim liberty to the captives, release to the prisoners and to announce a year of favor from the Lord." He rolls up the scroll, hands it back to the assistant, and sits down. Sitting down is the traditional sign that an important teaching is to come. The townsfolk are waiting with baited breath when suddenly he startles them by saying, "Today, this scripture passage is fulfilled in your hearing."

The word that got them was "today" because they had been trained to look to the future, some day in the future, for salvation. It's like us singing Snow White's song, "Some Day My Prince Will Come" and Jesus correcting us by saying, "But the Prince has already come. He is here today." Thus Jesus makes no long-range forecast, no promise that things will be different in the future. Rather, he claims the power to transform the present, to transform today. There are no good times coming. They are here now. The kingdom of God is among you, he declares. And, in fact, some eighty percent of all the recorded sayings of Jesus underscore that reality: that here and now, this day, God has broken into your life, *can* break into your life. Here and now is what counts. Today, all this is fulfilled in your hearing. Today grace abounds. Today, the kingdom of God can be realized. Today, God is revealed behind every episode of your life. Not another day, but today.

Listen to an old woman. She says, "First, I was dying to finish high school and start college. Then I was dying to finish college and start working. Then I was dying for the children to grow old enough to attend school so that I could return to work. Then I was dying to retire. And now, I am dying. Suddenly, I realize I forgot to live each day."

This in contrast to C.S. Lewis, probably the most widely read religious writer in the English language, who, in his book *Surprised By Joy*, talks about his being raised in Northern Ireland, taught his prayers, but not much religion. And, of course, when he went to college, he dropped out of religion altogether, had no use for it, became a convinced atheist. But, in spite of himself, he was bothered by the grace of Today, a here-and-now tapping on his shoulder. He writes, "Some days a little door would open to an unspeakable burst of joy, then it would slam again. The door would open, then it would slam, open and slam." Finally, one day when he was at Oxford, at Magdalen College, something happened. The One who had been pursuing him daily finally caught up with him. He writes: "You must picture me alone in that room in Oxford, feeling the steady, unrelenting approach of Him whom I earnestly desired *not* to meet. It was in Trinity term of 1929 that I gave in, and admitted that God was God and I knelt and I prayed, perhaps that night, the most rejected and reluctant convert in all of England."

That was his time of grace. *Today* the Scripture was realized in his hearing. And that's why this gospel challenged Jesus' neighbors and challenges us to live and to be open to the life of Christ here and now. Not tomorrow, not next year, not when the millennium comes, but today. Let me suggest three ways to discover this everyday grace.

The first is this. Try to live one day of acceptance. Dr. Gerald Jampolsky wrote a book a few years ago entitled *Love Is Letting Go of Fear*. In that book he asks this question, "Have you ever given yourself the opportunity of going through just one day concentrating on totally accepting everyone and making no judgments?" He goes on to say, "Everything we think or say or do reacts on us like a boomerang. When we send out judgment in the form of criticism, fury or other attack-thoughts, they come back to us. When we send out only love, it comes back to us."

So, I suggest that we try that one day this week. Suspend all judgments, spend one day of acceptance and see how, today, this Scripture will be fulfilled in your hearing.

Secondly, look for the opportunity in today, even if "today" is not quite what you had bargained for. A graduate student had just gotten his first job, a desk job, he felt—and probably correctly—that was much beneath his talents. He complained to his friend that he didn't do pencil-pushing. His friend was entirely unsympathetic. He just patted him on the back and said to him, "You know, the world is a better place because Michelangelo didn't say, 'I don't do ceilings.'" So it is. You go through the Bible and Moses didn't say, "I don't do rivers." Noah didn't say, "I don't do arks." Ruth didn't say, "I don't do mothers-in-law," David didn't say, "I don't do giants." Paul didn't say, "I don't do Gentiles." Mary Magdalene didn't say, "I don't do feet." Jesus didn't say, "I don't do crosses."

Look for the opportunity today. Even in things you'd rather not do and in places you'd rather not be, today's grace awaits.

☐The third suggestion is this: at least one day, take time to put things in perspective. A man, driving to work one morning, had a little fender-bender occasion with some woman. They both stopped. The woman got out to survey the damage. She was absolutely distraught. It was her fault. She admitted it. And her car was a new car, less than two weeks out of the showroom. She dreaded going home to tell her husband. The man felt sorry for her but, nevertheless, things had to be done. She had to get the license number, registration papers, and so on. So she went back to her car and reached into the glove compartment to get the documents and on one of the first papers to tumble out, written in her husband's distinctive hand, were these words, "In case of accident, remember, honey, it's you I love, not the car." He put things in perspective.◻

Perspective is the long view of today's grace.

A day of acceptance without judgment, a day of opportunity without complaint, a day of perspective without fear. These three things make our Scripture reading fulfilled in your hearing—today.

4. TRINITY SUNDAY

(Jn 16:12–15   Year C)

Listen to this prayer:
Dearest Lord Jesus,
Savior and Friend.
Three things I pray. To:
See Thee more clearly,
Love Thee more dearly,
Follow Thee more nearly,
Day by day.

Were I to ask you where this is from, most of you would raise your hands and say it's from the 1970 musical *Godspell*. You might even remember the song, "Day by Day." But you would be wrong, at least partly so.

The prayer I just read was written by a saint named Richard Chichester, an English saint who lived in the thirteenth century. The writers of *Godspell* simply lifted his prayer and put it to music. But it's a lovely prayer and a fitting one for today, Trinity Sunday, because its three petitions give us some insights into that mystery. So, let's take them one by one.

Three things I pray: *to see Thee more clearly*. The Trinity is such a mystery to us that we don't realize that it *is* meant for us to see God more clearly, not obscurely. What we see in this communion of Persons called Trinity is a God of closeness, of nearness, of community. What makes God God is intimacy. God is interacted closeness. To see more clearly is to see a God whose very nature is desire and communication and, therefore, love. This is an initiating God, an outgoing God, a creative, life-giving God who stamps his communal life on us. We are in relationship because God is, and, remember, we are made in his image and likeness.

☐Let me share an analogy. I was reading about a woman named Ann Weems who is a Southerner who happened to be in Wisconsin giving a talk. Before supper on the first night a man with a Southern accent came up to her and asked, "Where are you from?" When she said, "I'm from Nashville," he smiled and said, "I thought so. Who are your people?" he asked. And Ann recalls a surge of memories that swept over her. She saw faces and names and even smelled aromas associated with home.

She had answered that question before when she went off to college in Memphis, when she got married and changed her name. "I knew what he meant," she said. "'To whom do you belong?' is an ancient question," she remarked. "It's a means of identification, a claiming of ties. It can instantly open or shut doors in your face."

"My father is Tim Barr," she told the man. His face lit up with a look of recognition. He told all the people around him, "Hey, she's one of us. She's Tim Barr's daughter." And they gathered around her and led her to the table, talking about people they knew twenty-five years ago in Nashville. Ann comments, "We dashed back in time and it felt right. I belonged. I was accepted. I know who my people are."□

To see Thee more clearly is to know who we are: brothers and sisters to one another because we are all children of a God who is relatedness itself. Stamped with his image and likeness, we are born in community. To see Thee more clearly is to recognize the accent of God in our lives, is to call God "Father."

To love Thee more dearly. This tells us of a God, the Second Person of the Blessed Trinity, who wears our flesh. How much more dearly can he love us that that?

□It reminds me that recently Pope John Paul raised up Damien the Leper to beatification, the   step before canonization. Everybody remembers what a failure Damien's mission was among the lepers of Molokai, how each Sunday he would begin his sermon with "You lepers" to a mere handful of people. How coming back from an unusually unsuccessful missionary trek around the island, weary and footsore, he put his aching feet into a tub of hot water to refresh them and one foot didn't feel the heat. And he knew instantly that he had contracted the dreaded leprosy. And remember the dramatic moment when he got up into the pulpit the next Sunday and instead of beginning his sermon with the usual "you lepers," he began with "we lepers." And like electricity, that news spread around the island and the next Sunday the church was filled to overflowing and every Sunday thereafter. Father Damien had taken on their flesh, even their leprous flesh, and become one of them.☐

To love Thee more dearly is to love an incarnate God, one who who wears our flesh, even our leprous flesh.

☐Or, again, it's like the mother who told her children that there were a couple of families in their area who were very poor and would have no food or clothing and no tree this particular Christmas. So she told her sons not to give them, their parents, any presents this year but rather to give the money to these poor families. She then tells of her son who was a basketball manager at his college and on the road a good deal of the time. He had just been home for a short visit and as he was about to leave he reached out to his mother's hand, saying "Take this, Mom," and pressed some money into her palm. "Use it for one of the families so they can have a decent Christmas." A quick hug and off he went down the steps. The mother relates: "In my hand rested a crisp fifty dollar bill. With the little money Chris had to live on in college, he must have been saving for months. I stood still for a moment. Then down the stairs I sprinted. I opened the door of the car and I sat down next to him. He gave me a wonderful hug and, in an instant, I was no longer sitting next to my twenty-year-old son. I was sitting next to my five-year-old Chris who once forgave someone who had stolen his toy car because he said, 'Mom, he must need it more than me.' A part of me wanted my boy of five back. Then he spoke, 'Please get out of the car, Mom, before I start crying too.' I hugged him one more time, told him how happy I was. Because of his generosity a family was going to have a good Christmas. 'I love you, honey,' I said, 'and God will bless you for this.' And with that I climbed out of the car, leaving with a moment that I shall cherish forever: the moment I saw Christ in my son."☐

To love Thee more dearly is to know many God-incarnations, to call God "Father" and consequently each other brother and sister.

And, finally, *to follow Thee more nearly* is to be not a mimic, but a disciple. One who lives by the Master's values. One who has the Master's Spirit.

☐Frederick Wunderlich, because he was an ordained priest, did not have to be conscripted into the German army in World War II, but for some reason he enlisted. His commandant had enough sensitivity to realize that since he was a clergyman he would do better in the area of human relationships and so he sent him to the French town of Verdun to work with the occupied peoples. That meant providing food, medicine, and shelter for the people. This is not the usual image we have of a German officer in World War II. But he was a good man and he made a difference in their lives. He was determined to bring some humanity to the insanity of war.

Some twenty-five years later, the former Captain Wunderlich was now a bishop. He was on vacation in France and since he was near Verdun, he thought he might go back to the old village to see if the mayor, with whom he had once worked, was still alive. He found his house. He knocked on the door. An elderly man opened the door. Recognition was instant and effusive. He threw his arms around him. "Captain Wunderlich! You have returned. Welcome to my home!" He embraced his old friend—or his old enemy, depending on how you look at it—and the two of them spent the afternoon talking about old times and the new. What greater miracle than to make a friend of an enemy.☐

Truly, to follow Thee more nearly in love and reconciliation is the work of the Holy Spirit.

So, here we are on this feast of the Holy Trinity by which we signed ourselves when we came in and began Mass. It is a mystery, indeed, but it's a mystery of God's closeness, enfleshment, and inspiration.

A close God is Father.
An enfleshed God is Son.
An inspiring God is Holy Spirit.

Seeing more clearly is to know God the Father.

Loving more dearly is to know God the Son.
Following more nearly is to know God the Holy Spirit.

However you think about the Trinity, let this prayer from the
thirteenth century help you:

Dearest Lord Jesus,
Savior and Friend.
Three things I pray. To:
See Thee more clearly,
Love Thee more dearly,
Follow Thee more nearly,
Day by day.
Amen.

5. FREEDOM

(Jn 17:20–26 7th Sunday of Easter Year C)

This is a dense and intense gospel, but we can look for some clues to its meaning in some key phrases: "That they may be one . . . that their unity may be complete. . . . Father, all those you gave me I would have in my company . . ."

All those terms: oneness, unity, company, I-in-them, you-in-me intimacy. . . .This is the religion Jesus left us: a religion of connectedness, of community—with one another and with him.

Bret Easton Ellis's unsettling novel, *Less Than Zero*, offers a graphic description of the moral and spiritual disconnectedness behind the contemporary facade of wealth, success, popularity, and power. In a dramatically staccato way, he describes the life of sex, drugs, and violence among the teenage children of wealthy entertainers in Los Angeles. Between the lines you can sense that the cries that arise from all the decadence he portrays are the aching, unspoken questions of these kids:

Is there anybody who loves me?

Is there anybody who really cares?

Is there anybody who wants to stay home for me?

Is there anybody who wants to be with me when I am not in control, when I feel like crying?

Is there anybody who can hold me and give me a sense of belonging?

Feeling irrelevant and lonely is a common experience in our society. Crowds that go to see once more the tragic loneliness of Norma Desmond in *Sunset Boulevard* find much that echoes in them.

Ann Landers, in an interview, was asked, "What is the question that you are asked most frequently by your readers?" "That's easy," she replied without skipping a beat. "The question most asked by far is, 'What's the matter with me? Why am I so lonely?'"

But there's our problem. We are taught and conditioned to be lonely. Why? Because, we are told, that's what freedom is all about! Freedom has been interpreted as not needing anybody, as me, myself, what I want, apart from anyone else. "Be your own person" in the extreme, as if anyone could be a "person" without the love, care, and affirmation of someone else.

"One thing I like about living in New York," my friend said, as we left his apartment, "as opposed to where you live"—nodding at me—"is the freedom. Here there is freedom to live the lifestyle I choose: to eat where I want, and to dress as I like. Freedom!" he chanted once more. . . .

As he closed the door behind us, locked the latch, turned the dead bolt, and switched on the electronic alarm, he warned me, "Don't dare open that door without switching off the alarm or all hell will break loose and the cops will shoot you dead!"

Freedom?

We Americans have built a society that has given us an unprecedented measure of freedom. But, again, what we call freedom has been translated into a vast supermarket of private desires where citizens are treated as little more than self-contained, self-interested consumers.

According to a recent story in the *Wall Street Journal*, it is now possible for large marketing firms to know almost everything about people in any one of the 240,000 neighborhoods across the U.S. We know that. Just check the catalogues we get. This is known as "geo-demography" on the Information Highway. What it does is to break down towns and cities into small neighborhood groups in order to predict which consumers will be interested in certain products. It can, with a high degree of accuracy, describe the lifestyle and buying habits of most of us if given our addresses and zip codes. It is not accidental, for example, that in our parking lot there are more Mercedes than Chevolets. They know us all too well.

That we are seen as individual, disconnected consuming units seeps into our thinking and feeling and living. The pursuit of this kind of freedom—the relentless acquisition of things we absolutely must have—leads us *away* from our families and relationships, even though we rationalize as we flee out the door, "but I'm doing it for them!" while "them," whoever they are, would rather have a hug.

Jesus comes along with a different message. He has another view, one his true disciples adopted. The view, for example, that Dorothy Day adopted. Long before she became a Catholic, she had a sense of the gospel. She worked among workers and the poor and the victims of injustice. The church began to attract her because of the experience of piety and faith of her small community of fellow roomers, young women who like herself believed devoutly in God. She became a Catholic because of her need to be connected, to be a part of community. The institutional church was for her something she both criticized and loved. But to be a part of this community of faith brought her immense comfort, strength, and joy. Whatever its deficiencies, that church was a community she cherished. And within it she stayed voluntarily poor in order to be rich in relationships—with others and with God.

This is the point of the gospel. The point the gospel makes is the *priority* of relationships, of community. To trade off the development of relationships, it tells us, for a bigger house or larger car or world travel is to leave a lot of lonely people asking:

Is there anybody who loves me?

Is there anybody who really cares?

Is there anybody who wants to stay home for me?

Is there anybody who wants to be with me when I am not in control, when I feel like crying?

Is there anybody who can hold me and give me a sense of belonging?

The late Joseph Campbell said in an interview:

I have a friend who gave me a list of things which let you know you're getting old.

Number one: you sink your teeth into a juicy steak and they stay there.

Number two: the little old lady you're leading across the street is your wife.

Number three: your back goes out more than you do.

But the real killer is this one: You've arrived at the top of the ladder and found it's up against the wrong wall.

So, back to the gospel.

". . . that they may be one, as we are one, I living in them, you living in me . . . that their unity may be complete. So shall the world know that you sent me and that you loved them as you loved me."

Notice what Jesus says. Notice the force of that word "so." The only way the world knows God is around and that his love is present is when people touch each other and hold and make time for one another, when they practice "being one," when their unity is complete.

In other words, the revelation of God's love is discovered in relationships. Relationship *is* religion. And that takes time and sacrifice but this is the gospel priority Jesus preaches. Maybe the message of the gospel—unity, oneness, relationship, community—is best summed up in this old Christian legend:

❑A woman's happiness was shattered by the loss of her brother, a good man, dearly loved. Torn by anguish, she kept asking God, "Why?" But hearing the silence, she set out in search of an answer.

She had not gone far when she came upon an old man sitting on a bench. He was weeping. He said, "I have suffered a great loss. I am a painter and I have lost my eyesight." He too was seeking an answer to the question, "why?" The woman invited him to join her and, taking him by the arm, they trudged down the road.

Soon they overtook a young man walking aimlessly. He had lost his wife, the source of his joy, to another man. He joined in the search of an answer to the "why" question.

Shortly they came up a young woman weeping on her front doorstep. She had lost her child. She too joined them. Nowhere could they find an answer.

Suddenly they came upon Jesus Christ.

Each confronted him with their questions, but Jesus gave no answer. Instead, he began to cry and said, "I am bearing the burden of a woman who has lost her brother, a girl whose baby has died, a painter who has lost his eyesight, and a young man who has lost a love in which he delighted."

As he spoke, the four moved closer and they embraced each other. And they grasped Jesus' hands. Jesus spoke again saying, "My dominion is the dominion of the heart. I cannot prevent pain. I can only heal it."

"How?" asked the woman.

"By sharing it," he said. And then he was gone.

And the four? They were left standing holding each other.☐

That's a wall to lean your ladder against.

6. GOD NOTICES
(1 Kgs 17:10–16; Mk 12:38–44
32nd Sunday in O.T. Year B)

❏A life insurance salesman visited a woman who had recently been widowed. For 35 years her late husband had sacrificed much in order to sustain a substantial life insurance policy. So the salesman said to her, "Your husband often told me how determined he was that you would be well provided for after he was gone. And so here I am," he continued, "to present you, as the sole beneficiary, with this check for $500,000." The widow tearfully accepted the check. She wiped her eyes and said, "But nothing can replace that wonderful husband of mine who left me this $500,000. But I can tell you this for certain: I'd give at least half of it now to have him back."❏

Both our Scriptures today tell of widows but we should note that the stories reveal more than what they appear to be on the surface. For one thing, what escapes us, which did not escape the original hearers, is that the widow is also a symbol, a symbol of someone in the direst of needs. In a society that did not have such things as annuities, insurance, and social security, to lose one's husband was to lose one's livelihood, to become quite marginalized, and to be at the mercy of sexual and economic exploiters. Thus those who devour a widow's savings—who prey on the helpless—as Jesus put it, deserve the harshest of judgments.

Another thing to realize is what we do not note, namely, that the gospel story is not about virtue. It's not about a generous widow. After all, the widow receives no reward. Jesus does not directly praise her. Rather, more to the point is what Jesus does. *He notices her.* His seasoned eye does not take in the high and the mighty who have captivated everyone else. His seasoned eye picks out someone whom everyone else has overlooked. He observes this little invisible, nondescript human being from the bottom of the social ladder. He notices her quiet act of fidelity, kindness, and generosity, those acts that make a difference in this world. He notices that and comments about it.

And that, ultimately, is the point and a point for us, two thousand years later, to ponder. Jesus notices. Jesus notices us who are the uncelebrities of this world. Our small deeds are observed, cherished, and remembered. No one else may know them or comment on them, but Jesus notices.

❑A few weeks ago I was visiting a family whose father is a widower and has Alzheimer's disease. His married daughter, who is also widowed, is taking care of him. It's not easy, as many of you know. She struggles a great deal. After I left, she walked me to the car and said, "I don't know how much longer I can really do this. It's awfully hard going after him. He wanders out at all hours of the night thinking he's back in the city looking for a bus. I don't know how much longer I can lift him or take him to the bathroom. I'm getting tired. It's very hard." And I said, "You're right. It is hard. I don't know how you do it, but I know somehow you will continue to do it until it isn't needed any more." And as I drove away, leaving her to her father who is unaware of her devotion, I thought of this gospel. This is a poor widow who is giving all that she has and nobody really notices it except—except the One who counts. He notices.❑

❑On a priests' retreat a few years ago, there was one old priest there whom we all admired. He had been a wonderful pastor and great scholar. We got around to talking about how we got into the priesthood. When it got around to him, he said simply, "I'm a priest because of Widow Brown." "Who's she?" we wanted to know. A great scholar, a notable citizen, a treasured teacher? "No. She was a little old woman who always sat near us on Sundays when we went to church. During Mass when I would settle in with my parents, trying to get through a boring sermon, Mrs. Brown would smile at me, quietly reach into her purse and pull out a piece of the best tasting chocolate in the world. She would pass it to me. She always had it there and always had it for me. And each Sunday that was the most tangible, visible, sacramental expression of disinterested love that I have ever experienced. I'm a priest today, you might say, because of Widow Brown." Widow Brown blended into the scenery. No one ever noticed her. But two did. A little boy who became a marvelous priest. And Jesus. He notices. He noticed the widow's chocolate mite.☐

☐One of those terrible, sudden storms and cloudbursts fell upon a newly wedded couple on a remote country road. Unable to go any further, they got out of their car and wallowed through mud to an old farmhouse. They saw a light in the window. By the time they reached the farmhouse, there was an elderly couple there waiting for them with a kerosene lamp. They had seen them from the window. Meeting them at the door the young man explained their predicament. He pleaded, "Could you please put us up for the night until morning? Any place on the floor, a mat or something would do just fine." And, as he was speaking, a few grains of rice fell from the little hairpiece the bride had on. The elderly couple exchanged knowing glances and said, "By all means. Certainly. You can have the guest room."

So they used the guest room that night. They got up early, not wishing to disturb the old couple. They got dressed. The man left a ten dollar bill on the dresser. And as they came out of the bedroom, there sleeping on the couch was the husband and crumpled up in a chair was the wife. And the newly married couple realized that this poor couple *had* no guest room. But they had given freely to strangers. The young couple knew this now. So did Jesus. While the rest of the country was tuned into David Letterman or Jay Leno, he noticed this act of kindness.☐

All this comes back to our original point, the point of this gospel of the Widow's Mite that tradition saved for us. It is a wonderful story not about the widow as such, not about virtue, but about noticing, noticing the little people. It is therefore basically a story of encouragement, a little lesson plan with three simple truths:

Truth number one: we count.
Truth number two: what we do counts.
Truth number three, which is the greatest of all: Jesus notices.

7. THE QUESTION
(Jn 21:1–14 3rd Sunday of Easter Year C)

This is an extremely rich gospel. It helps to remember that it was written in a time of trauma and, to that extent, it speaks deeply to the human condition. Let us explore two provocative themes.

The first theme centers around the opening episode of the disciples at sea. They're confused, they're lost, they're empty. They are still reeling from the death of their Master. They don't know what to do with themselves and so, in a kind of reflex action, they revert to their old trade, fishing. The unprofitable night indicates that both literally and figuratively they are at sea.

"Have you caught anything?" asks a voice on the shoreline. The answer: "We've labored all night long and have caught nothing. " And we pause on hearing this. Aren't those frequently our words? How often have we, in one form or another, spoken them after fruitlessly trying to pick up the pieces of life after the death of a spouse, a sickness, a setback, the loss of a job, depression, a divorce, the empty nest? Nothing. We've caught nothing.

And so, like the disciples, we labor at familiar tasks. We keep busy. But it seems all day long and all night long we catch nothing. There's just an empty net. But then one day we're aware of the Stranger on the shoreline. We can't quite make him out, but one day there's someone there and this time something connects. A friend walks into our life or maybe we're struck by a Bible verse we're heard a hundred times before; there's a new and encouraging word, a sign or gesture that sparks, a slow sensation that things are beginning to move together. There's nibble in the net.

❑About 17 years ago, a woman named Velma Barfield became the first woman in the United States to be executed in 22 years. She had murdered four people, had admitted her guilt. But the Velma Barfield who was executed was very different from the Velma Barfield who was jailed in 1978. She had long periods of empty nets, of trying to put the pieces back together again. But one day she recognized the Figure on the shoreline. She wrote about it in her book, *Woman on Death Row*. She begins her story on her knees in her cell praying, "Could Jesus ever forgive me after the terrible deeds that I had just done? Could he ever love me again?" But there was no answer.

But then she writes that, after many years, something happened that she could only describe in the best language she could. It seemed to her that Jesus appeared to her and said, "Yes, I died for your sins on the cross. Won't you let me come into your life and give you a brand new life?" "Right then and there," she said, "I confessed my sins to him. I asked him to forgive me. He came into my life that night." After her execution her Bible was found. She had many notations written in the margins. She told a friend once that she could never get through the day without the Living Word.☐

Velma Barfield was a woman who had long periods of empty nets, but one day she heard a voice of the Stranger asking, "Have you caught anything?" She answered, "Nothing." But she followed his instructions and her net was full.

So many of us are "at sea." We labor all day and all night long and catch nothing. The gospel message is that, unknown to us, there stands a Stranger on the shores of our lives. He *is* there and one day you will hear his voice. This gospel is a message of hope for empty times.

There's another richness to this gospel. It's what I call the episode of the second chance. Now it is important that you remember who was there in those boats. Jesus' disciples. You know, the ones who fled when he was arrested. The ones who, when he needed a bit of comfort, fell asleep on him. The ones who, when the going got tough, abandoned him. And there, too, was Peter, the leader, who figures so prominently in this story. He was there. Remember, he denied even knowing Jesus.

It is to these that Jesus appears. And he has a question. And it is urgently important that you realize what the question is not. His question is *not* "What have you done?" His question is *not* "Who were you in the past?" His question is *not* "Have you reformed?" His question is *not* "Do you remember your sins?" His question had nothing to do with the past and everything to do with the present. His question is simply "Here and now, do you love me?"

"Do you love me?" That's all Jesus is interested in. Let bygones be bygones. Let sins be forgotten. Let mistakes be put aside. Let stupidities be buried. Let hurts be unrecorded. Let betrayals be unmentioned. All that matters is, "Right here, right now, do you love me?"

Can't you sense the drama of this very personal gospel, the absolute forgiveness implied in the question, the total love of the Questioner? Can't you sense that this gospel lives? That on this Sunday morning, at this liturgy, here and now, Someone is asking the only question that matters in your life and mine. He is asking, "Do you love me?" It's the gift of the second chance. Never mind the past. *"Today,* do you love me?" This is why this gospel was saved by the faith community. It was saved for people like ourselves who also needed to know that the Stranger is on the shore of our lives as we toil with empty nets and that, above all, the Stranger comes with but a single question.

"Do you love me?"

8. EVER SO WISE

(Epiphany Mt 2:1–12 Years A,B,C)

The gorgeous story of the Wise Men is among the favorites of the Christian people. It is colorful, rich, multi-leveled, inexhaustable in its meaning. We love to hear it. We love to see the Wise Men's appearance at our crib with their royal clothes, elegant servants, and precious gifts. We love to point them out to our children and grandchildren. We love to weave stories about them and even give them spectacular names: Casper, Melchior, and Balthasar. It's all so Eastern, so Arabian, so exotic. What, we wonder, did Matthew, the gospel writer, have in mind when he told this marvelous tale and embellished it so? What he had in mind, I suggest, is quite powerful and is of the essence of the gospel, for the Wise Men represent, for Matthew, three things—and richly so. They are, as he tells it, Outsiders, Seekers, and Latecomers. And they are still with us today.

First, they are Outsiders. They didn't belong. They were not Jews. They were from a faraway land. They were different. Tradition has even made one of them black. But, records Matthew, they brought their own unique gifts and they were welcomed. Do such Outsiders live today? They surely do. Are they welcomed? Not always. Yesterday's front page tells the story of Asian Americans organizing because of laws to keep them—the only ethnic groups so named—out of the country and because of the vast amount of prejudice they are encountering. Some still remember with humiliation how the United States government interned many Americans of Japanese descent in camps during World War II. They smart from bias and hate crimes against them because they are "different." That skin. Those eyes. Those clothes. Who can trust them?

As for the black community, listen to Pete Velander's story:

❑"I remember the day I learned to hate racism. I was five years old. The walk home from school was only about five blocks. I usually walked with some friends. On this day I walked alone.

Happy, but in a hurry, I decided to take the shortcut through the alley. Without a care in the world, I careened around the corner—too late to change course. I had walked into a back alley beating. There were three big white kids. In retrospect they were probably no more than sixth graders, but they looked like giants from my kindergarten perspective. There was one black kid. He was standing against a garage, his hands behind his back. The three white kids were taking turns punching him. They laughed. He stood silently except for the involuntary groans that that followed each blow. And now I was caught. One of the three grabbed me and stood me in front of their victim, "You take a turn," he said. "Hit the nigger!" I stood paralyzed. "Hit him or you're next.'" So I did. I feigned a punch. I can still feel the soft fuzz of that boy's turquoise sweater as my knuckles gently touched his stomach. I don't know how many punches there were. I don't know how long he had to stand backed up against that garage. After my minute participation in the conspiracy, they let me go and I ran. I ran home crying and sick to my stomach. I have never forgotten.

"Thirty-five years later that event still preaches a sermon to me every time I remember it. One can despise, decry, denounce, and deplore something without ever being willing to suffer, or even be inconvenienced, to bring about change. If there is one thing that Jesus taught us, it was how to suffer with and for others. Jesus walked the way of the cross. He taught us the meaning of suffering as a servant. Perhaps my first chance to follow that example came in the alley by a garage 35 years ago. I don't know if that black boy from the alley grew up, or where he lives, or what he does today. I never knew his name. I wish I did. I wish I could find him. I need to ask his forgiveness—not for the blow I delivered, for it was nothing, but for the blows I refused to stand by his side and receive. I think, that's what it takes.'❑

At the crib, there were no Outsiders, no racism, no beatings. Jesus received them all. Ox and ass, shepherds and Magi, poor and rich, Jews and Gentiles—he came for them all. He would reject no one, as he would accept the unique gifts of each. What a pity if his followers don't always treat Outsiders as he did. It's really a part of the gospel. That's why Matthew included it.

Secondly, the Wise Men are not only Outsiders, they are Seekers. They traversed the desert in doubt. They weren't sure. They were looking for signs, reading the stars, making inquiries. Perhaps at the end, after all, there was nothing. But they continued the journey in one another's company.

I meet people like that. I remember talking to a group of teachers at a Catholic school. One of them raised her hand and with some reluctance said, "To tell the truth, I feel like a hypocrite teaching those children. I'm not sure I believe everything the church teaches. I go to Mass but my mind wanders and I'm not into it. I have my doubts about a lot of things, about faith, about religion, about the church." My ear caught the word "hypocrite," because I knew that many people felt that way and were confusing the term with "seeking." Real hypocrisy, you see, means people not only do not practice what they preach, but they are calculating about it. But seekers are different. They are different. This is the person who practices what he or she preaches, but not out of total conviction or maybe with minimal conviction and comfort. This person keeps up appearances, maybe for the sake of the children or social pressure, says prayers, goes to Mass, but has some genuine difficulty about the faith or practice or is just spiritually lifeless and is just going through the motions.

This person says, "How can I believe in a God who allows babies to be born with AIDS? How can I prove God's existence? How can God or going to Mass mean anything to me since I lost my dad or my child? Since my spouse left me? Since my prayers for so many, many years have gone unanswered? I pray, such as it is, but it's like I'm talking to myself. I go through the motions: I go to church, receive Communion, but I'm not sure any more. I'm just not sure. So much has changed. So much has happened. I'm empty, dried up. What am I doing here? I feel like a hypocrite."

But this is not hypocrisy. This is journey and searching. This is the discipline of keeping up appearances, not to deceive, but to test; not to win applause, but to win some kind of a sign from God that God is there and really cares. This is the journey of the spiritually numb hoping for a thaw. This is the full routine of fidelity. This is quiet, joyless duty of people going through the traditional dark night of the soul. They are trying to be faithful even when they don't get anything out of it. Such people are not hypocrites. They are searchers after truth. They are beloved of God. They are Magi seeking and they are Magi accepted. Matthew wants us to know that.

Finally, the Magi are Latecomers. Not there from the first. Out-of-Steppers. The oddballs. The Different. The Dalliers. The flirters with religion. The duckers of religion. The intellectuals. The sophisticates with another agenda. Those of a different pace and orientation and drum beat. Not the usual path. Yes, these Wise Men are Latecomers. But they too are accepted. In Evelyn Waugh's novel, *Helena*, a story of the Emperor Constantine's mother, the empress is at the end of her life in Bethlehem, musing on the Wise Men. She prays out loud:

> . . . like me . . . you were late in coming . . . How laboriously you came, taking sights and calculating, where the shepherds had run barefoot! . . .Yet, you came and were not turned away. You too found room before the manger. . . . You are my especial patrons and patrons of all latecomers, of all who have a tedious journey to make to truth. . . .Dear cousins, pray for me. . . .For His sake who did not reject your curious gifts, pray always for the learned, the oblique, the delicate. Let them not be quite forgotten at the Throne of God when the simple come into their kingdom . . . .

So here we have the converts, the Good Thieves, the Augustines, the John Newtons, the Tom Mertons, and Dorothy Days, and all who, finally, exhausted by their mind games, gave in to the Hound of Heaven. And those who have nowhere else to go but to a simple baby in a manger. Piri Thomas in his book, *Down These Mean Streets,* catches it well. In a moving scene a prisoner is speaking:

> ☐I went back to my cell, the night before my hearing.
> I decided to make a prayer. It had to be on my knees. . .
> I couldn't play it cheap. So I waited until the thin kid was asleep.

Then I quietly climbed down from my top bunk and bent my knees.

I knelt at the foot of the bed and told God what was in my heart.

I made like He was there in the flesh with me. I talked to Him plain . . . no big words, no almighties. . .

I talked with him like I had wanted to talk to my old man so many years ago . . .

I talked like a little kid and I told Him of my wants and lack, of my hopes and disappointments.

I asked the Big Man to make a cool way for me. . . .

I felt like I was someone that belonged to somebody who cared.

I felt like I could even cry if I wanted to, something I hadn't been able to do for years.

"God," I concluded, "maybe I won't be an angel, but I do know I'll try not to be a blank.

So in your Name and in Cisto's name, I ask this. Amen."

A small voice added another amen to mine.

I looked up and saw the thin kid, his elbows bent, his head resting on his hand.

I peered through the semidarkness to see his face, wondering if he was sounding me, but his face was like mine, looking for help from God.

There we were, he lying down head on bended elbows, and I still on my knees.

No one spoke for a long while.

Then the kid whispered.

"I believe in Dios also.

Maybe you don't believe it, but I used to go to church and I had the hand of God upon me.

I felt always like you and I feel now warm, quiet and peaceful, like there's no suffering in our hearts."

"What is he called, Chico, this what we ask for?" I asked.

"It's called Grace by the Power of the Holy Spirit," the kid said.

I didn't ask any more.

There, in the semi-darkness
I had found a new sense of awareness.☐

A Latecomer, like the Magi, and welcomed. Matthew had that
in mind too.

So, this familiar and beloved story turns out to be our story,
doesn't it? Which is why it has such appeal. The Three Wise Men
are not Casper, Melchior, and Balthasar. They are the Outsiders,
the Seekers, and the Latecomers. Matthew knew that all along.
Just as he knew that the Wise Men offered quirky gifts. And *he*
offers a happy ending. For the gifts have been accepted. The
Givers have been embraced. The journey is over. They had found
what they were looking for. So will you if you treat the Outsiders,
the Seekers, and the Latecomers the same way.

9. HOPE

(Lk 1:39-45 4th Sunday of Advent Year C)

Many of you recognize this gospel scene as the second joyful mystery of the rosary, the Visitation. And many of you are familiar with those wonderful medieval paintings of this particular scene. Many a holy card has been reproduced from them. Two women embracing, in royal robes, with a retinue of servants to care for the messy details of life.

In reality, of course, they were two peasant women who journeyed on foot and who were sharing their hopes and their dreams. But the paintings do catch something. They catch them, these two women, in mid-embrace, very reminiscent of the ancient mythology of the Graces in a kind of mid-embrace dance; or those paintings of the angels who, also in a mid-embrace, dance before the throne of God.

So why were these two women rejoicing and dancing and singing, Elizabeth with her question and Mary with her marvelous Magnificat? In fact, have you noticed? In Luke's gospel, everyone sings. Zechariah sings when his tongue is loosed. Angels sing to shepherds. Old Simeon sings his Dismissal Song.

What is the cause of all of this singing? The answer is the Spirit. The Holy Spirit hovers over this new creation, these new children within the wombs of two cousins, just as the Spirit hovered over the world at creation. "The Spirit breathed on the waters and life came forth," intoned Genesis. And in both instances, you must note, there was chaos beforehand.

In the primeval story there was chaos and a void until the Spirit breathed and brought forth order. In the gospel story, there was the chaos of the two empty wombs: Mary, the virgin and Elizabeth, the sterile. There was chaos politically because these two women, like the rest of their countrymen, lived in a territory occupied by the Roman forces. There was the chaos of poverty and brutality they were forced to endure. There was chaos in that they, as women, were a minority within a minority people.

And yet, these two women sang and danced for they saw something in the upcoming births of their children. Mary sang of it. The lowly would be lifted up, she chanted. The mighty would be deposed, she intoned. The hungry would be fed, she echoed. Yes, here and now, in the midst of their personal chaos, it was a time of salvation, a time of hope. God is at work even in troubled times, is their message. That's why they sang. And that is why we must sing. We must pick up Mary's song and Mary's hope because, even in our chaotic times, the Spirit is at work.

In 1863, brother was raging against brother in the terrible Civil War. On Christmas Day in 1863, Henry Wadsworth Longfellow, the great poet, received word that his son had been seriously wounded. He wrote a poem that started out bitter but wound up sweet.

I heard the bells on Christmas Day,
Their old, familiar carols play,
And wild and sweet, the words repeat
Of peace on earth, good will to men.

And thought how, as the day had come,
The belfries of all Christendom
Had rolled along the unbroken song
Of peace on earth, good will to men.

And in despair I bowed my head.
"There is no peace on earth," I said.
For hate is strong and mocks the song
Of peace on earth, good will to men.

Then pealed the bells more loud and deep,
"God is not dead, nor does He sleep.
The wrong shall fail, the right prevail
With peace on earth, good will to men.

'Til ringing, singing, on its way,
The world revolved from night to day;

A voice, a chime, a chant sublime
Of peace on earth, good will to men."

That's what makes this Visitation scene so poignant. We need to sing in the chaos of Bosnia, in the chaos of Zaire, in the chaos of our mean streets. We have to sing songs of promise, songs of hope. Most of all, we must sing them to our children. Our children, who are so full of terror at the heritage we're leaving them. Our children, so full of the media's nihilism which tells them incessantly that there is, deep down, nothing that counts here and nothing that exists hereafter and fills the void with compulsive consumerism. To our children we must sing songs of hope, songs that reveal to them a Spirit who will bring order out of chaos.

☐Many of you remember the humorist Sam Levenson. Sam tells the story about the birth of his first child. The first night home the baby would not stop crying. His wife frantically flipped through the pages of Dr. Spock to find out why babies cry and what to do about it. Since Spock's book is rather long, the baby cried a long time. Grandma was in the house but, since she had not read books on child rearing, she was not consulted. The baby continued to cry until Grandma could stand it no longer and she shouted downstairs, "For heaven's sake, Sarah, put the down the book and pick up the baby!"☐

Good advice. Put down the busyness and pick up the baby. Put down the overweening career and pick up the baby. Put down all the material things and pick up the baby. In a survey done of fifteen thousand children, the question was asked, "What do you think makes a happy family?" When the kids answered, they did not list a big house or fancy car or new video games as the source of happiness. The most frequently given answer was "doing things together." When you do things together, it seems that then they can best hear the song of hope. Pick up the children.

So, back to our Advent-Visitation image of two oppressed women singing. And to Mary's song updated:

My soul magnifies the Lord and my Spirit rejoices in God my Savior, because He has looked upon me, the lowliest of the low, an oppressed woman in an oppressed territory, from a little nondescript town. He has looked upon me, his lowly servant, *with favor.*

All generations shall call me blessed—and we look around our parish church, called St. Mary's, and 2000 years later we are honoring that prophecy—and holy is his name.

His mercy is for those who fear Him. He has shown strength in his arm, so have confidence. He has brought down the Stalins and the Hitlers from their thrones of arrogance. He has lifted up the lowly like Mother Teresa and Dorothy Day and Jean Vanier. He has filled the hungry with Good Things as we prepare to receive the Eucharist. He has helped us to remember his mercy which is why we are here.

These are difficult times, but no more so than Mary and Elizabeth's times, these two nobodies who made a difference. These two nonentities who danced in the dust. These two nothings who sang a song we still sing today.

10. JESUS' PRAYER

(Jn 17:11–19 7th Sunday of Easter Year B)

Today, in these few gospel verses, we hear Jesus at prayer. And it's an intriguing prayer, for it includes three distinct petitions that touch our lives and invite us to pray the same way.

First, on this night before his crucifixion, he prayed for his friends. "O Holy Father," he cried, "protect them. . . ." He knew they would need that prayer in the coming days. He knew that the cost of being one of his followers in those early days would be high. He knew there would be times when his disciples' lives would be in danger. He knew there would be times when they would be tempted to run. So he prayed for them. But, notice, he did not pray that they would be released from these problems, but only that they would be strong. He did not pray for escape —no one escapes the trials of life—but victory. He prayed, "I am not asking you to take them out of the world, but I ask you to protect them from the evil one."

In his book, *Den of Lions: Memoirs of Seven Years*, Terry Anderson tells of his captivity in Beirut for those years. He admitted that he, a lapsed Catholic, was made strong because of prayer. About a month after his captivity he and the others were given Bibles. With nothing else to do, he read and reread it. He was especially drawn to the apostle Paul who struggled with his weakness, imprisonment, and pride just as Terry did. Through Paul's struggles Terry was able to express his love for God. His only prayer was to ask for patience and strength to endure whatever came, the precise prayer Jesus prayed for him. His trial went on for seven years. He did not escape it. He was made strong through prayer. Jesus had prayed for him.

That raises the first question. *Who in your life needs to be made strong? Whom do you need to pray for, not that they escape life's hurts, but that they be made strong?* Perhaps you might pause briefly and say their names to yourself and present them before God.

If the first thing Jesus prayed for was that his friends would be made strong, the second thing Jesus prayed for was that his friends would be united.

❑A man named Tony Campolo tells a story about being at a worship service where a man prayed aloud for a friend. "Dear Lord," he said, "you know Charlie Stoltzfus. He lives in that silver trailer down the road a mile. He's leaving his wife and kids. Please do something to bring the family together." The man prayed again, repeating the location: "the silver trailer down the road a mile." Annoyed, Tony wanted to say, "Enough already. Do you think God's asking, 'What's that address again?'" Anyway, after the prayer service, Tony was driving home when on the turnpike he noticed a hitchhiker. He decided to give him a lift. "My name's Tony," Campolo said. "What's yours?" "Charlie Stoltzfus," the hitchhiker said. Campolo was dumbfounded. It was the young man for whom the prayer had been offered. Campolo got off at the next exit. "Hey, where you taking me?" asked the hitchhiker. "Home," Campolo said. The hitchhiker stared in amazement as Tony drove right to the young man's silver trailer. That afternoon that young man and his wife gave themselves to each other and to God.❑

Who in your life needs to be united? Who is alienated from you or the family or their family? You might pause briefly and say their names to yourself and present them to God.

The third thing Jesus prayed for was not, this time, for his friends, but for himself. And that's significant. It was an important prayer. He said, "I consecrate myself for their sakes . . . so that they may be consecrated in truth." The word "consecrate" means to make holy and so Jesus in effect is praying, "I make myself holy *in order* that my disciples may be holy." He knew there was no other way. He himself must be grounded in virtue and truth if *they* were to be. It's as simple and demanding as that. And there's the impact for us. We must make ourselves holy *so that* our friends, our children, our family, our co-workers, our classmates may be holy. There's no other way. It's like what Booker T. Washington wrote in his autobiography, "The older I grow, the more I am convinced that there is no education which one can get from books and costly apparatus that is equal to that which can be gotten from contact with great men and women." So, too, there is no other way to instill virtue and holiness than to have contact with holy men and women. Consecrate yourself in truth.

The actor Jimmy Stewart once wrote in a *McCall's* magazine article that the center of his universe as a boy was the family hardware store and, more importantly, the man who ran it, his father. He said that all his life his father had a great influence on him. One example was when Jimmy's bomber squadron was preparing to go overseas during World War II. Before departure, Jimmy's father embraced him and slipped a letter into his pocket. It read, "My dear Jim boy. Soon after you read this letter, you will be on your way to the worst sort of danger. . . .I am banking on the enclosed copy of the ninety-first Psalm. The thing that takes the place of fear and worry is the promise of these words. . . .I can say no more. . . .I love you more than I can tell you. Dad." Those words of the ninety-first Psalm? "You will be safe in God's care; his faithfulness will protect and defend you. . . .God will put his angels in charge over you to protect you wherever you go."

His dad was holy—consecrated himself—so that his son might be holy, have values.

So, it comes down to this: Jesus' prayer is profound and a pattern for ours. Pray for those near and dear to you: first, that they may be strong; second, that they may be united. And, most of all, pray for yourself: that *you* may be holy. Consecrate yourself in truth—for their sakes.

11. Dependence Day
(Fourth of July)

Father Pedro Arrupe was a rather famous priest. For one thing, he was the head of the Jesuits. For another thing, he was a very holy and perceptive man and a great scholar. He died just a few years ago. Shortly before he died, he was reminiscing about some of the events of his life and one of them that stood out in his mind was when he was visiting a poor village in South America and celebrated Mass for the poor people there. He wrote: "The Mass was held in a small, open building in very poor repair. There was no door, the dogs came in and out of Mass freely, and Mass began with hymns accompanied by a guitar. The result was marvelous. The words of the hymn they were singing were 'Love is giving of oneself while seeking what will make others happy.' As they ended the hymn I had a lump in my throat and I had to make a real effort to continue the Mass."

He said that what struck him was that these people seemed to possess nothing, and yet they were ready to give of themselves and to communicate joy and happiness. After Mass, one of the villagers invited him to his little hut. He was reluctant to go, but some of the priests urged him to. He said, "The man had me sit down on a very rickety old chair, and from there I could see the sunset. And the man said to me, 'Look, sir, how beautiful it is.' And we sat in silence for several minutes until the sun disappeared." Then the host said to him, "I don't know how to thank you for all you have done for us. I have nothing to give you, but I thought you would like to see the sunset. You liked it, didn't you? Good evening." Father Arrupe remarked, "We forget the simple beauties of earth—the sky, the sun, and the trees. We don't need many things to make us happy. Only God and God's creation."

That's a good thought on this, our American holiday. We are so dunned with the bad news—and there is plenty of it from riots to child abuse, from drug dealing to drunken driving—that we forget the simple beauties and the simple truths. One of them is that we are here and God is here, and we need each other. And that is why, on this holiday, when we commemorate the signing of our country's Declaration of Independence, I am going to invite you to make a Declaration, not of Independence, but of Dependence— dependence on God.

☐Let me explain that dependence by telling you of a missionary bishop who visited us a while back. He had to celebrate confirmation for a group of severely handicapped children. They were all institutionalized and none of them were capable of even the simplest kind of academic work. The chaplain of the home warned the bishop not to speak more than two or three minutes for that would be beyond their capacity, and also to avoid any highfalutin language. The bishop was quite nervous about it. He spoke this message to the children: "Dear children, your Mom and Dad and brothers and sisters all love you. That's why they gently stroke your head and your hair and your cheeks. And that's what happens when you are confirmed. The Good Lord gently strokes you because he loves you so much. So when I make the sign of the cross on your forehead with the holy oil, our dear Father is stroking and petting you."

A few minutes later, as he touched a cerebral palsy victim's forehead, the little boy's face grimaced in a little contortion and with great difficulty he said the word, "stroke" while the saliva spilled out of his mouth and his mother wiped away the saliva and her tears with the very same handkerchief. But the boy had gotten the message. God was stroking him. The bishop remarked, "You know, I don't know how others might think about that theology, but basically this is what God does. God stroked the people of Israel. The father stroked the Prodigal Son. Jesus stroked the children, stroked and caressed the lepers, laid his hand on the eyelids and heads and ears of those who were handicapped and afflicted." In brief, the bishop had summed up the message of Christianity in one word: that God is love and we need that love and depend on that love if we are ever to be whole.☐

That's what believers celebrate on Independence Day: dependence, dependence on God that we and our country must have if we are to be truly free. When our declaration is so independent that we leave him out of the picture we court disaster, as individuals, as a nation. So, today is a glorious day for us Americans. It is an equally glorious day for us American Catholics. We celebrate freedom and the birth of our nation, a nation, as the Pledge of Allegiance reminds us, "under God," for freedom is not possible otherwise.

☐Let me present this truth in another way, in the form of this true tale of a bishop from Notre Dame Cathedral in Paris from the last century. He was a great evangelizer. He tried to make his outreach to unbelievers, scoffers, and cynics. And so he liked to tell the story of a young man who would stand outside the cathedral and shout derogatory slogans at the people entering to worship. He would call them fools and all kinds of names. The people tried to ignore him but it was difficult. So finally the parish priest went outside to confront the young man, much to the distress of the parishioners. The young man ranted and raved against everything the priest told him. Finally he addressed the young scoffer by saying, "Look, I'm going to make a deal with you. Let's get this over with once and for all. I'm going to put you on a dare and I bet you can't do it." And of course the young man shot back, "I can do anything you propose, you white-robed wimp!"

"Fine," said the priest, "all I ask you to do is to come into the sanctuary with me and I want you to stare at the figure of Christ and I want you to scream at the very top of your lungs, as loud as you can, 'Christ died on the cross for me and I don't care one bit.'" So the young man screamed as loud as he could, looking at the figure, "Christ died on the cross for me and I don't care one bit." The priest said, "Very good. Now do it again." And again the young man screamed, with a little more hesitancy, "Christ died on the cross for me and I don't care one bit." "You're almost done now," said the priest. "One more time." The young man raised his fist, kept looking at the statue, but the words wouldn't come. He just could not look at the face of Christ and say that any more.

The real punch line came when, after he told the story, the bishop said, "I was that young man. That young man, that defiant young man was me. I thought I didn't need God, but found out that I did.'☐

Think of him as a symbol of this country on this, our Fourth of July. We keep trying to say we're individuals independent even of God, that we don't need him. We, like the restored bishop, are here to say as American Catholics, "but we do." And that may be our greatest contribution to democracy.

So, please stand. Square your shoulders, shake loose the dust and cares from your minds and hearts, look at Jesus Christ, and declare your Declaration of Dependence.

"We believe in one God . . ."

12. BELOVED
(Lk 15:1–3,11–32 4th Sunday of Lent Year C)

The story of the Prodigal Son or, more properly, the Forgiving Father, is so familiar to us that we feel it has nothing more to say to us. But let me put a different spin on it and, to do this, let me invite you into a story—a story about a woman who had been poor all her life.

☐One day she met the man of her dreams, a wonderful person and very wealthy, and she could not believe her ears when he asked her to marry him. After the wedding they moved into a beautiful suburban residence and lived in surroundings she had only seen in the movies. God was indeed smiling on her. Then tragedy struck. One day she began to feel extremely ill. It was a feeling she had never experienced before. She eventually went to the hospital where the doctors diagnosed her illness as terminal. The impact that the diagnosis had on her, as you might well imagine, was devastating. She suddenly felt that God had withdrawn his love.

In a fury, she wanted to tell God off. So, in her hospital gown and robe, she struggled through the corridors on her way to the chapel. It was to be a face-to-face confrontation. She felt so weak, however, that she had to support herself by bracing against the wall as she moved along. When she entered the chapel, it was dark. No one else was there. She proceeded up the center aisle on her way to the altar. Through what seemed like an endless journey from her room to the chapel, she had been preparing her speech. "O God, you are a fraud, a real phony. You've been passing yourself off as love for two thousand years. But every time someone finds a little bit of happiness, you pull the rug out from under her feet and cancel your love. Well, I just wanted you to know that I have had it. You are fickle; I see through you!"

In the center aisle and near the front of the chapel, she fell. She was so weak she could hardly see. Her eyes could barely read the words woven into the carpet at the step of the sanctuary. She read and then repeated the words, YOU ARE MY BELOVED. Then she put her tired head down over her crossed arms and listened. Deep within herself she heard, "You are my Beloved." Finding her way back to her room, she slipped off into a deep and peaceful sleep.☐

Beneath the surface, we have here the gospel story retold. This woman, like the Prodigal Son, experienced great blessings. Like the Prodigal Son she turned against the Father when things went bad and she felt she wasn't loved any more. And, like the Prodigal Son, she turned back to the Father.

Beneath this woman's story and the gospel parable lies this deeper reality, the sense that when things go wrong, especially for good and faithful people, it means that God doesn't love them any more. They reason thus: if they are Beloved Sons and Daughters of God—which means that God loves them—and they remain faithful, they will never know hurt. But if things go wrong, then it is a sign that God has withdrawn his love.

Little do they know, the Prodigal Son and the woman of our story, that this issue had been dealt with before. For the parable of the Prodigal Son and this woman's story are the same as the first temptation of Jesus in the desert. Remember, Jesus had just been baptized and a voice from heaven had declared him "Beloved." God loved him and made this love public. He was Beloved fully and deeply in a way no one else had ever been. He now knew who he was: Beloved. Then he is led to the desert to fast for forty days and be tempted by the devil who plays on his newly under-stood identity and his hunger and tells him, well, if he is Beloved of God, then he should *not* be hungry. After all, whoever heard of a "Beloved by God" not being full? So the temptation is, "Unless you are always full, you are not loved. So turn these stones into bread."

But Jesus responds, "I *am* the Beloved and I *am* hungry, but that doesn't mean that I am not loved. Not every time something bad happens to me will I think Yahweh does not love me. I will not question that I am loved. I do not live by bread alone."

And there you have it. When you come right down to it, we all leave God in one way or another because we feel we are not loved. We leave especially in time of trouble and hurt because we feel that these "being hungry" states are a sign that God has withdrawn his love and we are not Beloved any more, for Beloved people do not go hungry and suffer life's hurts. Otherwise God would turn our stones of sickness and brokenness into the bread of wholeness and health. So we flee. We take our inheritance and take off for another country.

I suggest that we remember the experience of Jesus. I suggest that his parable for today is not only about returning home seeking forgiveness. It's about returning home because the Father never left. He never moved. You did. He has never ceased to call you Beloved. *Jesus* knew that. He wants you to know that too.

Yes, you are ill, but you are Beloved.

Yes, things are going wrong in your life, but you are Beloved.

Yes, you are fed up disgusted, hurt, but you are Beloved.

Yes, you are hungry—hungry for love and acceptance—but you are Beloved.

The story is about coming home again. Not from sin and alienation, but in your heart. The parable has a profound message. Whatever is happening to you, there is one constant: you are Beloved.

13. ABBOT MACARIUS: A PARABLE
(Lk 6:39–45 8th Sunday in O.T. Year C)

[Instruction to the people before reading the gospel: "You are about to hear the challenging word of Jesus about being judgmental, superior, hypocritical, so please attend carefully. To drive these points home, I am going to read the gospel twice. Once is from St. Luke and, after I'm finished, you will sit. The second is the same gospel in story form and, after I'm finished that, I will sit."]

❏Once upon a time, Abbot Macarius, a holy monk, was caught up into seventh heaven and talked with Jesus. When he returned to earth, so to speak, he was radiant and his disciples knew something unusual had happened, that he had a vision of the Lord. So right away they were pressing him, "What went on? What went on? What did you talk about?"

"Well," said Abbot Macarius serenely, "one of the things the Master told me was that I am going to enter the Kingdom of Heaven. And, not only that, but I am going to sit at the main banquet table right next to the Lord himself!" The disciples were ecstatic to know that their Master, the Holy Monk, Abbot Macarius, would be sitting right next to the Lord Jesus in the Kingdom because, as is well known, all Masters took their disciples with them. So naturally they were overjoyed, but also, at the same time, they were anxious. "This is not going to happen soon?" they asked. "No," smiled Abbot Macarius, "I don't think it's going to be for a while. You don't have to worry."

Nevertheless, as the days went by, Abbot Macarius began to wonder about certain things. More specifically, he wondered that, if he was going to be at the Grand Banquet sitting on one side of the Lord, *who* was going to be siting on the other side for all eternity? Not, mind you, that he thought he would get bored talking to the Lord, but still—still he wondered who *would* be sitting on the other side?

After a while he became quite obsessed with the issue and began asking Jesus who it would be. In the beginning, the Lord was not overjoyed with this question and simply said, "You don't need to know." But Abbot Macarius kept hammering and hammering at him until at last he said, "O.K., O.K., I'll tell you who it is." So he gave Abbot Macarius his name, the name of another monk, a hermit, far, far away. He in turn told his disciples and, for the next few months, they spent all their time tracking down this man. And as soon as they found out where he lived, the disciples told Abbot Macarius and Abbot Macarius decided he would go and visit him. And he would go during the Great Holy Week so they could celebrate the great mysteries together.

Well, it was a stormy night and it was getting dark and it was getting colder than expected. He found the house and he knew the man was home because smoke was coming out of the chimney. Abbot Macarius knocked on the door very loudly and listened. Not a sound. Nobody came to the door. He rapped again and shouted, "Let me in! Let me in!" Nothing. Then he heard some grunts behind the door, but nothing that sounded like a human being. He rapped on the door again and said, "I am a monk, an abbot! Easter is coming. Already the darkness is setting in. You must let me in!"

With that the door opened and Abbot Macarius beheld one of the biggest men he had ever seen. The man filled the whole doorway and had to bend to get out. He had a ragged beard and he was huge. Abbot Macarius had to squeeze himself in the doorway to get in and when he got in he noticed that the hut was very barren. It had a table and a chair and a bed, but nothing else except big cupboards and boxes of stuff. He said, "Are you Brother so-and-so?" The man replied, "Yeah." "Well," said Abbot Macarius, "I am also a monk, an abbot, the head of a monastery, and I have come to visit you." The Huge Monk said, "I know who you are." "Well, aren't you going to invite me in for Holy Week?" The Huge Monk said, "No. I don't celebrate Holy Week."

This shocked Abbot Macarius. He thought to himself, "This man is so holy that he is going to sit next to me in the Heavenly Banquet forever, but he doesn't celebrate Holy Week? This is interesting." And he said out loud, "Well, I'm going to. Do you want to join me?" The big monk said, "No. You can do what you want." So Abbot Macarius took out the missal, lit the candles, brought out the bread and wine, and began to celebrate Mass for Holy Thursday. Meanwhile, the other monk began to eat his meal. He opened up the cupboard and took out food. He opened up boxes and took out food. He laid the food on the bed, offering nothing to Abbot Macarius, and started stuffing himself. He ate everything in sight and he ate for hours. Finally, Abbot Macarius realized that if he was going to eat at all, he was going to have to take it. So he grabbed a little here and a little there, enough to keep body and soul together.

After they were finished and began putting away what was left, the Huge Monk suddenly said, "O.K., you've eaten. Now, get out. Get away. Go!" But Abbot Macarius exclaimed, "You can't get rid of me. This is Holy Thursday. You have to let me stay here for at least two more days, till Easter." "Well, all right," said the Huge Monk. "Find yourself a place to sleep." And with that he plopped himself down on his bed and went to sleep. Abbot Macarius watched him a while and then thought to himself, "Sometimes, you know, there are hidden saints who are so holy that they hide their holiness and their devotion from the rest of the people. They usually pray all night in the dark, doing penance for the world. Maybe he's going to get up while I'm asleep and spend the whole night in prayer. I'll just pretend I'm asleep and I'll watch."

So all night long Abbot Macarius struggled to stay awake seeing what the man would do, but all that he did was snore very loudly, turn over, whomp the pillow, and bang the wall. Abbot Macarius did not get much sleep, but the monk seemed to do pretty well. The next morning, the Huge Monk got up and the first thing he said was, "Get out!" Abbot Macarius protested, "I can't leave, It's Good Friday. I can't go till tomorrow, the Easter vigil." Well, there was a repeat for breakfast. Food came out of everywhere and the other monk stuffed himself again. Same thing at lunch and dinner and the next day as well. Nothing was offered to Abbot Macarius.

At this point he was definitely having second thoughts. This man was a clod. He was crude, rude, ignorant. He didn't keep

Holy Week, didn't fast, didn't pray. He felt he had wasted his time in coming. This *couldn't* be the man who would be sitting next to him at the Heavenly Banquet forever. Did he misunderstand the Lord? No, he didn't think so. So he was beginning to wonder about the Lord, that he would make these kind of decisions. But why? He, Abbot Macarius, deserved better than this. After all, he was the head of a monastery. He kept Holy Week. He fasted. He prayed. He observed the Holy Rule. He had devoted followers and he spoke with the Lord. But this other man, this huge oaf, was clearly an inferior breed, ill-mannered, selfish, and, worst of all, a non-observant monk. In short, a sinner.

Well, thank heaven, Holy Saturday came and the vigil was over and Abbot Macarius was about to leave—and gladly at that. He was anxious to get away from such an inferior human being. He spoke to the Huge Monk. He said, "I came here because the Lord told me—and he told me very clearly—that you are going to sit next to me at the Heavenly Banquet forever." "Oh, yeah?" said the Huge Monk, "That's only if you believe that there *is* a Heavenly Banquet that lasts forever!" That was too much for Abbot Macarius and confirmed his worst suspicions. He stepped back from the brother so he wouldn't be contaminated, held his ears and raised his eyes to heaven and exclaimed, "Enough! Enough! I'm going. But I need to ask you before I leave. Why do you *live* this way? Why do you not pray as I do? Why do you not celebrate Holy Week? And, most of all, why do you stuff yourself every day?"

There was a long silence. Then the Huge Monk looked at him with tears in his eyes and he said, "I'll tell you why. When I was very young, six or seven years old, I lived with my parents and my grandparents and my great-grandparents. And we were very simple. We farmed our land and did what we could. And then the Infidels came. They burned everything to the ground. They destroyed the fields. They killed everyone. I watched them slaughter my mother, my father, my brothers, my sisters. The only ones they missed were my old grandfather and me. They left us with nothing, even though we had begged God for mercy. We had been good Christians."

He said, "We lived as best we could. We cleared a plot of land that had been burned. We started to plant and to try to put our lives back together again. Every morning after we planted, my grandfather would send me down to the stream and I would bring back water. It was only two or three years after this that the Infidels came again. It seems they come in every generation at least once or twice to burn us out. But I was hiding in the bushes because I was bringing water back from the stream. And they got my grandfather, and they tied him to a tree and tried to make him blaspheme Jesus. And he wouldn't. He was a tiny wisp of a man, with straggly hair and poor—like the rest of us. And they threatened to kill him if he didn't blaspheme Jesus Christ. But he refused, praying aloud. And so they poured kerosene on him, and they lit him, and they watched him go up in flames. And I watched my grandfather. He went up so quick! Just like a flicker of a candle and he was out. And from that day forward, I swore to myself that when they came again—and they will—they'd find somebody who was so big and so fat that when they tied me to a tree and poured kerosene over me and lit me, I would burn so long, and so hot, and the fire would be so great, that they and the whole surrounding area would know that Jesus Christ has a witness and that God is still served."

And, as the tears continued to run down his face, the Huge Monk started to pray, "O Lord Jesus, Master of all, how long will you let your children kill each other?" And as the man continued to pray, Abbot Macarius started to inch his way out the door. As he closed the door softly behind him and listened to the man continuing praying, for the first time in his life, Abbot Macarius wondered whether *he* was worthy to sit at the table at the Heavenly Banquet next to that man.□

14. INTENT TO KILL
(Lk 4:21–30   4th Sunday in O.T.   Year C)

This is a "made for television" gospel. It has all the makings of a TV drama. As you heard, it goes from acceptance of this prophet, to doubt, to challenge, to rejection and, finally, to hate with the intent to kill. But he escapes mysteriously. A good script. But, of course, the gospel is not made for television. It is made for us. So we must look at it more closely.

We begin by noting that Jesus preached "a year of favor from the Lord." A year of favor is a technical term. It means a time of jubilee when the Roman yoke would be cast off and burdensome taxes would be lifted. And, indeed, that was good news, something to cheer about. But—and this is what riled the crowd—to include as also favorable to the Lord the Gentiles and to mention specifically Gentiles like Naaman the leper and the widow from Zarephath as being saved was too much for them. For several reasons.

First of all, such words shattered their notion of privilege. Secondly, they broke down the officially sanctioned barriers of hatred and challenged them to see others as also brothers and sisters under the same Lord. And they found that to be quite an unacceptable message. And so, they decided to kill the messenger.

Our reaction to this whole scene? "Those blind, stupid, narrow-minded people!" Jesus' reaction to this scene is to look at us and ask, "Those?" We are "those." The fact is, we reject our prophets all the time. We don't want to hear the truth. We're like the man whose doctor decided that he had to tell the truth about his condition. He said, "You're a very sick man. You probably won't live more than a couple of weeks at most. You should settle your affairs. Is there anybody you want me to call?" "Yes," replied the sick man, "another doctor." We call for another prophet when the real one challenges us. We reject the truth and the truth-givers. And we do this in three ways.

First, we reject the message of those prophets who do not conform to our preconceived ideas. That's what Jesus' congregation did. "How can he say anything worthwhile?" they asked one another. "Is this not the carpenter's son? How can he know anything? He's not our idea of a prophet."

❑When the devil saw a seeker of truth enter the house of the Master, he was determined to do everything in his power to turn him back from his quest. So he subjected him to every form of temptation—wealth, lust, prestige—but the seeker was able to fight off these temptations quite easily. When the seeker got to the Master's house he was somewhat taken aback to see the Master sitting in an upholstered chair with his disciples at his feet. "That man certainly lacks humility, the principle virtue of saints," he thought to himself. Then he observed other things about the Master he did not like. For one thing, the Master took little notice of him. "I suppose that's because I do not fawn over him like the others do," he said to himself. He also disliked the kind of clothes the Master wore and the somewhat conceited way that he spoke. And all this led him to the conclusion that he had come to the wrong place and must continue his quest elsewhere. As he walked out of the room, the Master, who had seen the devil seated in the corner of the room, said, "You need not have worried, tempter. He was yours from the very first, you know."❑

To accept the prophet, we must give up our preconceived notions of where we will find truth and to be ready to accept it in many disguises. We have a tendency to reject those prophets who do not conform to what we think they should be.

Second, we reject those prophets who come to us with demands. Remember the rich young man who went away because Jesus had urged him to sell his property and to give it to the poor and follow him? For that rich young man, good as he was, that was too much a of a demand. And so he turned his back on Jesus.

❑Abou Adam was wealthy according to every earthly measure. At the same time, however, he sincerely strove to be spiritually wealthy as well. One night he was aroused from his sleep by a fearful stomping on the roof above his head. Alarmed, he sat bolt upright in his bed and shouted, "Who's there?" "A friend," came the reply from the roof. "I've lost my camel." Perturbed by such stupidity, Abou screamed, "You idiot! Are you looking for a camel on the roof?" "You idiot!" the voice shot back. "Are you looking for God in silk clothing, lying on a golden bed?"☐

Sell what you have and give to the poor. That's a demand not too palatable. I remember in one of those Christmas issues of *The New Yorker* a cartoon that depicted some very wealthy gentleman at a very proper club lifting up a very proper glass to propose a toast: "Here's to the rich, the very rich, the filthy rich. Have I left anyone out?"

Have we left anyone out? To feed the hungry, to give drink to the thirsty, to clothe the naked, to visit the imprisoned, to comfort the sick . . . have we left anyone out? Is prophet Jesus making too many demands to the point where we reject him?

Third, we reject the prophets who disturb us. What did the prophet Jesus say? "If you love only those who love you back, what reward is that? Do not even the tax collectors do as much? If you greet only your kin, what more are you doing than others? Turn the other cheek if someone strikes you. Forgive your enemies. Pray for those who persecute you." Why did he have to say such things that disturb us?

☐He's like the prophet Elijah whom he mentions in the gospel. Elijah would go around, as was his habit, in disguise. He wanted to find out how people talked to each other, how people treated each other, how they acted toward each other. He would often give them a test. One day, he disguised himself with dirty, raggedy, beggar clothes and he went up to a big mansion. It just so happened that there was a big wedding party going on there. He knocked at the door. The father of the bride came to the door, opened it up, and saw this man in his filthy rags and said, "I don't know what you're doing here, sir, but if you think you're coming to this wedding, you have a second thought coming. You are not welcomed here." And he slammed the door in his face.

Elijah left. A little later on, he returned. But now he was dressed in splendor: white suit, satin vest, silk top hat, and a gold-handled cane. He knocked at the door. The father of the bride

came, opened the door, saw this elegant gentleman, and welcomed him with great honor. And with great honor he led him to
the head table. With great honor he laid before him the finest of
foods and the finest of wines. Elijah looked around. People were
looking at this well-dressed stranger. And then, all of a sudden,
he took the food and began to stuff it in his pockets, every pocket he could find. And then he poured the wine all over himself.
Well, the people never saw such a custom. Would he explain?
Elijah answered, "When I came dressed as a beggar, I was thrown
out. And when I returned in elegant clothes, I was welcomed and
given the place of honor. But I am the same person. All that has
changed were my clothes. And so, since my clothes were welcomed to the feast, why should they not be *fed* the feast?"

The people hung their heads in shame and, when they lifted
them up again, he had disappeared. All that was left was a gold-
handled cane on the chair.□

"Lord, when did we see you hungry and not feed you? Lord,
when did we see you thirsty and not give you drink? Lord, when
did we see you naked and not clothe you?" The response? "As
long as you did not do these things to the least of my brethren,
you did not do them to me." We hate prophets who make
demands like that and come disguised as the down-and-outers.

Jesus speaks hard sayings. There's no denying that. He challenges our preconceptions. He asks us to see him in the poor and
disenfranchised, among the Gentiles, so to speak. Shall we reject
the prophet who comes to us in that way? He comes with his
demands for brotherhood and sisterhood. Shall we rise up
against him? He disturbs us with difficult sayings. Shall we toss
him over the hill with the intent to kill? He has fashioned this
gospel. Is it really a gospel for "those" people of yesterday?

No, it is decidedly a gospel for the people of today.

15. OUR THREE TEMPTATIONS
(Lk 4:1–13 1st Sunday of Lent Year C)

It is worth noting that the first real lenten people were not Christians, but rather they were pagans on the way to be Christians. These learners, these neophytes, or, as we call them, these catechumens, publicly wore sackcloth and ashes and lived the days before Easter as open, repentant sinners. But something happened when the long-time Christians noticed something remarkable at the Easter baptism. They were struck by the joy and by the radiant faces of those just baptized and they were, to put it frankly, quite envious. Why should the catechumens have all the fun? They, too, longed once more to experience the thrill of a new birth and the strength of a new life. They realized that they had become somewhat ho-hum and routine in their faith and so they decided to do something about it.

Well, the following year, when the catechumens began their preparation for their baptism at Easter, the already-Christians joined them! They too put on sackcloth and ashes and they too traversed the forty days as repentant sinners. They did this so that once more they could rekindle their faith, apologize for luke-warmness, and experience once more the joys of rebirth at Easter. And that is how Lent got into our church.

Along with this development came the standard gospel that kicked off Lent and that Christians have heard on the first Sunday of Lent since the fifth century, the gospel you just heard, the story of the three temptations. It proved to be a good motivational point to get started on the common journey of renewal and repentance. It was kept since the fifth century because its motif was timeless, that is to say, because each generation of Christians had its own particular three temptations that had seduced them from their First Love.

So, here we are, some 15 or 16 centuries later, hearing the same gospel and dealing with *our* three temptations. They're not the same as they were in the fifth century or the tenth or the seventeenth centuries. We have our own peculiar ones. What might they be? I suggest these three.

The first temptation for modern people is the neglect of the inner life. This is probably our most severe temptation. In the newspaper the other day, there was an article on Marcia Clark, who was the chief prosecutor in the O.J. Simpson trial. It tells about her 14-year marriage dissolving and consequently their two little boys, ages three and five, getting scared early on in life. Her husband complains that she works so hard and so long that she never sees their children. She says in turn that in fact the children mean everything to her, more than anything else in life. Yet, last December, the paper pointed out, she worked a six- or seven-day week for as many as 16 hours a day. I have no comment about the divorce or the children or working mothers or anything like that. My comment is simply this: working seven days a week, 16 hours a day, with maybe four or five hours for sleep—what time is there for the inner life when one works like that?

This past week *Newsweek* had on its cover one simple word: "Exhausted!" The inside article relates how the syndrome of exhaustion is depleting Americans, from the president of Harvard all the way down; who, because of modern technology, are more enslaved than ever, not emancipated as was predicted. The article talks about one woman named Marge Sullins who worked up to 70 hours a week, leaving barely enough time for herself and her friends and her 20-year-old son. Finally she collapsed physically. Again, what time is there for the inner life?

The article comments about past days when life was hard but, as it says: "Grandpa clocked in long hours on the railroad or in the mines, but when he came home there were no faxes waiting for him to answer, no cellular phones or E-mail to interrupt his after dinner smoke. Home was home, not a pit-stop for data gathering before heading back to the office. Today there is no down time, no escape from other people. We have cell phones in the car and beepers in our pockets. We carry them to Disneyland, to the beach and to the bathroom."

All this means, says Boston Medical Center's doctor, Dr. Mark Moskowitz, "that a lot of people are working 24 hours a day, seven days a week, even when they're not technically at work. A formula guaranteed for breakdown." The article goes on to mention one thriving business I never heard of—or dreamed of: Rent-a-Mom. It's one of the booming businesses in the United States. Rent-a-Mom shops take care of kids and do all the things for parents who aren't there or can't be there because of the pressure of work or career.

The article ends with a photo of a young man named Brad Sharek and beneath the photo of him sitting at his computer are these words: "The California software executive fully accepts the pressures of his three-person job which means 15-hour days and eating at his laptop. The reason, he says, is 'that the potential pay-off is so big.'" By that he means he's going to make a lot of money someday. Fifteen hours a day? Eating alone at a machine? "There's never enough time!" is the American cry. True. Never enough time to cultivate the inner life and the life of relationships. This is our first and severest temptation. Do we recognize it? Is it ours?

The second temptation for moderns may sound strange at first, but the more you think of it, the more valid it is. And that is, the temptation to hang onto emotional garbage. With so many divorces today, broken relationships, fractured and mobile lives, people are tied into debilitating memories and experiences.

❑A woman was telling her new workplace friend how awful her former boss had been. And her friend just laughed and said, "So forget him. Why not just enjoy it here?" And she went on to tell a little story about herself. She said, "I'm reminded of the time that I moved a few years ago. I was making enough money to have a professional mover pack for me and so when he asked me what I wanted to have him pack, I just waved my arm and said, 'Everything.' So when I got to my new place I saw that he had taken me literally. Along with my furniture, he had packed up my trash bins and, well, there I was in my beautiful new place with all my old garbage, including old newspapers, empty ketchup bottles and grapefruit peels." She was trying to tell her friend something.❑

What emotional and spiritual garbage are you carrying around with you? The hurts, betrayals, the sin, the guilt? Lent is the time to hand things over to God and get on with your life, your spiritual journey. That's a temptation: to hang onto emotional and spiritual garbage. Let them go. Lent is renewal time, a time when sins are atoned for, forgiven, and new beginnings are at hand. You can't see the Easter ahead looking back.

The third temptation for us moderns is to think we're different. Years ago, on Ash Wednesday I received a call from a young man I had known from another parish. He was a struggling graduate student and was crying out for help. When I got to his apartment, I found a tortured soul, filled with self-doubt, and filled with booze. Well, eventually, I got him to an AA meeting. But even though he was an alcoholic, he told me that he couldn't go back to another meeting because "I'm not like those people." I've never forgotten that line. "I'm not like those people." It taught me how strong this third temptation is: convincing oneself that somehow you're different. You don't share life's pains and limitations. You don't need the help of Christ or Lent's journey or the support of the people making it. That Lent is for masochists and religious fanatics. "I'm not like those people—in need of redemption."

So these are the three temptations for us moderns: to neglect the inner life, to hang onto emotional baggage, and to declare we're different, above the common journey.

Today's Scriptures directly confront such temptations and boldly proclaim that for Lent we must go into the desert and face two realities: our temptations and our God.

16. DOUBTING JOHN

(Mt 11:2–11   3rd Sunday of Advent   Year A)

It is worth noting that the gospel story of Jesus Christ is bracketed by two doubters. At the beginning of the story stands John. At the end of the story stands Thomas. Like a living parenthesis, they introduce and end the story of Jesus. These two men have much in common. Both are in the gospel. Both started out as believers. Both wound up as doubters. Both had received a call. John was called by the Spirit and sanctified in his mother's womb. Thomas was called by Jesus himself, "Come, follow me," and there was indeed that initial fervor and commitment. As for John the Baptist, after all, he baptized Jesus and heard the voice from heaven declaring that Jesus was a Beloved Son; listen to him. John said of Jesus that he was indeed the one who was to come, whose sandal he was not fit to tie, that Jesus was the one who was to come after him but is greater than him, that he, John, must decrease and he, Jesus, must increase. It's all there at the beginning of the Jesus story.

And at the end of the Jesus story, there's Thomas, called, as we said, by Jesus, witness to his miracles, and companion on his journeys. That took a great faith. And yet, at the end, after it was all over, after Easter, Thomas doubted. Doubting Thomas. And John? Here he is: John with second thoughts. Doubting John. Perhaps because he's languishing in a filthy prison, perhaps because he's heard nothing about the man he baptized, except bits and pieces. In any case, he wonders if he made a mistake. So he, always a direct man, sends two of his disciples who had visited him in prison to seek out Jesus and forthrightly express his doubts: "Are you in fact the one who is to come, that is, the promised Messiah—I'm not so sure any more—or shall we get on with it and look for another?"

Thomas and John: faithful ones who wound up as doubters. Now, let's add a third: ourselves. Let's be honest. Who is innocent of doubt? Who has never started out as a faithful disciple and wound up asking John's question? Just one look at our world, one acknowledgment of the crime rate, the fear, the drug addicts, the child abuse, the too many people who need more than we can give, the slaughter in Bosnia and Rwanda and on our streets and, sooner or later, we ask: Where *is* the Kingdom Jesus came to bring? Just one look at our own lives—the anger, the hurt, the tragedies, the disappointments, the losses—and we ask, where is Jesus? Shall we look for another? asks John. Some have looked. We know that. Perhaps in our own family. Some have abandoned the church, switched religion, or just dropped out. Others in desperation for *something* buy into therapies and New Age stuff, crystals, angels, miracles, and after-death books. There's got to be a Kingdom out there *somewhere*.

Is there any way out of this? Yes. The way out is in the answer Doubting John receives, an answer, not a direct one, but a powerful one: "Go and tell John what you hear and see: the blind recover their sight, cripples walk, lepers are cured, the deaf hear, the dead are raised to life, and the poor have the good news preached to them." You see, John's problem, like Thomas's problem later on, was *distraction*. Thomas concentrated so much on the horrible crucifixion that he didn't see the resurrection. John concentrated so much on horrors of prison life that he didn't see the Kingdom. So they both slipped from faith to doubt. Remember, at this time John was in prison and knew only the bad news: the tragedies and crimes and squalor of his fellow prisoners, and too much bad news distorts reality. No wonder he lost his first fervor.

And we are in the same position. We are in the same position. We are inundated, are we not, with bad news as a daily diet. Our papers today, our TV newscasts fill us with endless images of child abuse, infidelity, youthful killers, royal scandals, celebrity divorces, war, torture, and moral mayhem. Our movies fill us with endless images of unbelievable garroting, slicing, blood-letting and brutality of every sort, from a man's head being squeezed to a pulp in a vise in *Casino* to the torching of a toll booth in *Money Train*. We have become desensitized to violence and enured to suffering. We take abandoned children—abandoned by the poor and the rich, the poor by poverty, the rich by careers—as normal, divorce as inevitable, and out-of-wedlock births as commonplace. We are subject to and forced to concentrate on life's horrors. No wonder we ask of Jesus Christ: Are you the one who is to come? Where are you in all this mess? Where is your kingdom? I have my doubts about you. Count me in with John and Thomas.

But I suggest we, like John, are the victims of too much bad news and *that's* why we ask his question, *Are* you the one who is to come? But I tell you, Jesus' answer still stands. Which comes down to, "Take time to look at the *good* news and you will perceive the Kingdom." Right now as I speak to you, there are endless, daily, routine instances of the blind seeing. Think of the countless catechists letting in the light of the gospel all over the globe. Catholic schools, with great hardship, for example, in Philadelphia or New York, are educating hundreds of thousands of minority children and many non-Catholic minority children through dedicated, underpaid staff and teachers. Converts to the church continue at a large rate, although you never hear about it. Millions of cripples are walking, hanging on the arms of orderlies and nurses all over the world. Lepers are cured and church-run leprosaria are among the largest in the world. The deaf are hearing the word of God from endless clerical and lay ministers who surround the globe. The dead are raised to life as people recover from addictions, accidents, illness, and depression at the hands of innumerable counselors, volunteer firefighters and first aid personnel, therapists, and healers. The poor have the good news preached to them in the way of comfort and aid. Catholic Relief Services is the largest single private charitable service in the world and the largest single caregiver of AIDS patients as well. Did you know that?

Every day the corporal and spiritual works of mercy are being carried out in hundreds of millions of ways, but they never make the media news. Virtue seldom does. Why, look around in this building where the church has met for worship. Look how you love your children, provide for their needs. Look how you care for one another. The gifts you bought to light up someone's life, the house you prepared to make life festive are small examples of daily decency and love. Look at the countless charities you take for granted.

Of course, there's the hitch. You take these things for granted. I have always maintained, for example, that all parents are guaranteed to get to heaven. Remember, there is only one place in the entire gospel where Jesus gives the criteria of who gets to heaven. It's in Matthew 25. When I was hungry you gave me to eat, when I was thirsty you gave me to drink, when I was ill you visited me, and so on. As long as you did it to one of the least of my brethren you did it to me. Enter into the joy of the Lord. You know, the corporal and spiritual works of mercy—*and*, they are built into family life by nature. You can't escape them, which is why I said that all parents are guaranteed to get to heaven: "Mom, what'll I wear?"—counseling the doubtful. "Dad, will you help me with my math?"—instructing the ignorant. The 2:00 a.m. bottle—giving drink to the thirsty. Changing diapers—clothing the naked. Preparing meals—feeding the hungry. The cat died—burying the dead. "Are you still in the bathroom?"—visiting the imprisoned.

Well, you say, I *have* to do these things. It's my job, my duty, as if *that* made it less wonderful, less meritorious, less the fulfillment of Jesus' criteria for heaven. But my point is, *these things go on all the time.* The Kingdom of Jesus is here. Goodness abounds. Love is given and received. People are faithful. Caring, courtesy, and good deeds are commonplace.

So heed Jesus' warning: "Blessed is the one who finds no stumbling block in me." That is, don't let the daily diet of bad news trip you up. When we look around at a world out of control, we all have our doubts at times and side with John and Thomas. It's only human to do so. But in Advent we are told to lift up our heads. For looking *down* at the ground too much distorts the truth. Looking *up* in expectation helps us perceive the Christ in our lives. The Kingdom of God is at hand, indeed, here among us. Every day, the blind see, the crippled walk, the deaf hear, the dead rise, and the poor have the Good News preached to them. Every day. Like now.

17. WHAT I HAVE FAILED TO DO
(Mt 18:21–35 24th Sunday in O.T. Year A)

❑Thomas Fleming writes of his father who, back in the 1900s in Jersey City, had to go to work right out of grammar school. He worked in a watch factory, owned by the ruling Blaine family, right next door to his home. It was dull, monotonous work but it paid a dollar a day, good money back then. His father told him, "Each morning they opened the doors and we filed in one by one. Sitting there behind a desk would be an old high-collared clerk. You'd get in front of the desk and he'd ask you: 'Protestant or Catholic?' If anyone answered 'Catholic' he was told, 'No openings today.' If you said 'Protestant' you were handed a slip and told to report to a certain section for work. Like many other immigrant Catholics in the line, I gritted my teeth and said 'Protestant' —we needed the buck that badly."

The Blaines and their like held the social and political dominance in Jersey City with a vengeance. Gradually, in a long and bitter battle at the ballot box, people like Fleming's father joined forces with Frank Hague in the 1920s to eventually unseat them. The 1929 crash sealed the defeat of the old Protestant guard and many were reduced to poverty, including old Mr. Blaine's son. One day, writes Fleming, in 1940 a man in a frayed coat with stains on it came up the icy walk to their house to see his father. His father came downstairs, held out his hand, and said, "Nice to see you, Mr. Blaine. What can I do for you?" "Mr. Fleming, I need a job. I don't know whether you can help me. I don't know whether you *will* help me. I know my family hasn't been on your side politically."

Fleming writes, "There was silence for a moment. Here, if ever, was the perfect moment for revenge. How easily my father could even the score for those days of humiliation in the watch factory by throwing the man out of our house. And in this same moment . . . I realized that I wanted him to do just that. In the most savage, burning way I wanted to savor the taste of revenge.

Now ask him, 'Protestant or Catholic?' I wanted to scream. Instead, my father's voice came up to me steady and calm. "What kind of work can you do, Mr. Blaine?" Fleming goes on to tell about his father's promise to help the man. He ends his story with these words, "Mr. Blaine disappeared into the windy night. I sat on the stairs, thinking of those ragged lines filing into the watch factory each morning to accept their humiliation. . . . They were a part of history now. . . . With five minutes of matter-of-fact kindness my father had healed the wound, and proved to me the ready power of his quiet faith.'❑

A lovely story of forgiveness, the very theme of today's gospel. But I would like to stretch that theme beyond the usual need to forgive what has been done to the need to forgive what has not been done. In other words, to talk in terms of forgiveness of our sins of omission. As our Confiteor at the beginning of Mass proclaimed, "for what we have done and for what we have failed to do." There are two omissions in particular that I have in mind: the omission of charity and the omission of honor. Both need deep forgiveness. And so, in a kind of examination of conscience, let me illustrate each of these needs by a story. One is a classic tale that you know so well and the other is not, but has its powerful point.

❑The classic tale is Oscar Wilde's *The Happy Prince*. You will recall that the happy prince is nothing more than an exquisite statue gilded over with gold leaf standing on a pedestal high above the city. He looked down upon it with his blue sapphire eyes and guarded his domain with his sword in which was embedded a priceless ruby. One night a small lost swallow landed wearily at the prince's feet to rest. But before he could fall asleep, he felt a cascade of water pouring down on him. He looked up and saw that it was the happy prince crying. For the prince could see from his lofty perch a sick child begging his mother for an orange while his poor mother worked with bleeding fingers embroidering the gown of a rich woman. "Swallow," said the prince, "please stay with me. Stay with me tonight and be my messenger. The boy is so thirsty and the mother is so sad." The bird agreed and, following the prince's instructions, took the ruby from the sword and dropped it on the table next to the thimble of the woman. The next day the prince saw a young writer in his garret which was so cold that his fingers were frozen and he could not write to finish his play. So the happy prince had the swallow pluck out one of his sapphire eyes and fly it to the young playwright. The next day it was a little match girl whose matches had fallen into the water. She would sell none and her father would beat her severely. Again, the prince had the swallow bring his other sapphire eye to her.

At this point the swallow knew that he could not leave the sightless prince alone and so he stayed to act as his eyes and to pull off, one by one, the gold leaf from his body to bring them to all those who were hurting. Finally, one freezing day, the prince was completely stripped of all his riches. He had given everything—his ruby, his sapphires, his gold leaf. The swallow, too, had given his all. The bitter cold that he should have left long ago, got to him. In a last effort he flew up to the prince's lips, kissed them, and fell dead at his feet. At that moment, the leaden heart of the happy prince snapped in two.

Finally, the townspeople, disgusted at the eyesore that the statue had become, tore it down and melted it in a blast furnace. But the broken lead heart refused to melt, so the townspeople picked it up and tossed it beside the body of the dead swallow.

Looking down on earth, God said to one of his angels, "Bring me the two most precious things in that city." The angel returned with the leaden heart and the dead swallow. "You have rightly chosen," said God, "for in my garden of Paradise the little bird shall sing forevermore, and in my city of gold, the happy prince shall praise me."◻

For the charity deferred, O Lord, forgive me.
For the heroism denied, O Lord, forgive me.
For seeing, but not acting, O Lord, forgive me.

◻My second story concerns an incident during World War II where a young sailor struck up a pen pal relationship with a woman he had never met. The way it happened was that one day he was in the library getting a book when he noticed that there were pencil notations in the margin. And they were so deep and loving that he decided then and there that he would have to meet the person who wrote such beautiful thoughts. He went to the librarian and got the name of the woman who had written those lovely words. The day after his introductory letter to her as pen pal he was shipped overseas. But for the next year the two corresponded regularly back and forth, exchanging a great deal of pleasure in revealing their deepest thoughts. At different times the sailor asked for a picture of his correspondent but he never received one. But still, their feelings for each other grew.

It was finally time for him to return to the United States. He and his pen pal decided they would meet at seven o'clock and a rendezvous was arranged for Grand Central Station. How would he know her? She wrote back that he would know her by the red rose that she would wear in her lapel. Well, shortly after entering the station, a tall, beautiful blonde, in a pale green suit, sauntered by. Almost magnetically, the lonely young man was drawn toward this woman and her alluring vitality and sensuality. She smiled at him and even murmured,"Going my way, sailor?" as she passed by. But her spell over him was broken when he suddenly saw behind her a woman wearing a red rose in her lapel. His heart sank because she was as plain as the blonde had been stunning. She was fortyish, roundish, grayish, but with two sparking eyes in a gentle face. As the blonde walked away, the young sailor hesitated for a moment, but then turned his back on her beauty and strode over to the simple woman who was wearing the red rose in her lapel.

Looking at her, he faced the disappointed realization that their relationship could never really be a romantic one. And yet, on the other hand, he was buoyed by the memory of their letters and of the prospect of having at least a lifelong friend, one whose wit and spirituality and intelligence he already knew from their correspondence. And so, the young sailor introduced himself and suggested that they go out to dinner. But the woman just smiled at him with amusement and told him, "I don't know what this is all about, son, but the young lady in the green suit who just went by begged me to wear this rose on my coat. And she said that if you were to ask me out to dinner, she's waiting for you in the restaurant across the street. She said it was some kind of a test."□

For the honor not kept, O Lord, forgive me.
For the distractions rooted in selfishness, O Lord, forgive me.
For the embracing of glitz over substance, O Lord, forgive me.

18. I HAVE A DREAM
(Mt 2:13–15, 19–23 The Holy Family Year A)

In my former parish we customarily added two items to the baptism ceremony, which always took place at Mass. This was sensible, baptizing at Mass, because the faith community now had a new brother or sister and it was only right to welcome them and be aware of them. The first custom was to invite an older member of the parish to come up and silently lay his or her hands on the newly baptized infants as a sign of passing on the traditions and dreams of the faith. Very moving, very touching.

The second was to invite the parents, at the end of the ceremony, to share with the congregation their dreams for their child. This was important, no small thing, because these parents were brave enough to bring children into a hostile world to begin with. They had no illusions about the King Herods out there, waiting to slaughter their precious Holy Innocents. Yet they persisted in their dreams and brought them into the world.

King Herod. Wicked King Herod. Yes, they are aware of him. Everyone knows of his existence and his terrible power that still exists. He was metamorphosed fivefold and we can take his name, Herod, H-E-R-O-D, and list the five ways he continues the slaughter of Holy Innocents.

The H stands for King Heroin. The drug culture that claims so many youth. This past Wednesday's *Asbury Park Press* lists James Burke, age 18, Ross Kosick, age 19, as killed in a car accident, a car with more than 20 bags of heroin in it. A third passenger, Joseph Britton, age 16, is in critical condition. They are not from New York or Philadelphia or Los Angeles. They are from Toms River. The same issue of the *Press* proclaims the headline, "Heroin use rises, say police in Brick." Frederick Clark, age 18, died of an overdose there the other day. The youngest victim in Brick was 15. King Heroin is out there: Toms River, Brick, Brielle, Manasquan.

The E stands for King Erotic. Everywhere you go, there is sex presented as recreational, not relational as God meant it to be.

This King claims one-fourth of the nation's children who are fatherless, over a million of them aborted, and soaring out-of-wedlock births. Lots of slaughter here.

The R stands for King Rage, for the violence we live with daily and incessantly presented and glorified in the media. The physical violence, the moral violence. Crime in the streets. Crime in the home.

The O stands for King Only. Only my clan, my tribe, my country, my color, my way. "Others" are suspect, inhuman. Hate and racism flourish where this King reigns.

The D stands for King Divorce, arguably the most common form of child abuse.

Again, in Wednesday's *New York Times* an Op Ed piece pleaded for the children hurt by too easy divorce. The author, a professor at the School of Public Affairs, cites the statistics that between 1960 and 1980 divorce in our country rose by 250 percent before stabilizing at the highest level in the world; that today more than 40 percent of all first marriages are projected to end in divorce and, of course, as everyone knows, that the divorce rate for second marriages is even higher. What was that item I saw the other day? Famous model Christie Brinkley, married on skis a year ago and now a mother, is suing for divorce. One year! Is anyone thinking of this latest fatherless child? Anyway, the author of the article reminds us that research shows that, for children, divorce correlates with poor academic performance, weaker attachment to the world of work, higher rates of crime, depression, suicide, out of wedlock births and—and this is so telling—"diminished propensity to trust others and form stable adult relationships." Which is why children of divorced parents tend to end up in divorce themselves.

So, King Herod lives, lives in his letters: as King Heroin, King Erotic, King Rage, King Only, and King Divorce. H-E-R-O-D. He lives scheming to slaughter innocent children. Well, the parents at our baptism are well aware of this and are nervous and apprehensive, but they have one thing that gives them courage: they have *dreams!* They have dreams. Dreams such as we heard in today's gospel. They have, in fact, three dreams for their children, dreams that will overcome: word dreams, will dreams, and worship dreams.

Word Dreams. They are determined to get to their children first and say, "We can, we *can* make our children's lives happier; we *can* keep our family strong; we *can* offer reassurance, support, and concern. From the beginning we will use words like 'Please' and 'thank you' and 'I'm sorry' and 'I love you'—over and over again till they catch their little souls."

Will Dreams. Dreaming of a good school system means that I *will* attend the parent meetings. I *will* see that homework is done. I *will* monitor TV. Dreaming of a better neighborhood means that I *will* recycle, I *will* keep the property clean, I will not litter. Dreaming of closer family ties means that I *will* put the family ahead of a career, material gain, and social climbing, for what does it profit my children to gain the whole world and suffer the loss of their own parents in the name of a higher standard of living? I *will* give them my most precious gift: time.

Worship Dreams. I will *pray*. I will *teach them* to pray. I will take my children *to church* from the beginning to let them know they belong to a larger faith community, that there is something more to life. Someone more to life. I will let them know of their privileged lives that they must share with the children of the world who go to bed hungry each night and many of whom do not wake up the next morning.

Such dreams, such dreams will overcome and outwit King Herod. Dreams inspired by God, carried by an angel, and fulfilled by those who dare to cherish and live by them.

All of you here are dreamers, else you would not be here. Continue to dream. Dream boldly. Dream openly. Dream loudly. King Herod is strong and that chills our hearts, but God's dreams are stronger and that warms our spirit.

19. CROSSROADS
(Mk 10:17–30 28th Sunday in O.T. Year B)

Four people at the crossroads of their lives express the theme of today's reading. Two turned back, one stayed, and the other is still under consideration. The first person is the man of our gospel. A good man, be it noted, and also, be it noted, expressly loved by Jesus. "Teacher," he said, "what must I do to gain everlasting life?" Although wealthy, he had the insight that wealth was not the answer to life. As I said, a good man. Jesus presents him with a crossroads decision. If you really want everlasting life, Jesus challenges, let go. Let go of your wealth, sell what you have, and be my disciple. The silence. The pondering. The hesitation. Decision time at the crossroads of his life. There was no question of choosing between good and evil. The issue was choosing between the good and the better. The road less traveled. Discipleship. Quietly, he turned around and moved away. He had chosen. He simply said no.

☐The second person also said no. He lived two thousand years after the first man. He was erudite, charming, profound. A good man. He hosted that splendid series on television, *Civilisation*. I am referring, of course, to Sir Kenneth Clark. He later wrote his two-volume autobiography in which he declared that he was in fact a dedicated secular humanist. He did not look down on religion or was indifferent to it. On the contrary, he says some beautiful things about religion, but he simply did not believe. But he does describe a religious experience he had.

It happened while he was sitting in the church of San Lorenzo in Italy. He writes: "For a few minutes, my whole being was irradiated with a kind of heavenly joy, far more intense than anything I have ever known." The whole event enthralled him and he said that he considered himself quite unworthy of such a beautiful experience and could not understand why it was given to him. But, as he reflected on the experience, he was faced with an awkward question. What should he do about it? He was not a religious person in any formal sense and he knew that, if he responded to this mystical experience, if he said yes at this particular crossroad of his life, his family and his friends would think that he had quite gone off the deep end. And so, like the first man of the gospel, he turned his back on it and said no. He wrote, "I think I was right. I was too deeply imbedded in the world to change course, but no doubt I had felt the finger of God and I am quite sure that, although the memory of that experience has faded, it helped me to understand the joy of the saints." Still, for all this, he turned back at a crossroad of his life.☐

☐The third person at the crossroad said yes, although a very reluctant yes. He, like the first two, was a good man. He had, however, no use for religion and in fact, when he went to college, he proclaimed himself an avowed atheist. But often to his dismay, he found himself several times unexpectedly at a crossroad. He writes, "Some days a little door would open to an unspeakable burst of joy, then it would slam again. The door would open, then it would slam, open and slam." Finally, one day in his college room, something happened. The One who had been opening and slamming the door, opened it and stood there and wouldn't let him go. He was at the crossroad. He writes, "You must picture me alone in that room in Oxford, feeling the steady, unrelenting approach of Him whom I earnestly desired *not* to meet. It was in Trinity term of 1929 that I gave in, and admitted that God was God and I knelt and prayed, perhaps that night, the most rejected and reluctant convert in all of England." That man who said yes was C.S. Lewis, perhaps the most widely read Christian writer in the world today.☐

I said this was an account of four people at the crossroads of their lives. Two, as we have heard, said no, one said yes, and the other is under consideration. The one under consideration is you and me. Like all the others, we are good people but always— always—we stand at the crossroad waiting to be not merely good people, but *disciples.* Surrender, heroism, sacrifice, a deeper spirituality, making a difference—they all beckon at the crossroads of our lives. Sometimes, the call is to quiet witness. The mystic Caryll Houselander said, "Sometimes it may seem to us that there is no purpose to our lives. That going day after day to this office or that school or factory is nothing else but waste and weariness, but it may be that God has sent us there because, but for us, Christ would not be there. If our being there means that Christ is there, that alone makes it worthwhile." Maybe we're called to that: to be "more" Christ where we are.

Sometimes, we're called to that minor martyrdom of being openly counted as good Catholics. Back the beginning of this century, the famed writer and staunch Catholic Hilaire Belloc decided to run for Parliament in deeply anti-Catholic England. He knew his Roman Catholicism would be a great obstacle, so when he gave his first campaign speech, he stepped up to the platform with rosary beads in his hand, told the crowd that he was a Roman Catholic, that he went to Mass every day of his life, and that he knelt down daily to say the rosary. He then told his listeners, "If you reject me on account of my religion, I shall thank God that He has spared me the indignity of being your representative."

How many times do we all stand at the crossroad? How many times does Jesus tell us he loves us . . . and then ask for a bit more? "Sell what you have—your time, your reputation, your fears, your hesitancy, your insecurities, your need to be one of the crowd—and, come, follow me." All of us know, deep down, that almost daily we stand at the crossroads. All of us are aware that Jesus has issued us an invitation.

True, we say, we have it under consideration. The gospel says, "Don't wait too long."

20. DOCTOR LIFE
(Jn 10:1–10   4th Sunday of Easter   Year A)

I ask you to come with me in your imagination to a calm suburb in Detroit, a suburb known as Waterford township. If you turn down Paulsen Street with me, a street that's attractive, surrounded by birch and elm trees that are starting to bloom, it seems like any other quiet piece of America. And yet the people in Waterford township call it the Street of Death. Four times, you see, a white van has pulled up in front of a brown two-story house on Paulsen Street. A slender white-haired man with glasses has emerged from the van and walked up to the door. Each time he has made his visit, someone in that house has died. Neighbors shudder when they see that van arrive. They know it's going to happen again. The white van belongs to Dr. Jack Kevorkian, one of the most controversial people of our time. He has assisted in some 20 suicides in recent years. He is known as Doctor Death.

Now I ask you to come with me in your imagination to a calm suburb in ancient Palestine two thousand years ago. I ask you to watch a man sit among the children and take them in his arms. I ask you to watch him as he reaches out to the sick and the dying, healing those that he heals and assuring those that he chooses not to heal. I ask you to watch him dying his own death and yet giving comfort to the thief next to him. I ask you to listen to his teaching about forgiveness, love, and resurrection. I ask you to attend to his words in today's gospel, "I have come that they may have life and have life abundantly." If Dr. Kevorkian is Doctor Death, Jesus Christ is Doctor Life.

Were we to scan the gospels for what life means as Jesus understands it, we would find three elements that stand out: relationships, trust, and simplicity.

The primary life-giving relationship is, of course, with God. This means prayer. Jesus often spent the whole night in prayer. He knew that without Abba, without a deep and abiding connection with God, all was futile and lifeless. "God," as he reminded

185

his hearers, "is the God of life." The inescapable other life-giving relationship that flows from the first is relationship with one's neighbor. Love of God and love of neighbor give life.

☐Charlotte often told me, when she was a little girl many, many years ago in Queens, about her crazy bachelor Uncle Lou who knew everything in the world about gardening and golf. She remembers fondly, "Not only me, but all the kids in the neighborhood—he would teach them the difference between a petunia and a zinnia and that sort of thing. And as many as could fit into the rumble seat of his old car, he would take to the golf course and tell us why it was important to keep your head down and your left shoulder behind the ball. But," she continued, "the best thing I remember was when we went to camp and I always got a letter from Uncle Lou and in it he would always enclose a crisp new one dollar bill—which was a fortune in those days. And he always added a P.S.: 'Don't spend it wisely.' He was crazy. A funloving, frivolous guy. Lightweight, but fun."

Charlotte continued. "I went back recently to the old neighborhood. I ran into an old neighbor of mine who told me about his son who way back had gotten polio. He said, "I don't know if you know about this or not, but your Uncle Lou paid my son's hospital bill. Did you know that?" "No, I didn't," said Charlotte. She ran into another neighbor who said that when he lost his job her Uncle Lou supported him and his family for a whole year till he got another job. Did she know that? And so it went. This funloving, frivolous Uncle Lou, who had given her dollar bills to spend foolishly, spent his life wisely, spent it giving life, spent it in relationship with God and neighbor.☐

If relationship is the first element of life, then trust is the second. Trust that the God who makes it rain on the just and the unjust and takes care of the birds of the air, also counts the hairs of your head. Trust that even in the midst of hurt and brokenness, there is a glory not to be denied.

☐Toward the end of Leonard Bernstein's musical work, *Mass*, there is a scene in which the priest is richly dressed in magnificent vestments. He is lifted up by the crowd carrying a splendid glass chalice in his hands. Suddenly the human pyramid collapses and the priest comes tumbling down. His vestments are ripped off and the glass chalice falls to the ground and is shattered. As he walks slowly through the debris of his former glory, barefoot and wearing only a T-shirt and jeans, he hears children's voices singing off stage, *Laude! Laude! Laude!* Praise! Praise! Praise! And suddenly the priest notices the broken chalice and looks at it for a long, long time. And then he haltingly says, "I never realized that broken glass could shine so brightly."☐

Life is trust, trust in a God who makes all things new again, who can make the brokenness of our lives shine brightly.

Relationship and trust give life, and so does simplicity. Simplicity unclogs what chokes us, the things we're addicted to that suffocate us. Simplicity—a simple, less crowded, less acquisitive lifestyle—opens up spiritual arteries.

☐Once upon a time there was a proud man named Carl who loved to ride his horse through his vast estate and to congratulate himself on his enormous wealth. One day he came upon Hans, an old tenant farmer, who had sat down to eat his lunch in the shade of a great oak tree. Hans's head was bowed in prayer. When Hans looked up he said, "Oh, excuse me, sir. I didn't see you. I was giving thanks for my food." "Humph!" snorted the rich man noticing the coarse dark bread and cheese that made up the old man's lunch. "If that were all *I* had to eat," he sneered, "I don't think I'd feel like giving thanks."

"Oh," replied Hans, "it's quite sufficient. But it's remarkable that you should come here today because I feel that I have to tell you something because I had a strange dream just before awakening this morning." "And what did you dream?" Carl asked with an amused smile. The old man answered, "There was beauty and peace all around, and yet I could hear a voice saying, 'The richest man in the valley will die tonight.'" "Ah, dreams!" cried Carl. "Nonsense!" He turned and galloped away and Hans prayed as he watched the horse and its rider disappear.

"Die tonight!" mused Carl. "It's ridiculous! No use going into a panic." The best thing to do, he decided, was to forget the old man's dream. And yet—yet, he couldn't forget it. He had felt fine, at least till Hans described that crazy dream of his. Now he wasn't sure that he felt all that well. So that evening he called his doctor, who was a personal friend. He asked him to come over right away for he had to speak with him. When the doctor arrived, Carl told him of the old man's dream, how the richest man in the valley would die this very night. "Ah," replied the doctor, "sounds like poppycock to me, but for your own peace of mind, let me examine you." A little later, the examination complete, the doctor was full of smiles and assurances. He said, "Carl, you're as strong and healthy as that horse you ride. There's no way you're going to die tonight." The doctor was just closing his bag when a messenger arrived out of breath at the manor door. "Doctor, doctor," he cried, "come quick! It's old Hans. He just died in his sleep!"◻

21. WE'RE ALL CONNECTED

(Jn 17:20–26 7th Sunday of Easter Year C)

❏Murphy and Clancy happened to be passing a church. "You know," Murphy said, " I haven't been to confession for a while. I think I'll just pop in and go." So Murphy went into church and into the confessional and acknowledged to the priest that he had had his way with a woman. "I know your voice, Murphy," said the priest, "and this isn't the first time that this has happened. I want to know the woman's name." "It's not proper you should be asking," said Murphy, "and I'll not be telling you." "If you want absolution," said the priest, "you *will* be telling me. Was it O'Reilly's sister?" Murphy refused to answer. "I'll ask again, Was it the widow Harrington?" Again, Murphy wouldn't reply. The priest said, "One more time, Was it the Flanagan girl?" And the third time Murphy said, "I'll not be telling you." "Then you'll get no absolution from me," the priest said. "Out with you!" His friend Clancy, who was waiting for him outside, asked, "Well, now, did you get absolution?" "No," said Murphy, "but I got three good leads!"❏

Today's gospel is difficult to follow. If we're honest with our-selves, we will admit that it rambles all over the place and it's hard to know what Jesus is saying. But perhaps the context will help. What we heard was a prayer on the night before Jesus died. He's upset, as indeed we would be. So he prays as one under stress. He prays a prayer that doesn't have to make sense or be coherent or even logical. It's something like a little child's prayer. "God bless Mommy and Daddy. Bless my sister. Bless the dog 'cause he's not feeling well. Bless my skateboard. Bless Jimmy except when he fights with me. Don't let Grandmom forget her present . . ." The kid rambles on until he falls asleep. That, I think, is the kind of stream of consciousness we're privy to in this gospel. But, as you listen carefully, it all comes down to a single theme. That theme is unity, that we are all connected, and that we should know it and live by that truth. "I pray," said Jesus, "that

189

they may be one in us." To reach that realization, I suggest, there are "three good leads."

The first lead is this: we are all connected by nature. More and more we are learning how physically interconnected we are, that in nature we form one ecology. An article from *Audubon Perspective* brings this home.

❑The Diaks tribe in Borneo were suffering a severe malaria epidemic. So the United Nations World Health Organization came to the rescue and sprayed DDT to kill the mosquitoes. It worked for a time but then, all of a sudden, the roofs of the Diaks' homes began to collapse and rats were overwhelming the village. It turns out that the DDT wiped out the parasitic wasps that eat the thatch-eating caterpillars. With no wasps around, the caterpillars proliferated and they literally ate the roofs off their homes. In the meantime the bugs that were poisoned by the DDT were eaten by the lizards which in turn were eaten by the cats who died and, with no cats, the rats proliferated. So the World Health Organization had to come back and literally parachute cats into the de-catted island.❑

All living things are indeed interconnected by nature. We are that nature. We too belong the complex chain of all things. Jesus would remind us of that fundamental oneness.

❑If the first connection we have is through nature, the second is through our shared humanity. The author, Nikos Kazantzakis, tells of an experience he had when he went back to visit the isle of Crete. As he walked along, an elderly woman passed by carrying a basket of figs. "She halted, laid down her basket, picked out two beautiful figs and presented them to me. I asked, 'Do you know me, old lady?' She looked at me with amazement. 'No, my boy. Do I have to know you to give you something? You are a human being, are you not? So am I. Isn't that enough?'"❑

Kazantzakis remarks, "The old lady was right. She is saying, 'You are a child. I am a mother. That's enough. You are a son. I am a father. That's enough. We are brothers and sisters. That's enough. I am your God. You are my people. That's enough." In the language of Jesus' prayer, we are one in God, children of the same heavenly Father. "That you may be in them and I in you.

That they may be one in us." Being "one in us" through our common humanity under one God allows, of course, for no prejudice, racism, or bias. We are one in God. That is enough.

After our common connection through nature and humanity, there is our connectedness through grace. God lurks behind everything in this world. We live in a grace-filled world if we would recognize it and, when we do, we know that we are embraced by the common Spirit that infuses all things. As the poet Gerard Manley Hopkins wrote:

The world is charged with the grandeur of God.
It will flame out, like shining from shook foil . . .
Because the Holy Ghost over the bent
World broods with warm breast and with ah! bright wings.

⬜In a more prosaic vein, you might remember J. D. Salinger who wrote the famed *Catcher in the Rye*. He also wrote another stunning story called *Franny and Zooey*. There's a powerful scene in this book in which Franny comes home from college a nervous wreck. Her well-intentioned but misguided efforts to explore the depths of religious mysticism have left her extremely tense. Bessie, her mother, is concerned and shows that concern by bringing her distressed daughter a cup of chicken soup. Even though Franny knows her mother is trying to comfort her, the offer of the chicken soup annoys her and she lashes out at her mother. Franny's brother, who's sitting at the table, jumps up and confronts her. He tells her that her approach to religion is all wrong. He says, "I'll tell you one thing, Franny. If it's the religious life you want, you ought to know that you are missing out on every single religious action that's going on in this house. You don't have sense enough to drink when someone brings you a cup of consecrated chicken soup, which is the only kind of chicken soup that Mom ever brings to anybody."⬜

We bump into grace all the time, every time we give the sign of peace, every time we do a kindness, every time we embrace, every time we prepare a meal, every time we comfort, every time we serve. Grace abounds in this world of ours and binds us together—to one another and to God.

We are one in nature so we must reverence our world. We are one in humanity so we must respect one another. We are one in grace, so we must acknowledge the Hidden God. These are "three good leads" that ought to form the basis of our spiritual lives. These are the "three good leads" that bring us close to realizing Jesus' prayer: "Oh, Father, that they may be one in us, as I in you and you in me."

22. NO GREATER LOVE
(Jn 15:9–17 6th Sunday of Easter Year B)

Jesus instructs us in today's gospel that we are to love one another *as* he has loved us. The force of the "as" is displayed by the crucifixion. *That's* how much we are to love one another. The heart of such love, of course, is choice. Jesus chose to lay down his life for us. "I lay down my life. No one takes it from me," he says elsewhere in John's gospel. He does it freely because there is no greater way to show that he loves us. There we are. Love is always a choice.

☐Christopher de Vinck in his book, *The Power of the Powerless,* tells a simple story to underscore this. He writes: "One spring afternoon my five-year-old son, David, and I were planting raspberry bushes along the side of the garage. A neighbor joined us for a few moments. David pointed to the ground. 'Look, Daddy! What's that?' I stopped talking with my neighbor and looked down. 'A beetle,' I said. David was impressed and pleased with the discovery of this fancy, colorful creature. My neighbor lifted his foot and stepped on the insect giving his shoe an extra twist in the dirt. 'That ought to do it,' he laughed. David looked up at me, waiting for an explanation, a reason. That night, just before I turned off the light in his bedroom, David whispered, 'I liked that beetle, Daddy.' 'I did too,' I whispered back." De Vinck concludes his story by saying, "We have the power to choose."☐

So we do. We have the power to choose how we will respond to every living thing that crosses our path. We have the power to love one another or not.

☐Let us count the ways some have exercised that choice. There was a college student named Tom who was well liked by his peers. Nothing unusual here, except Tom had a large red birthmark that ran from one eye, down his face, across his mouth, down to his neck, to his chest. One day, a close friend of his asked Tom, "Tell me this. How did you ever overcome the emotional pain of your birthmark?" "Oh," he answered quickly, "it's because of my dad. You see, he

193

always told me, 'Son, this'—and he pointed to my birthmark—'this is where an angel kissed you because he wanted to mark you out just for your dad. You're very special to me, and whenever we're in a group of people, I always know right away where you are, and that you're mine.' My dad told me that so many times that I even began to feel sorry for all my friends who *didn't* have birthmarks."□

□A woman named Mary Ann Bird tells her story. She says, "I grew up knowing I was different, and I hated it. I was born with a cleft palate, and when I started school, my classmates made it clear to me how I must look to others: a little girl with a misshapen lip, crooked nose, lopsided teeth and garbled speech. When my schoolmates would ask, 'What happened to your lip?' I'd tell them I'd fallen and cut it on a piece of glass. Somehow it seemed more acceptable to have suffered an accident than to have been born different. I was convinced that no one outside my family could love me. There was, however, a teacher in the second grade that we all adored—Mrs. Leonard by name. She was short, round, happy—a sparkling lady. Annually, we would have a hearing test. I was virtually deaf in one of my ears; but when I had taken the test in the past years, I discovered that if I did not press my hand as tightly upon my ears as I was instructed to do, I could pass the test. Mrs. Leonard gave the test to everyone in the class, and finally it was my turn. I knew from past years that as we stood against the door and covered one ear, the teacher sitting at her desk would whisper something and we would have to repeat it back . . . things like 'The sky is blue' or 'Do you have new shoes?' I waited there for those words which God must have put into her mouth, those seven words which changed my life. Mrs. Leonard said, in her whisper, 'I wish you were my little girl.'"□

□Do you know the tragic story of Princess Alice? She was the second daughter of Queen Victoria. She had a four-year-old son whom she loved very much. When he contracted the disease known as "black diphtheria," Alice was devastated. The disease was highly contagious and very deadly. The nurses continually warned the Princess, not being in the best of health herself, to stay away from her son. Naturally this would be difficult for any mother. Still, Alice knew she would be in danger if she ignored the warning.

One day as Princess Alice stood in a far corner of her son's room, she heard her son whisper to the nurse, "Why doesn't my mother kiss me any more?" That was more than Alice could bear. As tears streamed down her cheeks, she raced to her son's bed, held him in her arms, and smothered him with kisses. Tragically, this turned out to be the kiss of death. Princess Alice contracted the deadly disease and in a matter of weeks, both mother and son were buried. A foolish thing to do? Stupid? Dumb? Yes, of course, all of these things. But who ever said love was logical? To love as deeply as the cross: who ever said *that* was sensible?◻

And so it goes: a parent responds to a baby's cry in the night. A nurse gently bathes a bedsore patient. A teenager listens to a friend's tale of family tensions. A retired person volunteers to stuff envelopes for a charity mailing. An auto mechanic repairs a traveler's car. Ordinary, non-spectacular, run-of-the-mill behavior. But love has been chosen. These people have "laid down their lives," have "died to self." In short, they have loved as Jesus did, which means they chose to pay the cost.

◻There's an ancient legend that says that the devil, Master of disguise, tried to get into heaven by pretending to be the Risen Christ. He took with him his demons disguised as angels of light and had them cry out the traditional first part of the welcome psalm: "Lift up your heads, O ye Gates of Heaven, and lift up your doors and the King of Glory shall enter!" The real angels looked down on what they thought was their King returning in triumph from the dead. So they in turn shouted back with joy the refrain: "Who is this King of Glory?" The devil then made a fatal mistake. He opened his arms and spread his palms and declared, "I am!" The angels immediately slammed the gate of heaven and refused to let the imposter in. They saw right away that were no marks of the nails in his palms. The imposter had no wounds of love, had not paid the costs.◻

Authentic love costs. It cost Tom's dad, Mrs. Leonard, Princess Alice, Jesus. "This is my commandment: love one another as I have loved you. There is no greater love than this: to lay down one's life for one's friends."

23. TO WELCOME CHRIST
(Jn 1:6–8, 19–28 3rd Sunday of Advent   Year B)

The Scripture opens with a question, "Are you the one who is to come or shall we look for another?" That in turn prompts us to ask the stereotypic question that good people always ask this Advent time of the year. "Christmas," we say, "is so commercial, so stressful, so . . . secular. How can I reclaim it for myself and for my family as a holy time, a holy day, not just a holiday?" To answer that question, I want to share with you some homespun suggestions for reclaiming Christmas. My suggestions are twelve and I hardly expect you to remember them all. My hope is that one or two might catch you and help you approach Christmas with a new intent and spirit.

Suggestion number one: give homemade gifts. Homemade gifts, as everyone knows, means "heart-made." A poem, a story, a gingerbread house, a loaf of bread, a painting, a birdhouse. Homemade gifts tell of time and effort and love more than store-bought things. To that extent they are personal acts of love—precisely what Christmas is about.

Suggestion number two: give service coupons. That is, you will give some service as a gift to someone: plant flowers around someone's house, watch the baby for a day, walk the dog, visit the sick. One woman I know gave her mother a coupon to clean her oven. She hates cleaning ovens, but her mother hates it even more.

Suggestion three: give love in someone's name. "In your name, I am making a donation to this or that worthy cause," and drop a check to a charity. One man relates, "Christmas shopping for me was the most depressing time of the year. I don't know which part of me suffered more, my feet or my soul. I like the idea of giving. I like the sparkle in my children's eyes when they open up their presents. I didn't like the idea of what I gave: things, manufactured things, mostly made out of plastic, destined more for shelf-life than for usefulness, one more bit of junk making the rounds.

So last year I gave each of my children two gifts. One gift was a cataract operation that gave sight to a blind person in Nepal. I made donations for the four operations in my children's names. The other gift was something to wear or to use, made in a cooperative craft shop in a poor village in a third-world country." The fourth suggestion: make homemade Christmas cards. For those who have a computer and access to a copier, it's a very easy project to make and reproduce them. If you don't have these things, there's still crayons and paste. The children especially will delight in making their own cards. And surely believers in any case ought to send religious cards. Again, for believers, Christmas is not just another holiday with non-offensive, politically correct motifs. It is the birthday of the Lord and we should witness to that in our cards. The fifth suggestion: celebrate Advent with the Advent wreath and Advent prayers. The sixth suggestion is this: have a birthday celebration for Jesus. The seventh: have the creche in your home. The display of the Nativity scene should be a centerpiece for the Christian family.

Suggestion eight is to use a potted tree for Christmas and save both the forests and overpowering the garbage heap. The ninth suggestion is, by all means, keep Santa, but remind the family that Santa is the Latin word for Saint and that behind that jolly figure is a real saint, St. Nicholas, and behind Nicholas is the Child who inspired it all. The tenth suggestion is to read a religious book to your children or grandchildren. Children love to be read to, mostly because of the physical intimacy it provides. The eleventh suggestion is to limit your gifts. Draw names out of a hat and those one or two persons are the object of your gift-giving this year. It helps the budget and concentrates the gift. The twelfth and final suggestion is this: give *yourself* a gift. That is, give yourself the gift of time: time for prayer, refection, perhaps even a little Advent retreat. As you are centered in faith, so will you enable others to be.

Thus, my twelve suggestions to "Put Christ Back in Christmas," as they say. Whether you adopt any or all of these suggestions to keep the faith focus where it belongs during this hectic season, keep in mind what it's all about. It's about love, about showing it through gifts and service, about priorities, about relationships honored and cemented through giving. It's about passing on the traditions of love.

□There's a short story of childless couple who had raised their orphaned nephew who is now leaving them for college. They're at the railroad station. The story relates, "David looked at his aunt and uncle. She, with hands chapped and hard from selling fruit and vegetables outdoors in all kinds of weather, face ruddy and round and invariably smiling, the heavy body more accustomed to a half dozen sweaters at one time than a single coat, her hair the color of moonlight now, but the dark eyes still bright. He, with his slight, wiry body strong and bent from lifting too many fruit and vegetable crates for too many years, the wind-burned skin, the swarthy face, the wry mouth; the childless couple who had taken the orphan David into their home, rearing him since the age of seven yet refusing to be called Mamma and Papa for fear he would forget his real parents. David grabbed their rough peddlers' hands in his smooth student ones. 'How can I ever repay you two for what you've done for me?' His uncle spoke gently, 'David, there's a saying, "The love of parents goes to their children, but the love of these children goes to their children." 'That's not so,' protested David, 'I'll always be trying to . . .' His aunt interrupted. 'David,' she said, 'what your uncle means is that a parent's love isn't to be paid back. It can only be passed on.'"□

To pass on love is the real business of Christmas. To prepare for that passing on is the real business of Advent.

24. DID YOU MAIL THE INVITATIONS?
(Mt 22:1–14   28th Sunday in O.T.   Year A)

Today's gospel has all the earmarks of its author, Matthew. He is reflecting the tense times of the church of his day when traditional Jews were persecuting the upstart untraditional Jews, the Christians, as we now call them. The details of the parable as Matthew tells it are not to be taken literally; for instance, the notion of a God who retaliates with murdering those who refuse to come to his banquet does not set well within the context of the mercy of Jesus. But there's enough to make us reflect about the main image of a banquet: an old biblical symbol for being called to live the way God wants us to live, a joyous gathering of disciples who have accepted the call and have led the moral life. The parable focuses on those people who have refused an invitation to come to this banquet. There are three categories of people who refused and they are instructive for us.

First, there are those who simply refuse outright of their own accord. They want no part of the banquet, no part of discipleship, no part of God. Period. Their lives are evil. Their god is their belly, pride, greed, and lust, as Paul wrote some 30 years before Matthew wrote his gospel. So, we can dismiss them. But there are two other categories of people who also do not come to the banquet, not because they are evil, although at times they may do evil things, but because some of the servants the Master sent out to issue invitations did not do so. This morning we must reflect on them.

❑The first group are what we might call the Segregated. There's an off-Broadway play called *The Construction* that might shed some light on them. The play opens with a group of people who are gathered in a kind of other-worldly place. The actors don't know where they are or how they got there or, more importantly, what they're supposed to do. "Where are we?" they ask. "And why are we in this place? What's the purpose here? What are we supposed to do?" In the midst of these unanswered questions, somebody notices that on stage is a lot of building materials, so they conclude that they were brought to this particular place to build something, although nobody knows what. Somebody suggests a swimming pool, another a club house. But as they're discussing this, someone hears a sound in a distance, the sound of other people. After listening a while, they exclaim, "We don't know who they are or what they want." Someone cries out, "We can't afford to take chances. We should protect ourselves." So they decide that this construction material is obviously meant for them to build a wall to protect themselves from those strangers. In fact, the more they discuss it, the more they become convinced that they must build a wall.

After they work on the wall for some time—and indeed, it turns out to be quite formidable—they look up and see a stranger headed their way. The stranger tells them he is a builder. Not only that, but he has plans under his arms. And the stranger, looking at the wall, tells they that they got it all wrong. As he spreads the plans out he says, "See, you're not supposed to build a wall around yourselves. You're supposed to build a bridge to other people and invite them in."□

The point is that some do not come to the Lord's banquet because we exclude them by the walls of our attitudes, our superiority, our scandals, our lack of joy, and simply by not inviting them. Good News by its nature is to be shared. We don't actively share our faith, build bridges to it. The segregated are not at the banquet often because we, the servants of Christ, have built walls instead of bridges.

The second group that could be at the banquet but often aren't are the Labeled, those we have pigeon-holed and keep there. There's a story that illustrates this.

□It's about a man everyone called Old Governor Campbell. He was the undisputed chief of the village bums in a little southwestern town. He hung around the courthouse, knew many of the merchants and lawyers. He sponged quarters from them. With the money he'd get something to eat but more to drink, for he was the town drunkard.

In those days the revival people used to sweep through those little towns with great regularity. And each time Old Governor Campbell would go to the revival meeting and get converted. The news would spread from the courthouse to the barbershop and local bars that Old Governor Campbell got religion again. They would tell it as a great joke and the people would laugh knowingly. There would be Old Governor Campbell, with his clothes pressed, hair combed, face shaven, standing erect on the street, full of pride for a few days. But never beyond a few days. Soon you would see the stubble growing back on his face, the hair would be uncombed, the clothes would be dishevelled, and he would be back in his role as the town drunk. People would pass by and say to him, "How many times did you make it this time, Governor? How does it feel to be your old self again, Governor?" People would slip another quarter in his hand with a wink in their eye and, at the courthouse and barbershop would say things like, "That's the trouble with religion. Those preachers keep trying to convert people like Old Governor Campbell and there he is again, stiff as a billygoat. He'll never change."☐

And they never realized that the trouble wasn't with religion. It was with them. When they laughed at the old derelict, they became a party to his tragedy. They did not believe he could change and they didn't want him to believe it either. His trouble wasn't that he got converted too often. His trouble is the same as ours. He simply doesn't get converted often enough. The trouble is that we've labeled him and keeping him labeled satisfies our sense of superiority. If he changes, so must we. So it is easier to ridicule than encourage, easier to disenfranchise than invite. If the banquet has missing persons, the parable asks, "Are we to blame?"

If that weren't enough to think about, here's a final zinger to the parable. When it wasn't filled with people who should be there—some of whom, as we have seen, we are responsible for—the Master tells his servants to go out and get others, the good, the bad, and the ugly. In short, there will be some people at the Heavenly Banquet we'll be surprised to see.

❑A man tells his story. "It was outside of Schwartz's bakery on Fairfax Avenue that I first saw him do it while I sat in my car waiting for my wife to finish shopping. As I watched the crowds go by, my attention was drawn to a poorly dressed young woman, with two forlorn children, pushing an old supermarket cart with bundles of bags and rags and whatever else goes into living from hand to mouth. Coming in the opposite direction was this man I recognized and whom I did not like one bit. As he passed her, he turned around and called out something to get her attention. I didn't hear what he said but when he turned he pretended to stoop down and pick up some money. It was green and how much it was I did not know. He motioned to the woman that she had dropped it. He quickly put it into her child's hand and left.

"It was more than a month later when I was at the checkout counter that I saw that man again. He was standing behind an obviously poor person who was counting her money to pay for milk and bread. He didn't see me, but I saw him bend down and he came up holding a twenty dollar bill, all the while insisting that the woman had dropped it. She protested it wasn't hers but everybody in line urged her to take it and so she did."

The man concludes, "You know, when anyone is lucky enough to see an act of compassion in the crowd, it kind of makes for good feelings. And I don't even like the man. In fact, I hate him. But the suspicion is that he's going to be at the banquet and I am not."❑

25. CHRISTMAS CODE
(Lk 2:1–14 Christmas [Midnight] Years A, B, C)

For those with a mathematical or economic bent of mind, let me share with you what J. Patrick Bradley, who is the chief economist at the Provident National Bank in Philadelphia, calculates to be today's cost to what one's True Love would give to thee for the Twelve Days of Christmas. One partridge in a pear tree, he says, comes to $27.48. The partridge is $15.00. The pear tree is $12.48. Two turtle doves, $50.00. Three French hens, $15.00. Four calling birds, $280.00. Five golden earrings, $600.00. Six geese a-laying, about $150.00. Seven swans a-swimming, $7000.00. Eight maids a-milking, $30.40. Nine ladies dancing, $2417.90. Ten lords a-leaping, $2686.56—obviously, a stronger union. Eleven pipers piping, $947.70. Twelve drummers drumming, $1,026.68. If you wanted to give all these to your True Love for the Twelve Days of Christmas today, your grand total would be $15,231.72.

But, of course, that's the economist's point of view. He looks at the old song in terms of dollars and cents. We look at it as a pleasant holiday nonsense ditty. But in the past, others looked at it more profoundly because this seemingly harmless tune held a deep Christian secret. "The Twelve Days of Christmas" was written in the sixteenth century. Moreover, it was written by a couple of wily Jesuits who were playing a dangerous game. For, you see, this was sixteenth-century England and in sixteenth-century England anything Catholic was prohibited and, if found out, was punishable by imprisonment and death. The Catholic faith, as a result, was forced underground. Still, there was, as you can imagine, a desperate need to encourage the faith and, above all, to instill it into the next generation. So, these Jesuits came up with a way to teach the outline of faith—but in code. The code was our song.

It sounds harmless enough to us, but let us look at it more closely. The Twelve Days of Christmas, as everyone knew, was the Nativity celebration from Christmas Day to Epiphany. "My true love gave to me" is God speaking to the anonymous Catholic. "Twelve drummers drumming" are not, as you might guess, the twelve Apostles, but rather the twelve beliefs outlined in the Apostles Creed. The "eleven pipers piping" are the eleven apostles—Judas having left—who pipe the faith in an unbroken tradition. The "ten lords a-leaping" are the Ten Commandments. The "nine ladies dancing" are the nine choirs of angels. The "eight maids a-milking" are the eight beatitudes. The "seven swans a-swimming" are, of course, the seven sacraments; the "six geese a-laying" are the six precepts of the church; the "five golden rings" are the Pentateuch, the first five books of the Bible; the "four calling birds" are the four gospels that sing the Good News; the "three French hens" are the three gifts the Magi brought; the "two turtle doves" are the Old and the New Testaments; and, finally, of course, the "partridge in a pear tree" is the resplendent Christ reigning from the cross.

Now for the uninitiated sixteenth-century Protestant Englanders, the song was a simple holiday pleasantry. But for those who were playing hide-and-seek with their faith, it was a coded outline from which one could unfold the truths of faith, a kind of catechism chapter headings that teachers could secretly use to hang their teachings on.

People have always used imaginative ways to pass on the faith and to restate the basic gospel message and, in particular, the message of Christmas. Matthew and Luke certainly did that with their stories of the Magi and shepherds and choirs of angels. Others have added to the tradition, as evidenced in the Russian legend of Babushka.

☐It seems that old grandmother Babushka, a good woman, is about to retire for the evening when, out of the fierce winter night, comes a knock on her door. It's the Wise Men and they tell her excitedly about the King born in Bethlehem and they urge her to come and honor him. She peeks out the door. It's an awful night, cold and blustery. Babushka looks back at her warm bed, hesitates, and says, "I will see the Christ Child—tomorrow." She returns to her bed and, lo, another knock at the door. This time it's the shepherds urging her to come and, if not, at least to give them a basket of goodies to bring to the Christ Child. Again, she looks at the weather, looks at her bed, hesitates, but finally replies, "I'll bring them myself—tomorrow." Well, tomorrow comes and Babushka is as good as her word. She packs some food and off she goes to Bethlehem. But the stable is empty when she gets there. She is crestfallen, but determined. She keeps looking. In fact, she looks for the Child for the rest of her life, joining all the wanderers who have ever lived.

And in her endless journey she finds children, finds them everywhere. She finds many a manger. She finds many a cradle. She finds many a mother nursing her baby. She leaves gifts at each place hoping that it is the Christ Child. She is now very old and near death. As she lies dying, the Christ Child appears to her wearing the face of every child she has ever touched and offered gifts to. She dies happily knowing that, in spite of her first hesitancy, she did indeed find the Child, not in the manger where she expected him, but in the poor and needy where she never expected him.□

Again, a story of hiddenness just like the song that hid the faith. A story that says that people too, like words, are codes behind which the image of God is apparent if we but knew the key to get at it. The message of Christmas is that love is the key.

26. THREE QUESTIONS FOR CHRISTMAS
(Lk 2:1–14 Christmas [Midnight] Years A, B, C)

Have you ever noticed that the entire Christmas story begins with a lot of questions? When the angel appeared to old Zechariah telling him that Elizabeth, long past her child-bearing years, would have a son, he asked, "How will I know this is so?" When that son grows up to be John the Baptist, he will ask the crowds that come to him, "Who has taught you to flee the wrath that is to come?" When the angel appeared to Mary to announce that she was to conceive a child, she too had her question, "How can this be, since I do not know man?" When she traveled in haste to visit her cousin, Elizabeth greeted her with a question, "How is it that the mother of my Lord should come to me?" Later on, the Magi would ask wicked King Herod, "Where is the One that has been born King of the Jews?"

Thus there are questions that begin the Christmas drama and so they prompt me to ask you some questions, three of them in fact, each wrapped in a story, for Christmas is a time of story-telling. The first question is this: who brought you here? I don't mean, who physically drove the car tonight. I mean in the long run. I mean, who in your background is responsible for your being here every Sunday, or even if it's only once or twice a year? Who planted the seed of faith in you? In that sense, you have my first question: who brought you here?

❑He's not so much in the news today, but billionaire Ross Perot wasn't always a billionaire. He gave an interview a few years ago and he told the story of the depression years when he lived in Texarkana, Texas, and his family had to struggle to make ends meet. He recalled that, in those days, an awful lot of hoboes came and knocked at the door of their house looking for a hand-out. Ross' mother never turned them away, although she often wondered why so many of them came to her house and not so much to her neighbors. One day she learned the reason. One of the hoboes told her that on the curb in front of their house was marked a code known only to the hoboes. The code sign meant, "Come to this house. You'll get a meal." So Ross asked his mother, "Should I erase the mark?" "No," his mother said, "leave it there." Commenting on this in the interview, Ross said these words, "We are all what we are taught to be. You sat in that little house in Texarkana and you saw your parents doing things like that when you were a child, and that's the greatest lesson in the world."□

So, who brought you here? Who made the mark on your spirit? Whom are *you* marking?

□Or, if you want a story about those questions that's more current, consider the story of TV actor Henry Sanders. He's the black actor who plays the blacksmith on the popular series, "Dr. Quinn, Medicine Woman." When he was working in a little repertory theater in Alabama, a call came in from Hollywood offering him this part of the blacksmith. But he knew he was committed to this little rinky-dink theater. Most people, lured by Hollywood, would have just walked off and said goodbye. But not Henry. He wrote these words, "Some actors in this dilemma might decide that a network TV series was more important than a repertory play in a regional theater and would simply have walked out. But I had accepted that part in good faith. I signed the contract. I made a commitment, and people were counting on me. As I sat in my hotel room, I thought about who I was and what I believed in. I had been raised in a single-parent home by a mother who had a strong faith. And I remember she read to me from the Bible, 'Let your yes be yes and your no be no.' Well, I had given that Alabama Shakespearean theater my yes and it would have to stand. So, with a heavy heart, I called Hollywood and told them that I could not accept." It turned out that, later on, the producers were so impressed with his sense of honor and fidelity that they did offer him the part and were willing to wait till he was finished his commitment.□

So, we're back to my first question: who brought you here? Who was the faith-person in your background? Who marked you for Christ? Whose values are you living by? And, most of all, whom are you marking, introducing to the faith, passing on values to?

My second question is this: who holds you? Who holds you with love, encouragement, and affirmation?

☐In World War II a soldier was on duty on Christmas morning. It had been his custom to go to church every Christmas morning with his family, but now, in the service on the outlying districts of London, this was impossible. So, with some of his soldier buddies, he walked down the road that led to the city as dawn was breaking. Soon they came upon an old, gray, stone building over whose main door were carved the words, "Queen Ann's Orphanage." So they decided to knock and see what kind of celebration was taking place inside. In response to their knock, a matron came and explained that the children were orphans whose parents had been killed in one of the many bombings that took place in London. The soldiers went inside just as the children were tumbling out of bed. There was no Christmas tree in the corner. There were no presents. The soldiers moved around the room wishing the children "Merry Christmas" and giving them whatever gifts they had in their pockets: a stick of chewing gum, a Life Saver, a nickel, a dime, a pencil, a pocket knife, a good luck charm. The soldier who had gotten his buddies together noticed a little fellow alone in the corner and that little fellow looked an awful lot like his nephew back home. So he approached him and said, "And you, little guy, what do you want for Christmas?" The lad replied, "Will you hold me?" The soldier, with tears brimming in his eyes, picked up the little boy and held him in his arms very close.☐

Holding each other is among life's greatest blessings. Who holds you? That's my second question. Who holds you? Whom do you hold? Or should?

My third and final question is the deepest of all. It is this: who are you? Who *are* you? Because who you are is what you do. It's not the other way around. What you do doesn't make you who you are, but who you are determines the kinds of things you do. If you know you are nothing, with no past and no future and no God, just a bunch of impulses that need to be satisfied, then you will do nothing things, selfish things, hateful things. But if you know you are a child of God, full of dignity and worth, then you will do God-like things.

❏Robert Smith of Pennsylvania tells a boyhood story. "It's been many years since I saw her, " he relates, "but in memory she's still there every holiday season. I especially feel her presence when I receive my first Christmas card. I was only twelve years old and Christmas was only a few days away, and the season's first blanket of white snow magnified the excitement. I dressed hurriedly because the snow out there was waiting for me. What would I do first? Build a snowman? Slide down the hill? Throw some flakes in the air and let them flutter down?

"Well, our family station wagon pulled into the driveway and Mom called me over to help her with the groceries. When we finished that, she said, 'Bob, here are Mrs. Hildebrand's groceries.' No other instructions were necessary.

As far back as I could remember, Mom shopped for Mrs. Hildebrand's food and I delivered it. Our 95-year-old neighbor lived alone. She was crippled with arthritis, and she could only take a few steps with a cane. I liked Mrs. Hildebrand. I enjoyed talking with her. More accurately, I enjoyed listening to her. She told me wonderful stories about her life, about a steepled church in the woods, horse and buggy rides on Sunday afternoons, and her family farm that had no electricity or running water. She always gave me a dime for bringing in her groceries. It got so that I would refuse only half-heartedly, knowing she would insist, and five minutes later I would be across the street at Beyer's Candy Store.

"As I headed over with the grocery bags, I decided I wouldn't accept any money from Mrs. Hildebrand. This would be my present to her. So, impatiently, I rang the doorbell. 'Come in,' she said cheerfully; 'put the bag on the table.' I did so more hurriedly than usual because I could hear the snow calling me back outside. She sat at the table, picked up the items out of the bag and told me where to set them on the shelves. I usually enjoyed doing this, but it *was* snowing! As we continued, I began to realize how lonely she was. Her husband had died some 20 years before. She had no children. Her only living relative was a nephew in Philadelphia who never came to visit her. Nobody even called on her Christmas. There was no tree, no presents, no stockings. For her, Christmas was just another date on the calendar.

"She offered me a cup of tea, which she did every time I brought in the groceries. 'Well,' I thought, 'maybe the snow could wait a bit.' We sat and talked about what Christmas was like when she was a child. Together we traveled back in time, and an hour passed before I knew. 'Well, Bob,' she said, 'you must be wanting to play outside in the snow,' as she reached for her purse, fumbling for the right coin. 'No, no, Mrs. Hildebrand. I can't take your money this time. You can use it for more important things,' I insisted. She looked at me and smiled. 'What more important thing could I use this money for, if not to give it to a friend at Christmas time?' She placed a whole quarter in my hand. I tried to give it back, but she would have none of it. I hurried out the door and I ran over to Beyer's Candy Store with my fortune. I had no idea what to buy—a comic book, a chocolate soda, ice cream. And then I spotted a Christmas card with an old country church on its cover. It was just like the church Mrs. Hildebrand described to me, and I knew I had to buy it.

"I handed Mr. Beyer my quarter and borrowed a pen to sign my name. 'For your girlfriend?' Mr Beyer teased. I started to say no but quickly changed my mind. 'Well, yeah,' I said. 'I guess so.' As I walked across the street with my gift, I was so proud of myself. I felt like I'd just hit a home run in the World Series. I rang Mrs. Hildebrand's doorbell. 'Hello, Mrs. Hildebrand,' I said, and handed her my card. 'Merry Christmas.' Her hands trembled as she slowly opened the envelope, studied the card and began to cry. 'Thank you. Thank you very much,' she said in almost a whisper. 'Merry Christmas to you.'

"On a cold and windy afternoon a few weeks later, the ambulance arrived next door. My mom said they found Mrs. Hildebrand in bed. She had died peacefully in her sleep. Her night table light was still on when they found her and it illumined a solitary Christmas card with an old country church on the cover."❏

Who are you? Who you are is what you do. A kind boy, trained by his parents, did a kind deed. It follows. Are you a Christian? A disciple? Who are you?

So, in the tradition of the Scriptures, I have left you this Christmas eve with three questions the feast itself provokes: Who brought you here? Whom are you bringing? Or should? Who holds you in love and affirmation? Whom do you hold? Or should? Who are you? Does that cause you to act the way you do? Or should?

From the very beginning, Christmas raises questions. From the very beginning, Christmas offers answers.

Merry Christmas!

27. Time Marches On
(New Year's Day)

Daniel Boorstin, the historian, says that one of the most significant inventions of all times is the mechanical clock. To be sure,
there were sand clocks and water clocks and sun clocks and candle clocks for many millennia, but with the mechanical clock the
human race incorporated the night hours into its schedules. And
that was momentous. For, up to that time, night was a time to eat,
to tell stories, and to sleep. Jesus, living in the pre-mechanical
time, makes reference to that in one of his speeches. He says,
"Night time comes when no one can work." Now we say, "Work
and shop until you drop at the stores, and factories open 24 hours
a day."

The first mechanical clock depended on weights whose motion
was controlled by gravity to fall in a measured way to drive the
hand. You should know, by the way, that, as late as 1500 of our
era, there were no minutes or seconds on clocks. The clocks only
told the hours or, to be more precise, they *sounded* the hours
because the average citizen could hardly afford one of those con-
traptions so they depended on listening to the clock in the town
square that the town had erected. Which is why all those old
towns always had large clocks even when people owned their
own. You may recall, for instance, the prominent clock in the
town square in the *Back to the Future* movies.

Today we have atomic clocks that measure time in millionths
of a second. I often wonder how we would live with no second or
minute hands on our clocks. Would we live more leisurely? Be
more sensitive to the arc of the sun? The passage of the planet?
Would some of the pressure of our lives disappear? Would we
have a better day if we had only the hours and not the minutes
and seconds? Not likely, I'm afraid. We're too programmed to
work and "be on the go"—a badge of success—24 hours a day.

It comes as no surprise that the number of Americans holding
two or more jobs has grown 88 percent in 25 years. Some do this

out of dire need; for most, however, the primary motivation, as studies have shown, is consumption. Our society honors the four-job family that labors hard to provide a big back yard, lots of bathrooms, and plenty of automobiles. Americans, who today work more hours than ever before in history, spend nearly four times as many hours a year shopping as do Western Europeans. And while the average paid vacation in Europe, Sweden, and Britain is from four to six weeks, for Americans it is only two weeks.

This is why stress, a term borrowed from engineering, is killing more of us than AIDS. The doctors of the American Academy of Psychosomatic Medicine believe that 74 to 90 percent of all reported diseases are due in part to stress. We certainly must take note that three best-selling prescription drugs in America are Valium for relaxation, Inderal for high blood pressure, and Tagamet for ulcers. Depression too is widespread. The scientists, interestingly, give several reasons for its epidemic proportions. One, they say, is a decline in the belief in God and the afterlife. This means that time is never redeemed. Another, understandably, is broken families. A final reason they give is the fast pace of life which leaves no time for the human organism to repair itself.

All the more reason, then, to note that the mechanical clock, like most discoveries, was designed to meet quite a different need. In this case, the need was the duty of the medieval monks to pray at set times of the day: the third, the sixth, and the ninth hour, and so on. Ironically, the clock takes on a different role today. It does not summon us to prayer, but tempts us to fill every hour, every minute, and every second of our lives with a thousand bits of busyness that leave us no time for our God and for ourselves. And advertisers, like the Mad Hatter, add to the problem by rushing time for us. In July they advertise back to school sales; in September, Christmas gifts; on Ash Wednesday, Easter finery; in May, summer sales. They move us constantly round and round like squirrels on a wheel never giving us the time to savor the current celebration and mystery in the hot economic pursuit of the next. It is no wonder that "I never have enough time" is the universal American cry. As someone remarked, "Twenty-five

years ago, people were asking, 'How can I get to heaven?' Today
they are asking, 'How can I get through the day?'"

In this context, the digital clock takes on the deeper meaning of
disconnectedness. Digital clocks tell us what time it is *now*. They
don't tell us about the past or about the future like a watch that
has a face on it. It simply describes the present, right now. To that
extent it becomes a metaphor for the Now Generation: no past, no
future. Only now. People become what we call "digital livers."
They want it all now. They thrive on instant gratification. They
are a rootless, hurried people looking at a digital watch that gives
no clue to the past or future. As someone wrote in a rather cynical poem:

This is the age of the half-read page,
The quick hash and the mad dash.
This is the age of the bright night
And the nerves tight,
And the plane with a brief stop.
This is the age of the lamp tan in a short span,
The brain strain and the heart pain.
The catnaps till the spring snaps
And the fun is done.

So, our human question, our religious question: where do relationships fit in such a time-tyrannizing world? No place or in a
very little place?

☐Consider the story of the lawyer who lived 500 miles away
from her elderly father. They had not seen each other in a number
of months. The father calls her up and asks, "When are you going
to visit?" The daughter proceeds to tell him about the demands
on her time, her court schedule, meetings, and so on and so on,
that prevent her from visiting. So the father says, "You must tell
me something I've been wondering about for some time now.
When I die, do you intend to come to my funeral?" The lawyer
responds, "Dad! I can't believe you'd ask that. Of course, I'd come
to the funeral." The father replies, "Good. Let's make a deal.
Forget the funeral. I need you more now than I will then."☐

☐Raymond Camp, who wrote a column called "Wood, Fish and Stream" for the *New York Times*, tells of a letter he got from a boy. It read, "Would you tell me where I could find a place to fish that is not more than five or six miles from my house in Queens? I am 14 years old and have saved up enough money to buy a rod, reel and line, but do not know where to go fishing. My father sometimes goes with other men, but he's too busy for me so I have to find some place I can reach on my bicycle or the subway." The columnist managed to find out the father's name and send him his son's letter with a brief note. He received this reply from the father: "You handed me quite a wallop in your letter, but I am sorry you did not hit me harder and sooner. When I think of the opportunity I might have lost, it frightens me. I do not need to point out that I now have a new fishing companion, and we have already planned a busy spring and summer. I wonder how many other fathers are passing up similar opportunities?"☐

These stories make me think of Barbara Bush's address to Wellesley College in which she said to the graduates, "As important as your obligation as a doctor, a lawyer, or a business leader may be, your human connections with your spouse, your children and your friends are the most important investment you will ever make. At the end of your life, you will never regret not having passed one more test, not winning one more verdict or not closing one more deal, but you will regret time not spent with your spouse, your children or your friends."

So the clock, which started out as servant to the soul, has evolved into its demanding taskmaster. The mechanical clock which started out to intone the hours for prayer and solitude has evolved into a giant press squeezing out those very things from our lives.

New Year's Day has provoked these reflections, of course. But New Year's does mean that we have another gift of time, a finite gift to be sure. It won't always be there. We have 365 days ahead of us to . . . to do what? To rush, to run, to acquire, to abandon loved ones in the pursuit of what we call "the better life"? Or to be frequently summoned to prayer, wonderment, contemplation, and relationships? A New Year is an opportunity, not renewable, to become what we were meant to be, and it will be parceled out by clocks, mechanical, faced, digital; they are all there to measure time and to remind us what a limited and precious resource it is for us all. And so, let us pray:

Lord, you who live outside of time and reside in the imperishable moment, we ask your blessing upon your gift of time.

Bless our calendars, those ordained lists of days, weeks, and months, of holidays, holy days, fasts, and feasts.

May they remind us of birthdays and other giftdays, as they teach us the secret that all life is meant for celebrations and contemplation.

Bless, Lord, this New Year, each of its 365 days and nights.

Bless us with happy seasons and a long life.

Grant to us, Lord, the New Year's gift of a year of love. Amen.

28. WHO ARE YOU?
(Mk 8:27–35 24th Sunday in O.T. Year B)

Not many people are honest enough or brave enough to ask Jesus' question, "Who do you say that I am?" Think about that. Think about asking some friend—or perhaps, more courageously, some enemy—"Who do people think I am? What are they saying about me? What do you really think of me?" That's more than enough food for thought. But I would ask you to move to another, deeper level and ask you to ask yourself, "Who am I?" It's that question I would like to help you explore this morning. And I would like to present three stories that might help you to frame an answer.

☐"Who are you?" My first story comes from a doctor who relates how, as an intern, part of his work was to travel around in teams examining patients. He would notice their looks as the team entered, ranging from intimidated to apprehensive. He remembered one man in particular, a black man in his sixties, who was very mischievous and very sick. His complex condition brought many visits. But the doctor remarks how he always felt the man could see right through them. He would say, "Hey, boys," when they entered the room like they were a bunch of ten-year-olds. He always somehow seemed so pleased and amused and some of the team were nervous about him. But this doctor was intrigued. Now and then the man would get into serious trouble and they would rush him to intensive care. Then he would rally, to everyone's amazement, and ask them, "You guys here again?" as if he were surprised to find *them* alive.

One night there was an emergency and this doctor took the initiative and went to see him alone. The man looked pretty bad but a few seconds after the doctor's arrival, he gave him a grin and said, "Well?" like he expected him. Like he had come to know how much the doctor had come to love him. The doctor looked a little surprised and he just stood there and laughed a minute. And then the man hit the doctor with a single remark, half a question,

217

and half something else, "Who are you?" he asked, sort of smiling. Just that, "Who are you?" The doctor says he started to say, "Well, I'm Doctor . . ." and then he just stopped cold. It was hard for him to describe or sort out what went on in his head. All kinds of answers went through his mind. They all seemed true, and yet, somehow, they all seemed less than true. "Yeah, I'm this but I'm also that. Well, that's not the whole picture. The whole picture is . . ." The doctor's confusion must have shown because the black man gave him a big grin and said, "Nice to meet you." They talked a few minutes about this and that and at the end the doctor said to him, "Is there anything I can do for you?" He replied, "No, I'm just fine. Thanks very much, Doctor." He paused for the name and the doctor gave it to him. He grinned and that was it. He died a few days later.

But the doctor could not get him out of his mind. Nor this question, "Who are you?" he had asked. The doctor reflected that for years he had trained as a physician and realized he almost got lost in it. He realized that what that man did was to take away his degree and toss it back to him with an "and also?" And also? And also? And that story does the same for us. Who are you? Beyond the degree, beyond the title, beyond the role, beyond the house, beyond the car, beyond the facade, who are you?❏

❏"Who are you?" I ask a second time. My second story tells of a man who had his answer. He had begun a career in one of this nation's great corporations. He majored in business when he was in college and had had a real knack for it. No one was surprised when he was selected top choice for the corporation's executive training program. After a few months of training, his boss took him to the national convention. There he was to get a first-hand look at how things worked at the top and who the important people were for his career. He also got *too* good a look. He noticed some pretty heavy drinking among the executives and was urged to join in. He was told to get a woman from the supply of those who had been hired for the occasion. When he refused both, he got a clear message that this was not what was expected for an up and coming executive candidate. The boss called him in when they got home to discuss the matter. The boss said he was willing to overlook his strange behavior at the convention if it wouldn't happen again. He in turn replied that he would not engage in such behavior. When asked why, his straightforward and firm answer was, "Because I am a Christian."☐

This young man is not holier-than-thou, not a Bible reader, not a prayer group member. He's a businessman, husband, father, but beneath it all he knows the answer to the question, "Who are you?" His unspoken answer is simply, "A disciple."

He was fired, by the way, and has been out of a job for nearly a year but, with his abilities, he's confident he'll find something. He lost his job, but not his identity. But "a disciple of Jesus" is a pretty good answer to our question.

☐"Who are you?" I ask for the third time and suggest in my final story that the answer is planted there early, or not, as the case may be. The electric sign over the little grocery shop was getting rusty and grimy. The father asked his young son if he would paint the sign. The boy was happy to, so he got a ladder, put sandbags to hold it firm, and went up the ladder, a little terrified of the height, but too embarrassed to tell his dad. Anyway, all around the edges of the sign were little blue light bulbs that had to be removed in order to paint. So the boy went down the ladder, got a bucket, and climbed back up, taking out the bulbs one by one. However, when he took the bucket to bring it down, it slipped out of his hand and crashed 20 feet below on the sidewalk. Every single bulb was broken. Terrified, he knew he had to tell his father. Holding back his tears, he went in and told him that he had broken all the bulbs. The father had only one question, "Are you hurt?" When he said no, the father said, "Then I'm not worried. I can replace the light bulbs, but I can't replace my son." "Who are you?" That lad can answer, "I am someone worth more than many sparrows, many bulbs. I am loved. My father told me so."☐

Who are you beyond all the externals? "Who do people say that I am?" is one question—Jesus' question in today's gospel— and "Who are you?" is another. The gospel is simply a challenge to introspection, a call to reexamine values, a prodding to some humility.

❑When George Bush was president, he was doing his public relations thing by visiting a nursing home. He came upon a wizened old man hobbling down the corridor. President Bush took the man by the hand and said, "Sir, do you know who I am?" The man replied, "No, but if you ask one of the nurses, she'll tell you."❑

"Who are you?" If you ask one of the gospels, it will tell you.

29. EMMAUS: A THRICE-TOLD TALE
(Lk 24:13–35 3rd Sunday of Easter Year A)

This is surely one of the most elegant accounts that Luke has left us. It's a beautiful and moving story, a story, basically, of a journey: the joyless journey of some dispirited disciples and the stranger they encounter who transforms that journey. Because it is so rich in layers of meaning, this morning I would like to retell Luke's story in three different versions: a child's fairy tale version, an adult's version, and a poet's version.

□The child's fairy tale version goes like this. Once upon a time some grandparents were in a little gift shop looking for something to give their granddaughter on her birthday. Suddenly, the grandmother sees a precious teacup. "Look at this lovely teacup, Harry. Just the thing!" Granddad picks it up, looks at it and says, "You're right. It's one of the nicest teacups I've ever seen. We must get it." At this point the teacup startled the grandparents by saying, "Well, thank you for the compliment, but, you know, I wasn't always so beautiful." The grandparents, still surprised, said, "What do you mean you weren't always so beautiful?" "It's true," said the teacup. "Once I was just an ugly, soggy lump of clay. But one day a man with dirty and wet hands threw me on a wheel and started turning me around and around till I got so dizzy that I cried, 'Stop! Stop!' but the man with the wet hands said, 'Not yet.' Then he started to poke me and punch me until I hurt all over. 'Stop! Stop!' I cried but he said, 'Not yet.' Finally he did stop but then he did something worse. He put me in a furnace and I got hotter and hotter until I couldn't stand it any longer and I cried, 'Stop! Stop!' but the man said, 'Not yet.' And finally, when I thought I was going to get burned up, the man took me out of the furnace.

"Then, some short lady began to paint me and the fumes were so bad that they made me sick to my stomach and I cried, 'Stop! Stop!' but the lady said, 'Not yet.' Finally she did stop and gave me back to the man again and he put me back in that awful furnace. I cried out, 'Stop! Stop!' but he only said, 'Not yet.' Finally he took me out and let me cool. And when I was cool a very pretty lady put me on a shelf, right next to the mirror. And when I looked into the mirror, I was amazed! I could not believe what I saw. I was no longer ugly, soggy, and dirty. I was beautiful and firm and clean. And I cried for joy.'◻

"Did not the Messiah first have to suffer and so enter into his glory?" asked the stranger on the road to Emmaus. Did not the teacup first have to "suffer" and so enter into its glory? And so it seems that Luke's story, after all, is the same as the child's story of the teacup. The versions differ, the meaning is the same. And the meaning is the same for us. We go through life's journey taking some punches, taking the heat, as we say. Our losses and hurts are shaping us and we cry out, "Stop! Stop!" "Not yet" is often the answer and we wonder why. The story provides an answer. We are being molded into saints and, furthermore, we are reminded, we are not alone on the journey. The stranger is there, though unrecognized. At times, though, we do get a glimpse of that Presence.

◻The adult version of the Emmaus story concerns a young medical student who had to be away from his fiancée for a month to take the comprehensive exams in his last year of college. This was an agony for him, to be separated. He was sad and depressed. He was on a bus traveling from Ithaca, New York, to New Haven, Connecticut, and the bus stopped at the Greyhound station, a rather dreary place. He sat down on an unraveling revolving seat at a dirty counter. The counter was U-shaped so he found himself sitting across from an old woman. She saw him and said, "Honey, you sure do look depressed." He said, "I am," and before he knew it, he was crying. The woman reached across the counter to pat his cheek with a dirt-under-the-fingernail hand and he pulled back when he saw it. She simply asked, "What's wrong, honey?" And he told her about his fiancée and how much he loved her and how much he missed her. He showed the woman her picture. The woman said, "Oh, I've never seen such a beautiful young woman."

Then she began to tell him that she had been married to a traveling salesman who had since passed away. And she related how they used to weep, both of them, each time he had to go away, but how happy they were when he returned. She said, "Marriage is wonderful. You're going to have a wonderful marriage. Everything's going to be fine."And then she suggested he might feel better if he had something to eat, so she ordered a donut from under the scratchy plastic. And the woman took the donut, broke it, and she gave it to him. As she did, an announcement came over the loudspeaker and she said, "Oh my goodness! My bus is here." And she disappeared. Only then were his eyes opened and he recognized Jesus in the breaking of the donut.☐

The Emmaus story lives on that level too. Wherever goodness is shared, tears dried, comfort given, charity done, the Stranger, the Risen Christ, is present.

The final version of Luke's story is a brief one, from the poet's point of view:

They walked the highway, defeated, alone.
A Stranger joined them and lifted the stone.
He unfolded the scriptures, what prophets had said.
They shared life together, the cup and the bread.
Then they knew him, the Stranger, the man who was dead.
He gave them the answer when love broke bread.

This version gives us a clue of what we are doing here and why the Eucharist is so central to the Catholic experience. We are all on a journey. Our paths are uneven. Losses, at times, are heavy. We seem to be marching with no purpose while searching for some meaning to our lives and our deaths. We need the Eucharist—the Breaking of the Bread at Mass—to be reassured that Jesus has not left us alone. We need to recall that on the night before he died, he left us something. "My body given for you, my blood shed for you. Do this in remembrance of me," he said. And so Luke, who left us these words, is saying that in faith we will recognize Jesus the Stranger disguised under the appearances of Bread and Wine, and in that recognition, we will know that all will be well. In short, the Risen Christ is here in a unique way in every Mass to remind us that our lives are not purposeless, that we do not travel alone, that Someone cares, and that one day we too shall shine bright and beautiful with the fullness of his love.

30. SEEDS
(Mt 13:1–23 15th Sunday in O.T. Year A)

I have a very churchy question to ask you this morning. Do you know the difference between heaven and hell? Whatever answer you come up with, here's one I heard recently. Heaven is where the cooks are French, the police are English, the mechanics are German, the lovers are Italian, and everything is organized by the Swiss. Hell is where the English are the cooks, the Germans are the police, the French are the mechanics, the Swiss are the lovers, and everything is organized by the Italians.

Basically, of course, any difference between heaven and hell is grounded in the old truth that ultimately you will reap what you sow. And that brings us to the metaphor of today's gospel: the seeds we sow. And sow them we do and it is the point of today's reflection to make us both conscious of that and, hopefully, proud of that. The late Fred Hermann used to begin his speeches by asking his audiences, "Who was Jim Thorpe's coach? Who was Albert Einstein's arithmetic teacher in the second grade? Who was Ignace Paderewski's piano teacher? Who was Billy Graham's religion teacher in junior high?" You can see what he was getting at with his questions. Who planted the seeds of future greatness? How small the beginnings, how great the outcome. When Abraham Lincoln met Harriet Beecher Stowe, author of *Uncle Tom's Cabin*, he remarked, "So this is the little lady who started the big war."

And here's where the gospel hits home. What are we planting in our children, our friends, our co-workers? What "big war" are we seeding?

A while ago some reporters were interviewing Boris Yeltsin, asking him what gave him the courage to stand firm during the fall of communism in the former USSR. Interestingly, he credited the electrician from Poland, Lech Walesa, who started the downfall of communism there. When Walesa was interviewed and asked what inspired him he said it was the civil rights movement in the United States led by Martin Luther King. When Martin

Luther King was interviewed and asked what inspired him, he said it was the courage of one woman, Rosa Parks, who refused to move to the back seat of the bus. Is it too much of a stretch to say that a brave little woman in the South brought about the downfall of communism? Seeds are like that. And that is the moral lesson for us. How valuable the little things we do, the people we influence.

☐Alexei Peshkov lost his father when he was only five years old. His mother remarried and she sent him off to live with his grandparents. His grandfather hated the little boy and every night in his life he beat him. That little boy knew those beatings and the worst of poverty that Russia had to offer. As a result, when he got older, he changed his name. He called himself Maxim Gorky, the famous writer we now know. In Russian Gorky means bitterness and Maxim means what it sounds like: maximum. This man knew and lived maximum bitterness all his life. But then, he began reading the works of another famous Russian writer, Leo Tolstoy, and began to change. These were wonderful stories of faith and love and hope. One day when Gorky was walking along the seashore, he saw an old man there. He saw Tolstoy, his idol, sitting there, this man who had introduced him to life and joy. He turned to his friends and said, "So long as that man lives, I will not be an orphan upon the earth." Once more, the gospel asks, "Can we say the same?"☐

☐A grandson remembers fondly and indeed with awe a long-gone grandfather who influenced him deeply. He was a black man in the deep South, a kind of Uncle Remus figure to generations of children. He told them stories, taught them how to fish and hunt, how to fly a kite, and so on. He owned a little cabin and some land where he lived with his wife and continued to live there after she died. The grandson says that the fateful day came about a year later after his grandmom died. A very valuable deposit of copper was discovered running through his grandfather's property. Some of the business leaders in town came to his grandfather and offered to buy his land so they could start a mining enterprise. The old man, who had not been raised in a money culture, simply wanted to live out his days on the old homestead, so he declined to sell. Still, there was a great deal of money at stake, a great deal. It wasn't long before the atmosphere began to turn ugly. For when the businessmen could not buy him out they resorted to threats. And many of the people, whom as children he had befriended, began to turn on him. Finally, it came down to this. They let it be known that if he was not off the property by the weekend, there would be a lynching.

The grandson was terrified. He ran all the way to town to tell the local preacher. The old preacher told him not to worry. He sent the boy home and that night, under cover of darkness, he went to see the old man. The next morning, at the appointed hour, a band of executioners rode up hiding behind their white hoods and masks. They were surprised to see the old preacher come out with the old man and stand beside him on the porch. The preacher spoke. "Look," he said, "John knows that he is going to die and he has asked me to come out here, since he can't read or write, and make out his will, his last will and testimony. And now he wants me to read it to you." The preacher looked around at the crowd, held up some old pieces of paper, cleared his throat and began to read. "He wants to leave his fishing rod to Peter because he remembers the first bass that he taught him to catch with it. He wants to leave his rifle to James because he remembers how he taught him to shoot it. He wants to leave his net to Michael because he taught him how to catch catfish with it. And he wants to leave his hoe to Ethan because he helped Ethan raise crops when his parents were starving." And so, says the grandson, item by item his grandfather proceeded to give away things to the very people who had come out to take his life. One by one they began to turn away and leave until there was no one left. He went up to his grandfather and asked, "Grandpop, what kind of a will was that?" His grandfather laid his hand on his shoulder and replied, "The will of God, son. The will of God." If I am an upright man today, says the grandson, it was because of my grandfather.☐

Who *was* Einstein's second grade arithmetic teacher? I don't know, but we're all eternally grateful. Who seeded you, made you what you are, put value, meaning, and grace into your lives? I don't know, but it shows by your presence here this morning.

Whom are you seeding, quietly and effectively raising up caring, sensitive, and open-hearted people? Only you know the answer to that, as you surely know that, if you fail, there simply will be no crop.

❏Upon Jesus' arrival in heaven, a vast host of angels greeted him. After the formalities, they asked him who he had left behind on earth to finish the work he had begun. Jesus replied, "Just a small group of men and women who love me." "That's all?" asked the angels, astonished. "What if this tiny group should fail?" Jesus replied, "I have no other plans."❏

31. A WEDDING HOMILY

It may strike you as odd that I, most likely the only professional bachelor in this church right now, am going to speak to John and Mary and to you about marriage. But I would not be so foolish to tackle something of which I have no personal experience, although I have learned a great deal about marriage over the years, and so, a while back, I sought out three couples of wit and wisdom, and asked them what they would say to a bride and groom on their wedding day. It is their insights that I would now share. And here are those insights. One couple said tell them that marriage is a gift; another couple said tell them that marriage is basically an ordering of their priorities, their value system; the last couple said tell them that marriage is a dedication.

So, let me share the marriage-is-a-gift of the first couple who happen to be Mitch and Kathy Finley who in fact do a lot of writing about marriage and family life. When they were married for ten years, Mitch wrote these words: "Two of the most famous quotations in English literature are found in the same book, one at the beginning, one at the end. 'It was the best of times. It was the worst of times. It was a season of light. It was a season of darkness. . . .It is a far, far better thing that I do than I have ever done.' The source, of course, is Dickens's *A Tale of Two Cities*, a novel about the French Revolution. Yet these familiar words come to mind as I pause to reflect on a marriage now ten years old. These years have been for me the best of times and the worst of times, mostly the best of times. The vows I spoke ten years ago were, in retrospect, a far, far better thing than I had ever done. The ten calendar years that my life companion and I have lived together mark seasons of light and seasons of darkness, mostly of light. These ten years stand as a witness to the truth of those words, that marriage is our last best chance to grow up."

To this extent, they say, marriage is indeed a gift: the gift of maturity gradually causing people to move away from "I want" to "I give," from "me" to "our," from pride to humility, from self-

centeredness to sharing. Marriage helps people be more than they
thought they could be. Marriage indeed is a gift, say the Finleys.
Tell the people that.

☐My second couple agrees, but because of their unique experience, they would place the emphasis on marriage as an ordering
of the couple's values. There's a reason behind that. Many years
ago, you see, they and their two young children were under
house arrest for a long time in China. They lived somewhat com-
fortably but were never allowed to leave their house. One day a
soldier unexpectedly came to the door and without any explanation, told them that they could return to America tomorrow but,
as he said, "You may take only 200 pounds with you, no more and
no less." Only 200 pounds! So they got out the large scale and the
arguments began. Must have this vase, must have these books,
must have these dishes, must have these toys, and so on. Back
and forth they argued. They put stuff on the scale. They took stuff
off the scale over and over again until, at last, they had exactly 200
pounds.

The soldier, as promised, returned the next day. He asked,
"Are you ready?" They said yes. "Are you packed?" They said
yes. "Did you weigh everything?" They said yes, pointing to the
boxes on the large flat scale. "Did you weigh the children?" A
dreadful silence as they looked at each other and then, after a
moment's hesitation, off came the books, off came the vase, off
came everything. And that's when they realized that they had let
things get in the way of people, that they had forgotten their priorities.☐

And they're convinced that many marriages break up because
secondary things like constant consumption replace primary relationships, care, and time for one another. We will hear their concern expressed, by the way, at the final nuptial blessing which has
these perceptive words, "May cares never cause you distress nor
the desire for earthly possessions dominate your lives." So,
understandably this couple says, "Tell the bride and groom and
the congregation to order their values. People first. It's the only
way."

My third couple giving insight is really half a couple. This is a woman, a widow, and a wonderful writer named Madeleine L'Engle. She was married for 43 years to Hugh Franklin, the soap opera star, who died of cancer. She wrote a book about their marriage and, in the course of that book, she has these marvelous words: "Our love has been anything but perfect, and anything but static. Inevitably there have been times when one of us has outrun the other and has had to wait patiently for the other to catch up. There have been times when we have misunderstood each other, demanded too much of each other, been insensitive to each other's needs. I do not believe that there is any marriage in which these things do not happen. The growth of love is not a straight line, but a series of hills and valleys. I suspect that in every good marriage there are times when love seems to be over. Sometimes these desert times are simply the only way to the next oasis which is far more lush and beautiful after the desert crossing that it could possibly have been without."

Lovely words and how true they are. If only some couples would only hang in there in their desert times—the times of their divorce—and hold out for the next oasis, the next stage, of their marriage which will be far richer than they ever imagined and which, to tell the truth, cannot be reached without the hard time, the death time, the purification time. In any case, Madeleine L'Engle says this takes dedication, to marriage itself and to one another. And she would want me to tell you that.

So, there you are. Three wisdoms from three well married people. Take your choice: marriage is a Gift, marriage is an Ordering, marriage is a Dedication. But there's no problem. Marriage, of course, is all three. It's just a matter of emphasis. Nor, beyond that observation, should we fail to notice something else, that the first letters of Gift, Ordering, and Dedication spell God. And that's a reminder that marriage came from God to begin with and we all remember his command that a man and woman were to leave father and mother and cling to one another, for now they "are no longer two, but one flesh." To that extent, marriage is a outward sign, a visible symbol, or, as we Catholics like to say, a sacrament of God being one with us in love. Which is to say, every forgiving marriage tells us of God's mercy. Every lasting marriage tells us of God's steadfastness. Every enduring marriage tells us of God's patience. Every faithful marriage tells us of God's fidelity. In short, we know God from the way people act. A good marriage is one of those clues.

Now we are ready to bring that God-sign called marriage into effect. We are ready, John and Mary are ready, to pronounce those words that will set them off on a new adventure. A new couple is in the making, a new unit of society, a new beginning. It's truly a momentous time. It's their chance to publicly accept the Gift, the Ordering, the Dedication that is marriage. Come, let us witness it.

32. THE TRANSFIGURATION
(Lk 9:28–36 2nd Sunday of Lent Year C)

[This "storytelling" homily, as noted in the introduction to these homilies, is a "synthetic," or patchwork, homily in that it is an illustration of how stories can be recycled to fit many themes. Here I've taken Mary Ann Bird's story in Homily 22, "No Greater Love," and the J.D. Salinger story in Homily 21, "We're All Connected," and the Mother and Son story in Homily 4, "Trinity Sunday," to work in a particular theme connected with the Transfiguration gospel.]

The most significant line in this familiar gospel is its opening sentence, "Jesus took Peter, John, and James up to the mountain to pray." Do you recall when we meet this same trio going apart with Jesus? Of course. In the garden of Gethsemane. They who beheld his glory on the mountain peak would witness his agony on the garden ground. Why? Because to endure the latter they needed the former. As today's preface puts it—and listen for it—"He revealed his glory to strengthen them for the scandal of the cross." Yes, he revealed his glory to strengthen them for the scandal of the cross. That makes sense, but it does raise a question: what about us? It is good and proper and fitting that the three apostles had a vision to sustain them in hard times but, again, what about us? After all, we too could put up with an awful lot if we had a Remembered Moment of glory to sustain us, a clear indication of the Presence of Jesus, some sign that when all was over, everything would be all right.

Where's *our* vision to hold on to?

The response is that we too do in fact have our moments of transfiguration, but simply fail to recognize them. It is, if you will, a matter of *seeing*. Our prayer and our practice must help us to see. Seeing is the great paradox in the Bible; those with two good eyes are blind, those who are blind see. The mystics speak of a "third eye," a seeing with the soul. How important that is, for they knew what modern psychologists know: what we see rules our behavior. Let me give you an example.

❏Steve Covey, the author of the best selling *The Seven Habits of Highly Effective People*, tells of an experience he had on a New York subway one Sunday morning. He says that people were sitting quietly. Some were reading newspapers, some were dozing, others were simply contemplating with their eyes closed. It was a rather peaceful, calm scene. At one stop a man and his children entered the car. The children were soon yelling back and forth, throwing things, even grabbing people's newspapers. It was all very disturbing and yet the father just sat there next to him and did nothing. It was not difficult to feel irritated. Steve could not believe the man could be so insensitive as to let his children run wild and do nothing about it. It was easy to see that everyone else in the car was annoyed as well. So finally, with what he thought was admirable restraint and patience, Steve said to the man, "Sir, your children are really disturbing a lot of people. I wonder if you couldn't control them a little bit more?" The man lifted his gaze as if coming into consciousness for the first time and said, "Oh, you're right. I guess I should do something about it. We just came from the hospital where their mother died about an hour ago. I don't know what to think and I guess they don't know how to handle it either."

Steve says, "Can you imagine what I felt at that moment? Suddenly I *saw* things differently. Because I saw differently, I *felt* differently. I *behaved* differently. My irritation vanished. I didn't have to worry about controlling my attitude or my behavior. My heart was filled with this man's pain. Feelings of compassion and sympathy flowed freely. 'Your wife just died? Oh, I'm so sorry! Can you tell me about it? What can I do to help?'"❏

Nothing changed in that subway car. All was the same: the same people, the same irritation, the same kids. What *did* change was a way of seeing it all and, with the seeing, a change of behavior. It was Steve Covey's moment of Transfiguration, a moment of revelation that sustained him in a difficult situation. The point is, we have to see differently, to recognize such revelations of God in our daily lives. Let me share three stories of seeing.

A woman named Mary Ann Bird relates, "I grew up knowing

I was different, and I hated it. I was born with a cleft palate, and when I started school, my classmates made it clear to me how I must look to others: a little girl with a misshapen lip, crooked nose, lopsided teeth and garbled speech. When my schoolmates would ask, 'What happened to your lip?' I'd tell them I'd fallen and cut it on a piece of glass. Somehow it seemed more acceptable to have suffered an accident than to have been born different. I was convinced that no one outside my family could love me. There was, however, a teacher in the second grade that we all adored, a Mrs. Leonard. She was short, round, happy, a sparkling lady. Annually, we would have a hearing test. I was virtually deaf in one of my ears; but when I had taken the test in the past years, I discovered that if I did not press my hand as tightly upon my ears as I was instructed to do, I could pass the test. Mrs. Leonard gave the test to everyone in the class, and finally it was my turn. I knew from past years that as we stood against the door and covered one ear, the teacher sitting at her desk would whisper something and we would have to repeat it back, things like 'The sky is blue' or 'Do you have new shoes?' I waited there for those words which God must have put into her mouth, those seven words which changed my life. Mrs. Leonard said, in her whisper, 'I wish you were my little girl.'"☐

Before Mrs. Leonard, she saw ugliness. After Mrs. Leonard, she saw beauty. Don't you think Mrs. Leonard's words remained a sustaining vision as this little girl hit the hard knocks of life? Right there with Peter, John, and James, it was her moment of Transfiguration.

☐J.D. Salinger who wrote *Catcher in the Rye* wrote also another stunning book, *Franny and Zooey*. There's a powerful scene in this latter book when Franny comes home from college a nervous wreck. Her well-intentioned but misguided efforts to explore the depths of religious mysticism have left her extremely tense. Bessie, her mother, is concerned and shows that concern by bringing her distressed daughter a cup of chicken soup. Even though Franny knows her mother is trying to comfort her, the offer of the soup annoys her and she lashes out at her mother. Franny's brother, who's sitting at the table, jumps up and confronts her. He tells her that her approach to religion is all wrong. He says, "I'll tell you one thing, Franny. If it's the religious life you want, you ought to know that you're missing out on every single religious action that's going on in this house. You don't have sense enough to drink when someone brings you a cup of consecrated chicken soup, which is the only kind of chicken soup that Mom ever brings to anybody!"◻

Franny was blind. She didn't see Christ in the ordinary, the grace in a soup consecrated by love. Her moment of revelation came and went and she didn't see it. She would look with envy on Peter, John, and James and never realize she had the same experience. Do we do the same?

◻A mother told her children that hard times had fallen on several families in town and so this year, they were not to give them, their parents, anything for Christmas, but to give the money to these poor families. She then tells of her son who was a basketball manager at his college and on the road a good deal of the time. He had just been home for a short visit and as he was about to leave he reached out to his mother's hand saying, "Take this, Mom." And he pressed some money into her palm. "Use it for one of the families so they can have a good Christmas." A quick hug and off he went down the steps. In his mom's hand rested a crisp fifty dollar bill. She realized that with the little money Chris had to live on in college, he must have been saving for months. She sprinted down the stairs, opened the door of his car, and sat down next to him. He gave her a wonderful hug and, in an instant, she relates, "I was no longer sitting next to my twenty-year-old son. I was sitting next to my five-year-old Chris who once forgave someone who had stolen his toy car because he said that he must have needed it more than he did." Then he spoke, "Please, get out of the car, Mom, before I start crying too." His mother hugged him one more time, told him how happy she was that some family was going to have a good Christmas. She said, "I told him, 'I love you, Honey, and God will bless you for this.' And with that, I climbed out of the car, leaving with a moment I shall cherish forever—the moment I saw Christ in my son."◻

That was her mountain experience. She saw differently. She saw not just her son, but Jesus. It was her time of revelation that sustained her through hard times.

We need not ask then, "What about us?" We *do* have our mountaintop revelations but simply fail to see them. We must remember what this gospel is telling us. If God is revealed in the human face of Jesus, Jesus is revealed in the human faces of those who touch us in love and whom we touch. We need only to open our eyes to witness the daily revelations of Jesus' sustaining and reassuring presence.

33. PROPHET JOHN
(Mt 3:1–12 2nd Sunday of Advent Year A)

Here we are, on this second Sunday of Advent, listening to this unpleasant prophet again as Christmas draws near. This prophet, John the Baptist, is obviously not a popular figure to work up in cheery ceramics. You won't find him as a character in the creche, as a sugar cookie figure, or on a Hallmark card. He, with his gaunt and stark visage, wearing a dusty camel's hair coat—not cashmere—reeking of locust and honey and smelling of poverty and desert discipline, is not one we embrace easily. How many Christmas cards have you received depicting John the Baptist? "Greetings from our house to yours. Our thoughts of you at this time of the year are best expressed in the words of John the Baptist, 'You brood of Vipers! The ax is laid to the root of the trees, and every tree that does not bear good fruit will be thrown into the fire.' Merry Christmas from the Smiths."

By and large, we prefer the round, jolly, overgrown elf in the red velour suit with a bag full of gifts for those who have too much already.

Yet, all three gospels have John the Baptist at the beginning of the Christmas story and so the message is clear: if you want to get to the joy of Bethlehem, you must get past the Jordan where John the Baptist is. The church has always demanded that, if you really want to see what's in Bethlehem's manger, you must first confront this crazy prophet out in the wilderness whose sermons are as bitter and wild as the terrain. In short, no Jesus without John. Not a pleasant prospect, but there it is.

There it is. That's why John comes ranting down every Christian church aisle today hurling invective, demanding to cleanse us of our delusions with a cold dip in the icy Jordan. "The Kingdom of God is at hand," proclaims John. "Good," we say. "At last God has come to give us what we deserve, to set us up, treat us right, soothe our pain, take our side."

"*Therefore*, repent!" cries John. Therefore? Do what? Repent. Turn around. Let go.

"You brood of vipers! Who warned you to flee the coming fire? Bear fruit of repentance!" And we say, "He's attacking street hoodlums, criminals, and perverts, not us." Then John turns to us, screaming: "And don't *you* say, We have Abraham for our father. Don't tell me that your family has always been members of this church, that you're kind to your spouse and children and support several important charities, and everyone thinks you're nice. Don't tell me that you give at the office at Christmas and use envelopes."

Repent, repent—not only of your sins, but of trying to *hide* them: the small-mindedness, backbiting, jealousy, adulterous affairs, minor embezzlements, self-centeredness, the sloth. Somewhere along the line, preaches John, you must do the A.A. thing, "Hi, there. My name is Mary and I'm an alcoholic." "Hi, there. My name is Andrew and I'm a sinner."

Beneath our Christmas card cheer, our Norman Rockwell image, we *are* fitting subjects for the preaching of John. Beneath our celebrations of our human potential, our glorious attainments, our cultivated self-esteem is someone worthy of the preaching of John the Baptist who comes calling us to account, measuring our lives not by what nine out of ten Americans think, but by what Almighty God commands.

Picture this very moment, this wild figure sprinting out of the sacristy and into the sanctuary and running up and down our aisles, looking into our very souls and stopping in front of different parishioners and crying, "Repent!" and all the others wondering what they might be repenting of. But *they* know. They know. Over there, fellow parishioner Saul repents of his part in a murder and knows in his heart that he will have to live and preach another gospel. John stands in front of another parishioner named Augustine, who lowers his head in the pew and thinks of his impurity. Over here, Ignatius, the military man, ponders his marauding. Over there, John Newton thinks of his shameful treatment of slaves and vows here and now to write "Amazing Grace." In the center aisle, Dorothy Day repents of her communism and promises to live and work amont the poor. Over at the side, Charles Colson, sitting there in the pew as he sat in the Oval

Office as a trusted advisor and fellow conspirator to the Watergate president, feels the keen look of John and decides that he, a convicted criminal, will minister the word of God to prisoners.

And now. Now John is in front of *us*, looking, pointing. Saying nothing. Just there with his unsettling, wild presence. And we lower *our* heads and promise . . . what? What? Repent. Repent. We know what we need to repent of. Or do we? Pause for a moment beneath his uncomfortable gaze and think. Think, for example, of the instances I used before: the minor embezzlements, the self-centeredness, the sloth. Sloth? Isn't that one of the seven capital sins? Why mention *that* one? Anger, maybe. Lust, yes. Pride. Yes. But sloth? If there's anything we're *not* guilty of, it's sloth. Sloth is laziness and we are a people who run around, commute, taxi the kids all over, belong to a hundred groups and organizations. We never have enough time. We're exhausted. No, sloth is the one thing we're not guilty of.

❏Oh? says John. O.K. Let's take that example. Did you know that sloth is a kind of living death? Let me explain. As a lad, Bruno Bettelheim lived in Germany and at that time the Nazi terror was starting to move through Germany, and the signs were clear that it was going to engulf Bettelheim and his Jewish family. He wrote a book called *The Informed Heart.* He tells in that book how he and his peers pleaded with the elder people to flee Germany, run away, because this terror was at their door. But the more they pleaded the more the old people said, "No, we can't leave our possessions, we can't leave our homes, we're settled here." And this went on week after week until finally the young people left and the Nazi terror came and swallowed up those Jews and killed them. This is an example of sloth.❏

Sloth is when one knows that one is setting upon a damaging or deadly course and somehow can't muster the courage, the hope, the faith to do something different. The man who detests his job but continues in it for a lifetime is guilty of sloth. The man or woman who sits at the Internet computer on-line for hour after hour, neglecting real life relationships, forgetting that life in the real world is far more interesting, far more important, far richer than anything they'll find on the computer screen. The woman who sees herself as a martyr to her family, the grownup children who never make a break with her. The married couple whose marriage is a lifelong hell, the teenager whose crowd is leading him or her into drugs or drink or premarital sex—they're guilty of sloth. They *know* they're on a damaging course. They *know* they're going to die from this. They know their behavior is utterly destructive to themselves and others, but they can't bring themselves to get out of it.

As a matter of fact, the one thing that the slothful have in common is the perfect alibi. If you should mention to some of these people, as I have done, that they might possibly have a different reaction and way of life, they come upon you with a ton of excuses and anger. The man who is in this terrible job he hates, which is giving him ulcers and is going to shorten his life by 20 years, will say, "But I've got to support my family." The computer addict who sits—and eats—seven, eight, ten hours in front of the screen says, "Yeah, but the payoff is so great: the money." The martyred housewife will say, "But how can my kids do without me if I'm not here every moment? How will they make the bed? How will they find the refrigerator? How will they work the microwave? How will they have clean clothes?" And you say, "Well, at some point, they've got to be on their own. How old is your little boy?" "Thirty-four." Teenagers know they are going to destroy themselves with drugs and drink, but the need of peer acceptance and popularity is so great they don't have the courage to move on. And that's sloth. We're guilty of sloth when we find ourselves continually depressed or in pain and can produce excellent moral and practical reasons why we can't improve our lot.

So, there you are. An example of the need to repent. There *he* is; you know, that terrible, unwanted, smelly prophet from the desert, still standing there in front of you. And the fact is, he is *going* to stand there blocking your view of the Christmas Crib when it's up because, as we said, that's his job; that's what he's about and what this gospel is about and what this liturgy is about:

No Jesus without John.
No joy without the Jordan.
No rejoicing without repentance.
Today, the prophet has spoken.

34. Deciding and Waiting
(Lk 21:25–28, 34–36 1st Sunday of Advent Year C)

As you can readily see from the banners and the change of vestment color, we have with Advent entered into the beginning of the church's year. Advent is not an especially connected time or clearly defined. It's rather a kind of neutral season of transition. We have other seasons of the church's year that have more definition to them. Christmas is garlanded with all kinds of motifs. Epiphany shines a powerful light on the call to the Gentiles. Lent is a strong time of readiness to celebrate the Easter mysteries. Easter is splendid rebirth. Pentecost is the fiery time of the Spirit. But Advent, even as a preparation for Christmas, seems to limp a little. It's a rest stop, if you will, a shutting-down time from the past before we begin again. Hence, all those end-of-the-world images in Advent's readings. Destruction before rebuilding. Devastation before renewal. Something's ending. Something's about to be born. But, first, death.

Some of us may remember the little kid's ditty we used to chant, "Ring around the rosy. Pocketful of posies. Ashes, ashes, all fall down!" There's a dark origin to that tune. The "ring around the rosy" refers to the Black Death of the fourteenth century. The sign of the dreaded disease was a black ring rash around a red spot. Hence, "ring around the rosy." "Pocketful of posies" refers to the people's use of carrying flowers with them, in the days before bottled perfumes, to try to cover over the terrible stench of decaying bodies and death. Finally, "ashes, ashes, all fall down" refers to the fact that the Black Death felled one-fourth of the population of Europe. Every family had a death. It was a terrible, terrible time. Because it was so horrible, people tried to cover it over, live with it, by transferring something deadly into a little rhyme and game. They sang "Ring Around the Rosy" to help cover up the despair they had to live with.

Advent is just the opposite of this rhyme's intent. It covers up nothing. On the contrary, Advent insistently remembers. It remembers things that *should* die, should be destroyed in order that

243

something new will arise. That's why this season will play on the twin motifs of deciding and waiting.

Deciding. Since Advent, we said, deals with endings—the stars falling, the moon refusing to give light, the sun dimmed—and the anticipation of something new arising from all this destruction, then it demands that we come to certain decisions. Of all the decisions it asks us to make for a new time is the decision to make inner space. The past was too cluttered and needed to be torn down. We all know that. We need space.

☐Henri Nouwen, the spiritual writer, spent a couple of years in Peru among the poor. He was, however, quite taken with their simplicity and the utter happiness of their lives, even though they were living in abject poverty. He could not help but feel the contrary when he returned to the United States with all its wealth. He wrote in his diary, "What strikes me about being back in the United States is the full force of restlessness and the loneliness and the tension that holds so many people. The conversations I had today were about spiritual survival. Many of my friends feel overwhelmed by the many demands made on them. Few feel the inner peace and joy they so much desire."☐

And most of us probably can answer, "Amen to that."

Nouwen sees that more and more. He comments further: "To celebrate life together, to be together in community, to simply enjoy the beauty of creation, the love of people and the goodness of God. These seem such far-away ideals. There seems to be a mountain of obstacles preventing people from being where their heart wants them to be. So painful to watch and experience. The astonishing thing is that the battle for survival has become so normal that few people believe that there can be a difference. Oh, how important is discipline, community, prayer, silence, caring presence, simple listening, adoration, and deep, lasting, faithful friendship. We all want it so much, and still the powers suggesting that it is all fantasy are enormous. But we have to replace the battle for power with the battle to create space for the spirit."

If Advent's first demand is about deciding, then it suggests what to decide: more space in the new church year for one another, for cultivating friendships, for family, for God.

Advent's second demand is that we must wait. Wait till the destruction is over and the debris is settled; wait patiently for something else to be born. Give it time. Waiting is not our strong suit, especially since we have been culturally honed to instant responses.

□A man was telling me recently about trying to work through some new variations on his computer. It took a little time to resolve and crank out the work on his laser printer. So he said, "As I waited, I went into the kitchen to make myself a cup of tea. I filled the cup with hot water and put it in the microwave." He said he was not only frustrated because he had to wait for the printout, but also for the cup of tea. Then he adds, "I find myself flashing back to about 35 years ago when I was a kid and lived on a farm and we had neither typewriters nor computers. If I wanted a cup of tea I would have to go out to the yard and walk to the well and I would have to pump the water and bring it back and put it on a wood-burning stove. It would have been a half hour before I could have my tea, and here I am, frustrated because it's taking two minutes to get my tea and to have my computer turn out what it should."□

Waiting, as I said, is not our strong point. Most people equate waiting with waste, a waste of time. In a land where time is money, we don't want to wait. So we build Concordes, drink instant coffee, fax our messages, drive with our cellular phones, drops squares of sod for instant lawns, and eat fast foods at fast food places. If life asks us to wait, we get nervous—and guilty. We should be *doing* something.

But Advent asks us to wait. In fact, Advent is the season of waiting. One woman, with good insight, likens Advent to pregnancy. She writes, "Waiting is an impractical time in our thoughts, good for nothing, but mysteriously necessary to all that is coming. As in a pregnancy, nothing of value comes into being without a period of quiet incubation. Not a healthy baby, not a loving relationship, not a reconciliation, a work of art, and never a transformation. Rather, a shortened period of incubation brings forth what is not whole or strong or even alive. Brewing, baking, simmering, fermenting, ripening, germinating, gestating are the processes of becoming, and they are the symbolic states of being that belong in a life of value necessary for transformation."

That's why Advent's chief figure is Mary. Mary had to decide and gave her answer, "Let it be done unto me according to your word." Mary had to wait. Patiently, she had to create space for the child in her womb, in her life. She had to wait nine months to look into the face of her Savior and ours. She had to let it happen.

This season, then, is strongly suggestive. What's destructive in your life that should be itself destroyed? Let them, like Advent's sun, moon, and stars, fall. What needs to grow? Family unity? Friendships? Inner peace? Rushing is the enemy of the spirit as it is of relationships. Like Mary, we need to sit quietly in prayer and let the Spirit do what it will.

35. CHRIST THE KING
(Lk 23:35–43 34th Sunday in O.T. Year C)

For you and me, Americans living in the waning years of the twentieth century, the image of Jesus as King is troublesome. Kings are something Americans rejected over 200 years ago. We're uncomfortable with the trappings of royalty. We live in a democracy, after all, and don't resonate with kings, even Christ the King.

But it may help us to appreciate what it's all about if we look at the feast's origins. It was created fairly recently by Pope Pius XI in 1925. Why? Because the church *needed* the image of Christ the King at that point. On its first celebration, Mussolini had been head of Italy for three years, a rabble-rouser named Hitler had been out of jail for a year, his Nazi party was growing in popularity, and the world lay in a great Depression. Secularism and atheism were rearing their heads. In such a time, Pius XI asserted that, *nevertheless,* with all of those new dictators and false values, *Christ* is King of the universe.

The feast, then, was basically a language thing, a symbol, a metaphor, designed to be a statement of life's fundamental question for broken times: who exercises dominion over you? Who or what rules our lives and how? If we pick up on *that* theme, then the feast of Christ the King makes sense for us today with its questions of dominion. Who rules our lives? Who dominates the culture?

Let's get uncomfortable—and I apologize for the uncomfortability—and take a look at the legacy America leaves its kids, and see who and what rules *their* lives. According to the Children's Defense Fund in *one day* in the life of American children, that is, each day:

3 children die from child abuse.

9 children are murdered.

13 children die from guns.

30 children are wounded by guns.

101 babies die before their first birthday.

202 children are arrested for drug abuse.

248 children are arrested for violent crimes.

427 children are arrested for alcohol abuse or drunken driving.

2781 teenagers get pregnant.

1115 teenagers have abortions.

1234 children run away from home.

2860 children see their parents divorce.

3325 babies are born to unmarried women (25 percent of America's children are living without fathers).

10,988 public school children are suspended each school day.

100,000 children are homeless.

1,200,000 latchkey children come home to a house in which there is a gun.

These are the realities that have dominion over our children.

And these are not abstract figures. Only this week in our papers, you recall, we read where one 12-year-old shot and killed another lad, and a six-year-old, Alicia, born with cocaine in her blood, died a horrible death from abuse. Last week the papers announced that crime continues to decline but, and I quote, "Experts warn of the coming 'storm' of juvenile violence since there are now 40 million kids 10 years old and under who will become teenagers—not normally a big problem beyond the usual stress of growing up—but the catch is, as Professor John DiLulio at Princeton said, many of them are 'fatherless, godless and jobless,'" a proven formula for crime.

Fatherless, godless and jobless—these three evils, like the witches of Endor, will have dominion over their lives and society will suffer for it. We need a better dominion than that. Many kids *are* born into a scary world that offers no meaning. So they wind up killing time, themselves, and one another. They take to drugs to kill the pain or to find *some* moment of transcendence. In the absence of real values, a real hero such as Jesus, they are prey to media moguls, trend setters, script writers, and corporate executives who profit enormously from the violent meaninglessness adolescents are attracted to.

The secular culture has ruled out from the public forum the

one thing that could help them and us: the need for a belief in a God who loves them unconditionally. A Christ who is King. On the contrary, the culture dictates that our kids can't be redeemed, they can only be programmed.

They can't be saved, they can only be incarcerated.

They can't be forgiven, they can only be psychoanalyzed.

They can't be judged, they can only be sentenced.

They can't be prayed for, but only made to feel good.

They can't be introduced to repentance, but only introduced to therapy.

They can't be told of an all-embracing love that went to the cross for them, but only told to "have a nice day."

Not for them to be the prodigal children falling into the arms of a forgiving Father; rather they can only be adolescents sitting across the desk from their social worker. It's good, but not good enough. Not good enough.

☐The nation was sickened last week when a woman, Deborah Evans, was killed with her innocent ten-year-old daughter, Samantha, and her eight-year-old son, Joshua, and her baby torn from her womb. She wasn't married. She had a current live-in boyfriend. One of the murderers was the father of the infant she was carrying. The other two accomplices were not married. One of them, a woman, already had two children and she and her live-in boyfriend couldn't have their own, so they ripped open a womb to get a baby. What a history, what a future that surviving infant has!☐

Imagine when he reads about his origins and the deaths of his mother and half sister and brother. Even allowing that the mother was trying to get her life together, we have here a microcosm of everything that is chaotic and wrong: casual and conscienceless murder, fatherless children, multiple living out of wedlock, which is so fashionable, and mutilation.

In our society we live with another sickening irony in all this; taking a full grown baby from the womb could have been done legally if the mother wished it so. Think of the partial-birth controversy in which a six-month-old baby can be partially delivered alive before having her skull punctured with scissors and her brain sucked out. Pro-abortionists, like President Clinton, seek to protect this in spite of the testimony of two abortionist doctors, in yesterday's paper, Drs. Martin Haskell and James McMahon, who admitted that a significant number of such babies they abort are alive and healthy. But they are legally murdered. Our culture of death, as the Pope calls it, has dominion.

I saw the same moral chaos in civilized dress when I watched a segment on "60 Minutes." Mike Wallace was interviewing the famous and lionized Ben Bradlee, former editor of *The Washington Post*, who just wrote a book. It struck me: here was four- or five-times-married Mike Wallace interviewing three-times-married Ben Bradlee, a total of seven or eight wives between them. In his book Bradlee boasts of the women he's had sex with. He has a delightful son of 13 from his third marriage. I wondered what the boy thinks. I wondered if he will try to outdo his dad in sexual partners and marriages some day. That's the context of his life.

Yesterday's paper reported an increase of AIDS cases among men between 27 and 35, which, given its long incubation, means some contracted it when they were in their teens. The culture of death has dominion.

Well, with all these hard and unsavory things we'd rather not talk about in church or hear in church, you can see the symbolic impact of today's feast of Christ the King. It *still* has the same meaning as when Pius XI instituted it. It's meant as a challenge. *Who exercises dominion over you? Over society? Who rules your lives and how?* It says that evil and God, sin and redemption, good and bad, light and darkness, angels and demons, mercy and justice, repentance and forgiveness, heaven and hell—all are still viable metaphors that the Kingdom of Christ offers.

Look. It took millions of selfish choices to create our culture of death. It will take millions of unselfish choices to create a culture of life. In making real the Kingship of Christ, his rule in our lives, I think it all comes down to one fundamental reality: the priority of relationships. The priority of relationships, which form the dominion of Christ the King, involves three things: time, stories, and shared experiences, which is the basis of community.

Let me go back to the children as an example. One teacher at a high school says that the teachers are always asking, "How much time do parents spend with their children?" She writes, "One of the saddest comments I've ever heard was from Joe, a student, who was sharing his answer to a reflection question, 'What's the happiest time you've had in your life?'" He responded that a year ago he and his father went to dinner and stayed in the restaurant for three hours, just talking. It hadn't happened before, and it hasn't happened since, but Joe held on to that memory and hoped that his father, a busy professional, would find time for him again.

There it was all together: time together, stories told, and a shared experience—and the resulting moment of close community.

The teacher goes on. "Everything I've heard in the classroom, she says, tells me that deep down, kids are hungry for more attention from their parents. . . .A colleague of mine once commented on the number of girls who would stay after school to talk with her, pouring out their hearts and dreams and fears. 'They must have no one at home to listen to them,' she mused."

Christ's dominion begins with parents' dominion and friends' dominion. We reverse the culture of death by our decisions to give time, tell stories, and share experiences. All the busyness that takes us out of the home; all the busyness that makes us work, work, work all day long so we complain that we never have enough time, in order to live a certain lifestyle; all the busyness we convince ourselves is necessary to give our kids "advantages," when that advantage does not include ourselves—all that busyness is counterfeit. It produces a dark kingdom of lots of toys, lots of cars, and lots of bathrooms, but not the kingdom of heaven where Christ the King reigns, he who ruled by serving others and washing feet.

That is why you deserve such praise for being here, for bringing your families, for giving witness to the need for something more in your lives, for gathering in prayer and worship, for honoring Christ the King. I know the message has been a hard one, but remember, the feast was founded to face hard times and raise harsh realities. Pius XI was right to institute this feast and raise the question of who has dominion over us and our society.

The bottom line to this feast is this: as we approach a new millennium, if there is to be a future, there's a deep sense that things will only get better, *can* get better, if we submit to the teaching, the mission, and the life of Christ the King.

36. TRINITY IMPRINTS
(Mt 28:16–20 Trinity Sunday Year B)

I have a question that is entirely reasonable to ask in church. And the question is this: do you know the difference between heaven and hell? Well, I recently heard that heaven is where the cooks are French, the police are English, the mechanics are German, the lovers are Italian, and everything is organized by the Swiss. Hell, on the other hand, is where the English are the cooks, the Germans are the police, the French are the mechanics, the Swiss are the lovers, and everything is organized by the Italians!

I mention this because that's about the image we have of today's feast of the Holy Trinity. Everything's backward, out of order, and unintelligible: three-in-one, nature and person, Father, Son, and Spirit. What does it all mean and what does it really have to do with us? Like our story, it's a heavenly feast with a hellish twist. To answer that, I'd like to share with you three quick stories and then we'll see what they have in common that sheds light on the mystery of the Holy Trinity.

❏The first story is this: Once there was an elderly man, and one evening he was taking his usual walk. He was enjoying the crisp night air and the wind blowing gently. But suddenly he heard a voice crying out, "Help me! Help me!" The man looked around and saw no one and so he continued his walk. Again he heard a tiny voice, "Help me, help me!" This time he looked down and he saw a small frog. He gently lifted up the frog and looked at it intently. The frog spoke, "I am really a very beautiful princess. If you will kiss me, I will turn back into a princess and I will hug you and kiss you and love you forever." The man thought for a moment, placed the frog in his top pocket, and continued walking. The little frog looked up out of the pocket and asked, "Why don't you kiss me?" The man responded. He said, "Frankly, at this stage of my life, I'd rather have a talking frog."❏

❏Then there's this passage from *Zorba the Greek*. Zorba is speaking. He says, "One day when I was a child, an old man took me on his knee and placed his hand on my head as though he were giving me a blessing. 'Alexis,' he said, 'I'm going to tell you a secret. You're too small to understand now, but you'll understand when you are bigger. Listen, little one. Neither the seven stories of Heaven nor the seven stories of Earth are enough to contain God, but a person's heart can contain God. So, be careful, Alexis—and my blessing be with you—never to wound another person's heart.'"❑

❑A final story, a true one, comes from a priest friend of mine who was summoned one day to the chancery and told, "Father, we are sending you to this old, inner-city parish. There are some wonderful people there; yet they are old and the church and the parish have been in decline for the past 20 years. Just a handful of people left now, so they won't expect much ministry from you. Just go there and visit and do what you can." His heart sank. This is not what he wanted and he told the parish council when he got there—three elderly women—that he really wanted to work with young children and families. He told them, "I really prayed to God whether I should come here. How can I have a fruitful ministry here? But I'll give it a try."

A few months later, he happened to be visiting the hospital and stopped in to visit a mother with her newborn son. She talked to him of the experience of childbirth. "But worst of all," said the young mother, "is that we had this baby all by ourselves." "What do you mean?" he asked. "Oh," she said, "our parents are way across the other side of the country and since this is our first baby, it's a little scary for us. We have no one to ask what to do next. We have no grandparents. Most of the people in our neighborhood are young couples like ourselves. I wish this baby had some grandparents."

And suddenly, as you can guess, a light came on. "Grandparents!" he thought, "My God, the parish is full of grandparents! The whole tiny congregation is grandparents." So he talked the congregation into visiting the home of a couple whose baby was born into the neighborhood. Well, the baby visitors, as it soon turned out, were great in evangelizing. The young couples were looking for somebody to be excited about the birth of their children. The church had a surplus of grandparents and the two got together—and the church was reborn. Where once there was solitude, there was now community.☐

So, there are my three stories. What do these stories have in common? What these three stories have in common is their testimony to every human being's greatest drive, greatest urge, and greatest need: and that is union, togetherness, even if it is with a frog. To put it simply, to be whole, people need union. To be whole, people need relationships. To be whole, people need to have someone in their lives. That is self-evident. Think for a moment. Think of the most satisfying moments of your life. Now think deeply. Such moments, I guarantee you, were when you sat . on your mother's lap, when you were held, when you were hugged, when you were embraced, when you were loved, when you were affirmed, when you were simply in the silent presence of someone who loved you, when you had someone in your life.

By the same token, think of the worst moments of your life: when you were rejected, when you were divorced, when you peered out the window watching couples hand in hand going out while you sat alone, when you were cut off from family and friends, when you ached for a hug and it was not forthcoming, when you were scared and wanted someone to hold you and no one was there for you, when you were betrayed by a friend, when you felt isolated. We don't even like to go to the movies or out to dinner by ourselves, do we? Why is solitary confinement such a horrible form of punishment?

You see what I'm saying? You see what the bottom line is? It's that we human beings are in desperate need of union—even promiscuous sex at bottom is such a misguided search—in such a need for togetherness, for communion, that our whole life is one large search for love. Our hearts are made for one another and for God. Rejection is such an intolerable hurt because we need desperately to be connected. But my question is why? Why this existential, driving need for union? Why do the young flock to malls and singles bars? Why those best moments when union occurs and the worst when it is absent? Why?

The answer, simply and profoundly, is in today's feast. We are made in the image and likeness of God and *God is communion*. That's it. God's image is writ large into our very natures, imprinted on our neurons, coded on our brain cells, and burned into our hearts. The feast of the Holy Trinity says that God is communion, is relationship, and *therefore*, so are we. God's own inner self is to "be with," to be in connection, to be family: Father, Son, and Holy Spirit. What makes God God is intimate relationship and no wonder we can't help it if we have to be the same way. We have no choice. That's why the apostle says that God is Love and that we are most God-like when we are in love, give love, and receive love.

Every striving of our souls for union, every reach out for companionship, every urge for a hug and an embrace, every act of love gives indirect testimony to the Trinity. The Trinity says that God is community and so we seek. The Trinity says that God is relationship and so we search. The Trinity says that God is love and so we love. We can't help ourselves. We're made to that image and likeness. We mirror our origins. We are who we are because God is who God is.

So this is what we're celebrating today. In very simple terms, this profound feast tells us why we are what we are, why we are who we are, how we are who we are, and makes ever more real those famous words of St. Augustine, who knew a thing or two about love, "You have made us for yourself, O God, and our hearts are restless till they rest in you." Indeed, the Trinity is a mystery all right, but it's a mystery about us too, a mystery of love and our quest for it, a mystery of the Triune community we shall both recognize and enjoy in heaven.

37. FUNNY, YOU DON'T LOOK LIKE A PROPHET

(Lk 1:1–4; 4:4–21 3rd Sunday in O.T. Year C)

☐There's an old cartoon showing a damsel tied to a stake and a balding, stout, middle-aged Superman is flying through the air to rescue her. She is saying, "Actually, I expected a much younger man."☐

We have here, to put it mildly, a question of image. Images, as we know, are important. Politicians and pundits, movie stars, and media moguls spend millions of dollars to improve their public image. A whole multimillion-dollar industry exists precisely to work on a culturally honed and acceptable image. Whether there is any substance behind the image is irrelevant. It's what you see that counts.

In today's gospel, what the people saw wasn't much. A local boy returned, so-so parents, a mere carpenter's son. He was not acceptable. He didn't project "image." As a result, he was not only rejected, but made a target for murder. This Messiah, heralded by John the Baptist, called by his Father "Beloved Son," anointed by the Spirit—he was a disappointment. He didn't look like a Messiah.

And that scenario gets repeated in our lives, but with a different twist. Let me explain. At our baptism, we, like Jesus, have been heralded by our parents, called by the Father "Beloved Son" or "Beloved Daughter," and anointed by the Spirit. We have been chosen, inaugurated into the Kingdom, and made disciples of the Lord. We have been elected to be saints, witnesses, and prophets. In short, we have been made Messiah. And, don't we have the same problem that plagued Jesus, the problem of image, but, as I hinted, in a different form? It's not that others say, "Funny, you don't look like a prophet." The difference is that *we* say that to *ourselves*. True enough, we admit, we have been called in baptism. We do pray; perhaps we have even had some kind of mystical experience (they're more common that we think). We have felt

God's presence. To this extent we would and should openly witness to the love of God in our daily lives, but, and here's the hitch, we're not the type. We're not into heroism or going around asking, "Have you been saved?" or wearing our faith on our sleeves. We don't look prophetic, and really don't want to.

With that self-conviction, we fall into what I call "reverse hypocrisy." That is, we put forth to the public a different image of ourselves, a poorer image, a lesser image, a conforming image. We appear *worse* than we are. We speak surface, culturally accepted things, and not the deeper things of faith that occupy our hearts. We brag of sins we wouldn't think of committing. We speak a language that belies our sensitivity. In short, there's a cultural image out there of what a regular guy or regular gal should look, dress, and sound like and, under social and peer pressure, we put on that image. And, to that extent, we bury our gift.

And we justify this spiritual downsizing on the pretext that, after all, we don't look prophetic. We don't look saintly or commanding or charismatic like Charlton Heston as Moses or Jennifer Jones as Bernadette. We're not the type. Like Uriah Heep, we're too "humble" to even think of being public saints. Of course, the wonderful payoff is that if we are not the type to be open disciples of Jesus, we are relieved. It gets us off the hook. Let the others, made of sterner stuff, do the public witnessing thing. Let the others who have the properly noble saintly image speak up and speak out. By appearing worse than I am, I don't have to be better than I am. And there it is.

So, the bottom line is that once I convince myself that I have an image problem, I can settle for being a "basically good person," which means that I can be a minimal, bland, closet disciple of Jesus Christ. But the gospel would challenge that. It would challenge that on the very basis of image. What *does* a prophet, a saint, a disciple, look like? The people in today's gospel thought that whatever it took, Jesus didn't have the look. And they were wrong. Tragically wrong. Two women from neighboring countries in Europe, one with an image, the other not: glamorous Zsa Zsa Gabor and wrinkled Mother Teresa. Who's the disciple? Immanuel Kant was a short, dried-up creature. Beethoven was deaf and wild. Novelist Flannery O'Connor was homely and crippled. Mohandas Gandhi was a small, skinny man. Rachel Carson was a nondescript woman quietly working at her nondescript job in the Fish and Wildlife Department of the Interior when she wrote her book in 1951 alerting us to the whole subject of ecology. St. Bernadette could neither read nor write. Pope John XXIII was a fat old man. Funny, they didn't look like they could or would make a difference. Funny, too, that none of these people took their lack of image as an excuse to put themselves down and reject their gift, their status as disciples.

But we? We spend an awful amount of time cultivating a poor spiritual image in spite of the rich goodness that's there within us, usually in proportion to the time we spend in cultivating a culturally acceptable image of the right clothes, the right car, the right neighborhood, the right look, the right celebrity copycat. And so we suppress the deep, moving, powerful image of the Christ within us, the sensitive thoughts, the shared prayer, the invitations of grace, the religious questions, the real depth we have and are afraid to reveal. I have always been amazed in talking one on one to adolescents to hear them sooner or later admit to a cutting-edge prayer life, noble aspirations, and generous desires. But they must hide these from the public. In adults, it is less understandable and more tragic. Too many secular images sooner or later suppress the image of God within us.

☐Former Congressman Tip O'Neill tells a story of a man named "Honest Jake." Honest Jake became well known in the Boston area because of his assistance to three generations of immigrant families. He owned a little variety store and would extend credit to the poor immigrants to help them get started in their new land. As Honest Jake neared his sixtieth birthday, a group of people he had helped decided to give him a party and a generous gift of money. Jake received the money gratefully and began to use it for his own makeover. He had his teeth capped. He bought a hairpiece. He invested in a diet and exercise program and lost a lot of weight. He purchased a whole new wardrobe. Then he boarded a plane and a few hours later the new Honest Jake hit the beach at Miami. He met a beautiful young woman, asked her for a date, and she accepted. But before they could go out on the date, a thunderstorm came up, and Honest Jake was struck by a lightning bolt and died instantly. In heaven, he said to God, "After all those years of hard work, I was just trying to enjoy myself a little. Why? Why me?" And God said to him, "Oh, is that you, Jake? I'm sorry, I didn't recognize you."☐

We smile, but what a chilling story when taken seriously. Is that us? We figuratively cap our teeth, put on our hairpiece, don the acceptable clothes, and overall change our spiritual image to conform to what the world expects, and sooner or later we don't recognize ourselves any longer as God's child. And, sadly, neither does God.

I guess the lesson for today is the question, "What does a prophet, a baptized disciple of Jesus, look like?" The gospel today is telling us one simple truth: a prophet looks like you and me.

38. THE LOOK

(Lk 22:14—23:1-49 Passion Sunday Years A, B, C)

☐Two men are facing each other. One is only ten hours away from death. The other has just told a group gathered around a fire that he did not know the Man who was going to his death. "No, no," he protested, "I do not know him. I have never been with him. I swear I haven't." And just then a cock crowed to greet the dawn. The Prisoner, apparently being led from one room of the palace to another, passed through the yard where the fire and the denial still burned. He looked at the man who stood there. Just a look. Suddenly, the gate slammed shut and out into the cold dawn fled the man who had been so loud and so brave a moment earlier. He ran away into the silent streets to hide himself in a corner of the great city. And, as he ran, tears flowed down his face. They were hot and bitter, washing away something that was like dirt on his face and blood on his soul.☐

This scene frames a profound question: just what is this religion we call Christianity that has fascinated the world for the past 2000 years and still, battered and torn today, commands the allegiance of so many today? Some over the course of history have said that it is essentially a vast system of doctrine to be whole-heartedly believed. If you know the doctrines and believe them, you are a Christian. Others have said, no, Christianity is a way of life, like a philosophy. It's living in a Christian culture. Both these definitions are incomplete. The scene of two men in silent confrontation in the palace courtyard tells us the real meaning of Christianity. It is, when you come right down to it, a living relationship with a living Person. It is always and forever the relationship of redeemed human beings with the person of Jesus Christ in faith, trust, forgiveness, and love—in all the ways that one person is bound to another.

In this context we can understand what happened in the court-yard. As Peter was standing by the fire, lying for the sake of safe-ty and human respect, swearing falsely in order to capture a moment of warmth and acceptance from the world, he had broken his relationship with his Lord. He saw that he had thrown it away. He had turned against his Friend. And when that Friend turned and looked at Peter, he suddenly realized what he had done. He saw what he had just thrown away, what he had forgotten, what he had denied, what he had betrayed. He had not denied a doctrine. He had not embarrassed his culture. He had hurt a relationship. There was nothing left to do but to stumble out into the dark, blinded by burning tears, afraid and alone, never, never to forget his moment of shame. Yet he was destined to hear a few weeks later the voice of that Friend again, compelling, warm, and healing, saying to him by the lake, "Simon, Son of John, do you love me?"

What are we to do with this whole incident but apply it to ourselves? We haven't denied any doctrine or offended any philosophy or embarrassed the culture, but we have broken that bond of personal friendship between Jesus and ourselves. We, too, have stood by the fire, so eager for the world's approval, and bought it at the price of denying that we even know our Friend, Jesus the Christ, our Brother, our Savior. Denials such as Peter's, such as our own, always have four parts.

First, it always begins with a bad situation. Peter should never have been standing there by the fire to begin with. It was a fire harboring unsympathetic people, a fire surrounded by the "beautiful people," the pace-setters, the in-group, the sophisticates and their hangers-on. Only an unusual person could have held his own in the face of such collective and engaging paganism. Peter could not. Neither can we. And putting ourselves in a bad situation—the wrong company, the callous and destructive drinking buddies, the porno movie house, the religious mockers, the greedy social climbers—is the first step to denial.

Second, there comes a moment of forgetfulness. We want so bad to be accepted, so much to be a part of the crowd that we forget our own weaknesses. Sometimes we even assist ourselves in forgetting by popping pills or drinking to let down our defenses. It is common knowledge that drugs and alcohol are behind most crimes.

Third, the break always comes. We finally say something, or, more likely, *do* something that by its very nature is a betrayal of our Lord. We take that pill. We take that drink. We steal that cash. We repeat that joke. Or, worse, we *fail* to say something, to do something, and so our silence gives consent and evil rolls on, unopposed by us.

But then, there is the fourth and final step. Always and at all times, without fail, there is the Look. There is the look of Jesus Christ. It may take a long time in coming and it may take a long, long time in being recognized, but Jesus is standing there gazing, gazing, gazing—with eyes warning, pleading, longing, loving. Sometimes he looks at us in our silent moments when we passingly wonder what we are doing with our lives, what we are becoming. Sometimes he looks at us in past remembered innocence, seeing our child baptized or making her First Communion, which we have neglected for too long. Sometimes he looks at us in our brokenness: our shattered marriage, our failing health, our financial setback. Sometimes he looks at us through the closed eyes of death, in our experience of the death of someone we know and love. Sometimes he looks at us in the face of a friend, the example of a neighbor, a word from the Bible. In some precious and sudden way, one time or another, Jesus looks at us all—in the midst of our busyness, our activity, our money-making, our careers, our traveling—and in that look he is telling us that we are playing with fire, that we are dragging the sorrows of the ages across his soul once more, that we are hurting him, the best Friend we have.

And if we heed that look and if that look leads us to open our eyes, to shed tears of regret, shame, and repentance, then we are on our way to a new dawn and have a soulful answer to his question, "Mary, John, do you love me?" And when in tearful sorrow, like Peter and Magdalene and Paul and Augustine and all the rest, we nod yes, he is once more there, no longer as betrayed Friend, but as close Friend, Lord, and Liberator. For the look of Christ, as Peter found out, is one of understanding love. It is this look, never forgotten, that led Peter to wander around the Mediterranean Sea preaching about Jesus. It is this look that led

Peter to Rome where in the year 64, 30 years after this night, a fire broke out in Rome. But around *this* fire: Peter did not deny Jesus but proclaimed him and so died crucified upside down in a Roman arena, true this time to his Friend. And if, as they say, the dying see their lives pass before them, then I am sure that Peter recalled that night: his betrayal, his tears, and most of all, the look of his Friend. It was the power of that look that brought him to this ridiculous position with the world upside down and tears in his eyes once again. But this time these were tears of joy and expectation. Jesus his Friend would come, would be there, now and forever, with his forgiving look and soon, very soon now, there would be no more tears, no more betrayals, no more night.

There would be only Jesus, the Friend who once looked at him.

39. LOVE AMONG THE RUINS
(Mt 13:24–30 16th Sunday in O.T. Year A)

Our gospel confronts us with the age-old mystery: so much evil in the world! So much hurt, and racism, and abuse, and slaughter. So many wicked weeds, so to speak, among the society's wheat. Our television sets and newspapers never let us be unaware of the latest crime, the latest shooting, the latest celebrity divorce. A cartoon at Christmas time catches it well. There's a Santa Claus waiting to receive the children on his lap with his eyes glancing toward the line of waiting little ones who must pass through a metal detector! That says it all. But today, we want to pull back from all that and concentrate rather on the wheat, on the unheralded goodness that is insistent, quiet, and making all the difference in the world. Today we want to share "wheat" stories because we need to hear them lest we become discouraged.

❑Our first story concerns a letter a pastor received. It was marked, "Please give to Harry the Usher." It was handed over to Harry and this is what it said: "Dear Harry. I'm sorry I don't know your last name, but then you don't know mine. I'm Gert, Gert at the 10 o'clock Mass every Sunday. I'm writing to ask a favor. I don't know the priests too well, but somehow I feel close to you. I don't know how you got to know my first name, but every Sunday morning you smile and greet me by name and we exchange a few words: how bad the weather was, how much you liked my hat, and how I was late on a particular Sunday. I just wanted to say thank you for taking the time for remembering an old woman, for the smiles, for your consideration, for your thoughtfulness. Now for the favor. I am dying, Harry. My husband has been dead for 16 years and the kids are scattered. It is very important to me that when they bring me to church for the last time you will be there to say, 'Hello, Gert. Good to see you.' If you are there, Harry, I will feel assured that your warm hospitality will be duplicated in my new home in heaven. With love and gratitude. Gert."❑

I don't know how many Manny, Moe, and Jacks are out there

doing evil, but I do know the world is peopled with Harrys.

☐Our next story comes from Charles Kuralt who, you may know, has been roaming the back roads of our country for over 25 years, telling us extraordinary stories about ordinary people from places like Gnaw Bone, Indiana, and Lizard Lick, North Carolina. About what he has discovered, he writes, "I keep reading that . . . America has turned inward, that its people have become . . . selfish, but I see mighty little evidence of it. I have found a lot to be confident and reassured about: more decency and compassion and public spirit, less greed and arrogance and hostility. . . .Even in a complex, technological society, it turns out, it is one man or one woman with an idea who touches the national conscience—a Rachel Carson or . . . a woman who says no, she believes she will not move to the back of the bus today as the law requires, because she is tired from her work and tired of that law—and soon, not without pain, everything changes. These ideas don't originate in Washington. They spring from the land, which is the way it was supposed to work in the first place."☐

There's a lot of goodness in Lizard Lick, North Carolina, and throughout the land.

☐My next story concerns two people from Holland, Meip and Henrick Gies. You may remember their names as the ones who every day went up secret stairs with food and news for Otto Frank and his family who were in hiding from the Nazis. It was she who baked the holiday cake and brought Anne Frank her first and only pair of high heels. It was she, in the end, who rescued Anne's one-day-to-be-famous diary. She insists that she and her friends were just "ordinary" Dutch people. Concerning the occupation, Mrs. Gies wrote, there were "just two kinds of Dutch people: those who collaborated and those who resisted."☐

There's a lot of resisters among the collaborators in evil.

☐My fourth story concerns a doctor I know. On the back of his hallway door hangs a tattered, out-of-style coat with one sleeve patched and pockets frayed. On certain days, like Thanksgiving and Christmas, or when, as he says, he begins to feel proud or well off, he wears it with reverence. I asked him about it and he told me its history. Many years ago, he said, he was a young intern serving the poor in a crowded city. One night in midwinter he was awakened by the frantic cries of a child at his door, calling for him to come to an apartment down the street. He trudged through the snow and biting wind to a dingy building, then followed the small girl up a grimy set of stairs to a dimly lit room. He rushed inside to find a distraught father and mother bent over a limp figure on an old iron bed. Frantically he worked to save the life of their son, but the best of his skill was not good enough. As the boy died, the doctor suddenly began to shiver in the poorly heated tenement house. The grief-stricken father took off his coat and gently wrapped it around the young doctor's shoulders. "You need this more than I do. You keep it. Thank you for trying to save our boy." The doctor knew that this was the only coat the poor man owned. It had braved many winters at the little open-air vegetable stand on the corner. But he would not have dared to refuse it tonight, for it was given to him as a sacrament of love and gratitude.☐

There's a lot of such coats out there.

☐Finally, a scene from the musical *Man of La Mancha*, the story of the ridiculed Don Quixote who lives with the illusion of being a knight of old, battling windmills that he imagines are dragons. Near the end of the musical, Don Quixote is dying and at his side is Aldonza, a worthless slut he had idealized by calling her Dulcinea—Sweet One—much to the howling laughter of the townsfolk. But Don Quixote had loved her in a way unlike anything she had ever experienced. When Quixote breathes his last, Aldonza begins to sing "The Impossible Dream." As the last echo of the song dies away, someone shouts to her, "Aldonza!" But she pulls herself up proud and responds, "My name is Dulcinea." The crazy knight's love had transformed her.☐

And there's a lot of crazy knights out there.

So, our reflection for today. The weeds and the wheat parable is also a parable of the human condition and so often the weeds seem to be taking over and choking out all decency and civility. But, as we heard, the Lord lets them grow together. There *will* be a separation some day, but our message is that we shouldn't be surprised to see how much bigger the wheat stack is.

40. HOLY THURSDAY
(Jn 13:1–15 Years A,B,C)

"Jesus, knowing that the Father had given all things into his hands. . . got up from supper." So begins John's gospel for tonight. "All things into his hands"—from galaxies to grains of sand—and yet, he emptied those hands of such glories to take into them our feet. Why? That he might wash them. Why? "Afterwards you will understand," he said.

Gradually, the Christian community did understand. It understood when it reflected whose feet they were and on the fact that Jesus resolutely did not look up. He did not look up because he didn't want to know whose feet they were, for his love was indiscriminate. He would not play favorites. He would wash all of them. But he knew, he knew that among those feet there were:

Fishermen. He could tell. Their feet were rough, buffeted by nature and salt water. The feet of workers, the poor, the tired, the oppressed. Just like, he remembered, his father's feet when he was a little boy. Peter, James, and John had feet like those. He knew he was washing honest feet. Perhaps he tried to guess which of the three owned them. One pair of feet gave him pause, however. They seemed, somehow, indecisive, not quite on the ground like the others. The kind that might give in to pressure. The kind whose owner would mouth a denial? No, maybe not. Still . . . He paused a moment and then went on to another.

A Zealot. He knew he must be at the feet of the zealot, Jude. The feet were not still. They were tapping on the floor. Nervous feet. Eager feet. Eager for reform, overthrow. Perhaps a little terrorism thrown in. He washed them, hoping to reveal the man underneath the temper.

A Doubter. Who is this one? The feet were pulled back, not out front like the others. Someone hedging his bet? Someone not sure of what? Jesus? The mission? The Kingdom?

A Tax Collector. Refined feet, used to sandals, not burned like the others. Obviously spent a lot of time under the table where taxes are collected. And therefore an undesirable. A Quisling. An exploiter of his own people. A toady for the enemy. These feet need washing.

A Simple Soul. Soft feet. Innocent. Without guile. Must be Nathaniel's. Will he be equal to the task ahead?

A Traitor? Is it possible? One foot firmly planted in defiance, the other leading out ahead like it's ready to bolt. Are these feet going somewhere tonight? Who is this? He washed these feet with extra tenderness.

"Do you understand what I have done?" he asked when he was finally finished and straightened up. Not really. They did not understand at the time. As I said, it took time for the message to sink in. It took time to appreciate the love that was freely and equally given to sinner and saint, that the Master would repeat this washing, this loving, time and time again till time ran out.

For there would be a modern-day Peter, one with power in the church, with denial in his heart of what was around him. But one day Jesus washed his feet and Archbishop Oscar Romero died in the cause of the poor.

There was a Zealot, too. A woman of communist leanings and bohemian ways with her live-in boyfriend and illegitimate child. But Jesus washed her feet and made this woman, Dorothy Day, hot for justice.

The Doubter was reluctant. Saucy and intellectual, too bright to believe, a gadfly of the books and colleges. But Jesus washed those feet with great love and Thomas Merton surrendered to it.

The Tax Collector walked the corridors of power. He sat at the right hand of Presidential Power. And he bled his own people. But Jesus slowly uncovered his feet and washed them, and Charles Colson found himself a willing prisoner of the Lord.

This Traitor didn't get away. Oh, he denied everything with his sharp wit and sophisticated pen. He mocked religion and laughed at the church. That is, till his feet were washed and Malcolm Muggeridge found himself a new man and an apostle for Christ.

That's what time has taught. What happened on that Holy Thursday night was a summary of Jesus' whole mission. He would love without condition and wash the feet of all, Peter's and Nathaniel's, Dorothy's and Thomas's, yours and mine, without looking up; that is, without regard to position or prestige or power; without regard to shame or sorrow or sin. All would be embraced, cleansed.

In case the message was still not clear, Jesus went on to make one final statement of his desire to cleanse us of our sins and remain among us as a servant. He took what was meant by the washing of the feet and found a way to remind us of it. For after he returned to the circle of apostles, he took bread and broke it, declaring it was his body "given for you." And then he took the cup and blessed it, declaring that it was his blood "shed for you." Different act, same message: Jesus serves. Jesus washes, Jesus forgives, and Jesus remains among us through the ages ready to wash feet. The washing of the feet explains the Eucharist. The Eucharist explains the washing of the feet.

This is a holy night, awesome—full of awe. It bridges Passion Sunday and Easter Sunday and throws a light on them both. It offers us a challenge about the entire meaning of Holy Week. Jesus asked then and Jesus asks now, "Do you understand what I have done?" Do you? The answer to that brings us into the mystery.

41. CHRISTIAN ADVERTISING
(Mk 8:27–35 24th Sunday in O.T. Year B)

☐Nine young soldiers had received overnight passes from their base camp. When morning came, not one of the nine was present. An hour after their absence was noted, the first soldier straggled back into camp. He was immediately taken before his company commander. "I'm sorry to be late, sir," the soldier said, "but I had a date, lost track of time, and missed the last bus. I wanted to make it back on time so I took a taxi. About half way back to camp, the cab broke down so I went to the nearest farm and bought a horse. As I was riding on the horse, the animal suddenly fell to the ground and died. So I did the last miles on foot and here I am." Although he was skeptical about the chain of weird excuses, the company commander let the young man off with a mild lecture on the virtues of punctuality. Thereafter seven more stragglers reported in, one by one, each with the same story! They had a date, lost track of the time, missed the last bus, took a cab, cab broke down, bought a horse, horse fell dead. Finally, the ninth and last soldier arrived. Now totally exasperated, the commanding officer growled, "What happened to you?" The ninth man replied, "Sir, I had a date, lost track of the time, missed the last bus, hired a taxi . . ." "Wait a minute! Wait a minute!" cried the officer." Are you going to tell me that the cab broke down?" "No, sir," the soldier replied. "The taxi was fine. The problem was we couldn't get through. There were so many dead horses on the road."☐

And *that's* our theme for today: we have a message, a Christian message, words of wisdom, a great tradition—but nothing gets through. Nothing gets through because the Good News comes out bad news. Think, for example, of the commercials you see all day long. Look at the people in them: neat, well-dressed, smiling, happy with their product, smelling great, hair gleaming, underarms sterilized, bodies firm, homes comfortable, and lives stress-free. Thanks to the product touted, there is no blemish untouched, no breath unscented, no fingernail unpolished. Laughter, joy, and the good life abound in commercial land.

And then here comes Christianity. We all know what its Founder said. It's all there in the gospel. Jesus says, "The one who saves his life will lose it." Again: "They will manhandle you and persecute you. . . .You will be delivered up even by your parents, brothers, relatives and friends, and some of you will be put to death." Again: "Unless you take up your cross and follow me, you are not worthy of the kingdom." And about Paul: "I will show him how much he must suffer for the Gospel's sake." So, it comes down to this. Christianity is perceived as saying, "We offer you pain, suffering, rejection, sorrow, imprisonment, and death. Our heroes are Peter on the cross, John in boiling oil, Lawrence on the grill, Linus on the rack, and John of the Cross in the looney bin. We guarantee that you will get tortured, garroted, quartered, and killed. Won't you join us?"

I ask you, when people say, for example, that such and such a priest is so holy, what do they mean? They usually mean that he looks emaciated, irritated, and constipated. His eyes are rolled upward and he is thin, wan, and frail because he is "spiritual," that is, he's far from earthy, fleshy things and near to expiration, the realm of the pure soul. And if that weren't enough, often as not Christian art offers us models of saints who look undernourished, piqued, and tubercular. Again, would you join such a club, one whose chief product is the cross? Not when you have Club Med staring you in the face.

There's something wrong, and that something is the way we read the cross. "Unless you take up your cross daily and follow me, you are not worthy of me." The cross here means commitment. And *that* we can understand because that's the way we live. If, for example, you want to star in the Olympics, you must take up your cross daily, every day. There's no doubt about that. And you suffer. You forgo entertainments, certain foods, leisure time, and commit yourself to an unrelenting routine of practice and self-discipline. If you want to be a doctor or lawyer or whatever, there are the crosses of commitment to bear: long hours of study and practice and internship and so on. If you want your marriage to be successful, you take up your cross daily: patience, forgiveness, attentiveness.

And if you want to be a disciple of Jesus you take up your cross, the price of your commitment: fidelity in a world of institutionalized infidelity, ethics over job advancement, compassion over greed, forgiveness over revenge. There is a "cost" to such commitments; hence, the cross. But there is, of course, the by-product, too often neglected in our advertising: joy. The joy of receiving the gold medal, the joy of the degree behind your name, the joy of a loving partner, the joy of achievement, the joy of being a whole person, the joy of integrity, the joy even of hardship. How many couples, looking back over the first years of their marriage when they had nothing but each other, exclaim wistfully, "Those were tough years, but we were happy." You see, testimony to the "cross," to the pain that commitment always brings, but also to the joy that it brings.

Not the least of which is the love of God. The saints were happy in it. Mary, who knew hard times, spoke of it: "My soul magnifies the Lord and my spirit rejoices in God my Savior." Paul and Barnabas actually sang in prison. Francis chanted his canticle to Brother Sun and Sister Moon. Thomas Aquinas—all 300 pounds of him—wrote hymns of exquisite joy. Saints knew happiness even when disdained for their commitment to beauty and truth. They knew laughter in dispute, contentment in adversity, and inner peace in distress. St. Teresa of Avila told jokes on her detractors, John Bosco danced with the children, and G.K. Chesterton wrote witty verses and clever stories.

The point is that Jesus is saying nothing more than what human nature knows: no gain without pain, no crown without the cross, no humanity without commitment—and commitment always brings the cross as it always brings joy. Which is why Jesus also said, "So you have pain now, but I will see you again and your hearts will rejoice, and no one will take your joy from you."

Christianity has suffered from poor advertising. The cross has been downsized to mean depressing hardship for its own sake.

Joy has not been placed in the forefront where it should be. But we Christians should reverse that. It's not, "Come and join us and die." It's "Come and join us and live!" for Jesus has come to give life and give it abundantly.

42. ST. JOHN LATERAN:
MOTHER CHURCH
(November 9)

Today's feast, November 9, which this year has displaced the usual Sunday, may seem strange to us with its strange name: Dedication of St. John Lateran. Who was he? What could St. Mary's in Colts Neck, U.S.A., have to do with an almost 2000-year old church in Rome? The answer is: a great deal.

First, some background. You will recall that for the first three hundred years Christianity was illegal. It was an off-again, on-again persecuted religion with penalties of torture and death. In fact, the Roman Empire unleashed some ten persecutions against it catching not only Peter and Paul but all those names we will mention in the first canon. The Christians, during this time, had to go underground. They had no temples, no churches, no public places of gathering and worship. They met secretly in homes, barns, cemeteries. But in the year 313 the Roman emperor, Constantine, became a Christian, even though a heretical one. He granted religious tolerance to Christianity and eventually his successor granted it freedom.

Once Christianity was politically free to worship openly and publicly, it needed to build its own churches, especially when it became the national religion. Now there was a palace in Rome, formerly owned by the Laterani family which was now used by Constantine and his mother, St. Helena. He turned a wing of that palace over to the church, making it the first public church in Rome that was Christian. More precisely, he gave it to the bishop of Rome, Pope Melchiades, along with an adjacent basilica There the pope presided and resided as did all the popes after him—except for a 40-year hiatus when the popes were in Avignon, France—until 1871 when Pope Pius IX, during the Italian Revolution, fled to the Vatican Hill where the popes have lived ever since. Most of the popes have been crowned at St. John Lateran's. To this day, restored many times over the centuries, it remains the pope's official church in his capacity as bishop of Rome and to this day the Holy Thursday ceremonies are held there. It is called St. John Lateran's basilica in honor of St. John the Baptist and the original Laterani family name. It has inscribed over its door the words, "The mother church of Rome and of all the churches in the world."

We celebrate this feast of St. John Lateran, then, because it is the first Christian church, the mother church. But that is only the surface reason. We celebrate this feast because it reminds us of our origins. Rome was evangelized by Peter and Paul and countless missionaries. In turn, Rome, being the world center at the time, the heart of the Roman Empire, sent missionaries out to the west. Most of us are European in origin, although that is fading, and so the faith comes to us by way of Rome. Not directly from Jerusalem where the faith started, nor from Antioch in Syria which sent missionaries to the east, to the Balkans, and to Turkey, but from Rome and we celebrate that fact. We have been evangelized from Rome, the mother church.

"To be in union with Rome," as the saying goes, does not necessarily mean to take commands from Rome or have the same system of government as Rome or use the same liturgy, style, dress, and customs—although we surely are influenced in these matters and perhaps too narrowly so—but it does mean to be in union with our origins, with that faith proclaimed by Rome's imports from the mid-east, Peter and Paul. Rome is where Peter eventually lived and died and passed on the faith. The Lateran Palace or St. John Lateran's is the place where Peter's successors have lived and died and passed on the faith. It's our Christian equivalent of the Governor's Palace in Williamsburg or Independence Hall in Philadelphia. It's an historical sign and symbol of our deep rootedness, our connection with the past, our touchstone of faith with the long line of popes who have presided there.

St. John Lateran basilica, therefore, reminds us of our catholicity, our relationship with the center and from the center to the rest of Christianity. It reminds us here in our little parish in Colts Neck, New Jersey, that, through our connection with that mother church, we belong to a vast brotherhood and sisterhood both vertically to the past and horizontally to the present. And in these days of almost pathological individualism, of atomistic existence, this is no small thing indeed. We're part of a wide community. We are Catholic with both a small and big "C." St. John Lateran tells us that.

There's another reason why the Catholic world celebrates a church building in another part of the world. We are reminded that the building of temples and churches is a natural, poetic instinct we humans have. We need symbols and rituals in order to live and would sooner do without food and water. The poor of France know the Eiffel Tower could be melted down and the money given to them, but they would resist, knowing they do not live by bread alone. The Dome of the Rock for the Arabs, the Wailing Wall for the Jews, Westminster Abbey for the Anglicans, Sancta Sophia for the Turks, are all more than buildings. They enshrine national history and aspirations and house celebrations and rituals. They give identity and cohesion. Which is why tyrants' and invaders' first act is to destroy a people's shrines and literature. Without them, the people are nothing.

At times, people have lost their moorings and declared that all buildings are human vanity. The Puritans wrought terrible havoc by destroying many masterpieces, smashing stained-glass windows, and burning priceless works of art. They forgot that churches and cathedrals were not the products of human vanity, although at times they were, but truly the expression of human faith. Men, women, boys and girls, people from all walks of life, the whole town, for example, helped build Chartres Cathedral, stone by stone, love by love. This feast reminds us that our church, however grand or humble, is a sign of transcendence, a gathering for us to worship and say out loud what we are pressured to deny openly: Jesus Christ is Lord!

A final reason we celebrate this feast of our mother church, St. John Lateran, is that it reminds us that we ourselves are unfinished temples. We indeed have a great history of grandeur. Over the centuries the church has been responsible for more good and decency and help than will ever be realized. The constant media focus on our failings should not blind us to the enormous good we have done throughout the ages, and still do. Realize that Catholic Relief Services is the largest private relief service in the world. Think of all the Mother Teresas there are, the countless Catholic hospitals, schools and clinics, leprosaria. Perhaps the biggest assistance to AIDS patients is the Catholic church, although you would never know it. We have taught people to read and write and sing. We have healed, consoled, buried, and converted. We're in every part of the globe ministering to others, day and night, endlessly. We have done Christ's work.

But, of course, we are, as I said, unfinished. Just as St. John Lateran had to be restored many times throughout the centuries because of the ravages of time and vandals, so has the whole church. We have sinned and we have constant reforms and renewals to call us back to our origins. This is the reason we celebrate this feast. It recalls struggles, countless martyrs, sacrifice, Peter and Paul, missionaries, and it challenges us to see how far we have strayed from the message they left us at so great a price. To that extent, this feast beckons us to reform.

St. John Lateran. It's a shame many people, many Catholics do not know it and are perplexed as to why it's a weekend feast day and why we take the time to celebrate it. But now *you* know and in the knowing you should have pride and resolve: pride in our ancient heritage that keeps us grounded to the truth and resolve that our spiritual ancestors will not, as one of our Presidents said, have died in vain.

APPENDIX

Here you will find references to over 130 story-homilies scattered throughout my previous homily books as well as this one (all published by Twenty-Third Publications).

For your convenience, I have listed each homily according to liturgical season and Lectionary reading, and have noted the book and the page where it may be found. The code is as follows:

Timely Homilies	TH
Telling Stories, Compelling Stories	TSCS
More Telling Stories, Compelling Stories	MTS
Storytelling the Word	STW

ADVENT

1st Sunday	Year B	Mk 13:33–37	TSCS, 132
1st Sunday	Year C	Lk 21:25–28, 34–36	STW, 243
2nd Sunday	Year A	Mt 3:1–12	TSCS, 32 and STW, 238
2nd Sunday	Year C	Lk 3:1–6	MTS, 110
3rd Sunday	Year A	Mt 11:2–11	TW, 170
3rd Sunday	Year B	Jn 1:6–8, 19–28	STW, 196
3rd Sunday	Year C	Lk 3:10–18,	MTS, 120 and TH, 74
3rd Sunday	Year C	Phil 4:4–7	MTS, 32
4th Sunday	Year B	Lk 1:26–38	TH, 41
4th Sunday	Year C	Lk 1:39–45	STW, 143 and MTS, 110

CHRISTMAS

Christmas	Years A,B,C	Lk 2:15–20	TSCS, 5, 55
Christmas	Years A,B,C	Lk 2:1–14	STW, 203, 206 and MTS, 130
Holy Family	Year A	Sir 3:2–6, 12–14	MTS, 148
Holy Family	Year A	Mt 2:13–15,19–23	STW, 179
New Year's Day			STW, 212
Epiphany	Years A,B,C	Mt 2:1–12	TSCS, 59, MTS, 66 and STW, 137
Baptism of the Lord	Year A	Mt 3:13–17	TSCS, 69
Baptism of the Lord	Year B	Mk 1:7–11	MTS, 55

LENT

1st Sunday	Year B	Mk 1:12–15	MTS, 21
1st Sunday	Year C	Lk 4:1–13	STW, 166
2nd Sunday	Year C	Lk 9:28–36	STW, 233 and TH, 24
3rd Sunday	Year C	Lk 13:1–9	TSCS, 41
4th Sunday	Year B	Jn 3:14–21	MTS, 38
4th Sunday	Year C	Lk 15:1–3,11–32	STW, 154 and TSCS, 16
5th Sunday	Year A	Jn 11:1–45	TSCS, 127, 155
5th Sunday	Year B	Jn 12:20–33	MTS, 94
Passion Sunday	Years C	Lk 22:14—23:1–49	STW, 261
Holy Thursday	Years A,B,C	Jn 20:1–18	TSCS, 169
Holy Thursday	Years A,B,C	Jn 13:1–15	TH, 144 and STW, 268

EASTER

Easter Sunday	Year A	Jn 20:1–9	TSCS, 161
2nd Sunday	Year A	Jn 20:19–31	TSCS, 110
2nd Sunday	Year B	Jn 20:19–31	MTS, 26
3rd Sunday	Year A	Lk 24:13–35	TSCS, 150 and STW, 221
3rd Sunday	Year C	Jn 21:1–14	STW, 134
4th Sunday	Year A	Jn 10:1–10	STW, 185
4th Sunday	Year B	Jn 10:11–18	MTS, 152
4th Sunday	Year C	Rev 7:9–17	TH, 93
5th Sunday	Year B	Acts 9:26–31	MTS, 134
5th Sunday	Year B	Jn 15:1–8	TSCS, 63
6th Sunday	Year B	Jn 15:9–17	STW, 193
7th Sunday	Year B	Jn 17:11–19	STW, 147
7th Sunday	Year C	Jn 17:20–26	TH, 37 and STW, 126, 189
Ascension	Years A,B,C	Acts 1:12–14	TSCS, 6
Ascension	Years A	Mt 28:16–20	TH, 45
Pentecost	Years A,B,C	Acts 2:1–11	MTS, 156
Trinity Sunday	Year B	Mt 28:16–20	STW, 253
Trinity Sunday	Year C	Jn 16:12–15	STW, 121

ORDINARY TIME

2nd Sunday	Year A	Jn 1:29–34	MTS, 115
2nd Sunday	Year B	1 Sam 3:3–10,19	MTS, 44
2nd Sunday	Year C	Jn 2:1–12	STW, 113 and TH, 102
3rd Sunday	Year C	Lk 1:1–4; 4:4–21	STW, 117, 257 and TH, 129
4th Sunday	Year C	Lk 4:21–30	STW, 162

5th Sunday	Year B	Mk 1:29–39	MTS, 89
5th Sunday	Year C	Lk 5:1–11	MTS, 161
7th Sunday	Year A	Mt 5:38–48	TSCS, 98
8th Sunday	Year A	Mt 6:24–34	TH, 79
8th Sunday	Year C	Lk 6:39–45	STW, 157
10th Sunday	Year B	Mk 3:20–35	MTS, 6
10th Sunday	Year C	Lk 7:11–17	TH, 58
13th Sunday	Year B	Mk 5:21–24,35–43	TH, 98
14th Sunday	Year A	Mt 11:25–30	TH, 52
14th Sunday	Year C	Lk 10:1–12	TH, 140
15th Sunday	Year A	Mt 13:1–23	STW, 225
15th Sunday	Year C	Lk 10:25–37	TH, 31
16th Sunday	Year A	Mt 13:24–30, short form,	TSCS, 41 and STW, 265
16th Sunday	Year A	Mt 13:24–43, long form,	TSCS, 93
16th Sunday	Year C	Gen 18:1–10	TH, 148
17th Sunday	Year C	Lk 11:1–13	TH, 1
19th Sunday	Year B	1 Kgs 19:4–8	TH, 21, 123
21st Sunday	Year B	Jn 6:60–69	MTS, 15 and TH, 152
22nd Sunday	Year A	Mt 16:21–27	TH, 135
23rd Sunday	Year B	Mk 7:31–37	TSCS, 1 and TH, 110
24th Sunday	Year A	Mt 18:21–35	STW, 174 and TH, 17
24th Sunday	Year B	Mk 8:27–35	STW, 217, 271
24th Sunday	Year C	1 Tim 1:12–17	TSCS, 138
25th Sunday	Year A	Is 55:6–9	MTS, 50
26th Sunday	Year B	Mk 9:38–43,45,47–48	MTS, 1
28th Sunday	Year A	Mt 22:1–14	TSCS, 52 and STW, 199
28th Sunday	Year C	2 Kgs 5:14–17	TSCS, 26
28th Sunday	Year B	Mk 10:17–30	STW, 182
29th Sunday	Year B	Mk 10:35–45	MTS, 98
30th Sunday	Year B	Mk 10:46–52	TSCS, 11
30th Sunday	Year C	Lk 18:9–14	TSCS, 115
31st Sunday	Year A	Mt 23:1–12	TSCS, 36
31st Sunday	Year B	Mk 12:28–34	MTS, 61, 83
31st Sunday	Year C	Lk 19:1–10	TSCS, 21
32nd Sunday	Year B	Mk 12:38–44	STW, 131 and MTS, 78
34th Sunday	Year A	Mt 25:31–46	MTS, 72
34th Sunday	Year C	Lk 21:1–28	TSCS, 115
34th Sunday (Christ the King)	Year C	Lk 23:35–43	STW, 247

FEASTS & OCCASIONS

All Saints Day Years A,B,C	Rev 7:2–4, 9–14	STW, 110 and TSCS, 89
All Saints Day	Rev 7:1–8	TH, 115
Dependence Day		STW, 150
St. John Lateran		STW, 275
Environmental Sabbath	Mt 6:25–29	MTS, 104
Seven Beauties: An Entertainment		MTS, 166
Funeral	Mk 16:1–8	TSCS, 174
Funeral	Lk 7:11–17	TSCS, 178
Funeral	Mk 15:33–39	MTS, 139
Funeral	Jn 11:32–45	MTS, 143
Funeral	Lk 24:13–35	TH, 157
Wedding	1 Cor 13	TSCS, 168
Wedding	Jn 6:60–68	TH, 152
Wedding		STW, 229
Golden Jubilee	Gen 18:1–10	TH, 148

NOTES

Homily 4. The story of Ann Weems can be found in her book, *Family Faith Stories,* Westminster Press, Philadelphia, 1985.

Homily 5. Some of the initial thoughts came from Fr. Joe Nolan and his homily helps.

Homily 6. I omitted the first part of the longer form gospel in brackets and read just the widow's mite section (verses 41-44) so I could keep a single focus.

Homily 7. This homily can well be adapted to a Communal Penance service. I stopped this gospel at "Feed my Sheep" and omitted the verses beginning with "I tell you solemnly, as a young man you fastened your belt..." Again, to avoid another distracting thought from my main point.

Homily 9. For development purposes, I extended the Scripture beyond the stated verses to verse 56 (the Magnificat).

Homily 12. I stopped the gospel reading at the line, "He was lost and is found." The added lectionary verses about the elder son's dialogue with his father were a distraction from my main point.

Homily 13. I omitted the first and the last verses and read only the short section on seeing the speck on my brother's eye because hypocrisy was the main and only point I wanted to explore and didn't want the distractions of the other verses. This homily, as I explained in the first section, is one of those rare times when the whole story is explanatory of the gospel thrust. This story, by the way, is rooted in an old Jewish story and is likely a Christianized version of it.

Homily 16. Like some others, this homily has local or timely references, such as the names of persons and towns. The homilist is encouraged to substitute and personalize his or her own local tragedies and injustices, of which, unfortunately, there are no lack of examples.

Homily 19. I deliberately deleted the original story and substituted the C.S.Lewis story I used in Homily 3 in order to demonstrate that the same story can be effectively modified to fit different points.

Homily 27. The introductory idea about clocks comes from Father George J. Dyer's audiotape, "The Three Minute Theologian."

Homily 33. "Prophet John," is a good example of writing a homily. It is an amalgam of introductory remarks, expressions, and thoughts from William Willimon; a reflection on sloth from Monica Furlong—developed, expanded, and synthesized by myself—a story, plus my own insights. I offer it as an example of the process of writing a homily: drawing on others and adding your own creative touches, story, and contemporary notes to build a coherent message. This homily begs for gestures when different people are mentioned sitting in various parts of church.

Homily 38. "The Look," has origins I can no longer recall. It seems to me that the general thrust was described in some magazine article but it's been so long that I can't recall the source of the thoughts or expressions.

RESOURCES

In addition to those I've mentioned in this book, there are some resources that I have found very helpful. They are, of course, supplements, not substitutes, a fruitful source for references, quotations, insights, and stories. The list is personal, not exhaustive.

HOMILY SERVICES
Lectionary Homilies
Building 2, Suite 105
13540 East Boundary Road
Midlothian VA 23112

> Nicely provocative, giving not only pastoral implications but also references from the arts.

Good News
Liturgical Publications, Inc.
2875 South James Drive
New Berlin WI 53151

> Fr. Joe Nolan gives insightful liturgical notes, resources, notes, and often offbeat, intriguing homiletic insights.

Homiletics
Communications Resources, Inc.
4150 Belden Village Street, 4th Floor
Canton OH 44718

> Well done.

Pulpit Resource
Logos Productions
P.O. Box 240
South St. Paul MN 55075

> This one's by William H. Willimon, who is a daring preacher, wearing the mantle of Will Campbell. Some compelling insights from a master.

Dynamic Preaching
Seven Worlds Corporation
321 Troy Circle
Knoxville TN 37919

> An evangelical style production reflecting Protestant concerns, and often exciting.

The Living Pulpit
5000 Independence Ave.
Bronx NY 10471

Dedicated to one theme an issue, e.g., Prayer, Hope, Evil, Faith, Love, etc., with rich articles and quotes from the best writers.

The Christian Ministry
407 Dearborn Street
Chicago IL 60605

A Protestant publication with good homilies.

Stories. A magazine of short stories published three times a year.
Box 1467
East Arlington MA 02174

BOOKS
Stories
Arcodia, Charles. *Stories for Sharing* (E.J. Dwyer).
Aurelio, John. Any of his books of stories.
Bausch, William J. *Storytelling: Faith and Imagination; Timely Homilies; Telling Stories, Compelling Stories; More Telling Stories, Compelling Stories* (Twenty-Third Publications).
Canfield and Hansen. *Chicken Soup for the Soul: 101 Stories to Open the Heart and Rekindle the Spirit* (HCI Press, Deerfield, Florida). Have a second volume out, *A Second Helping of Chicken Soup for the Soul.*
Cassady, Marsh. *Storytelling Step by Step* (Resource Publications).
DeMello, Anthony, S.J. Anything by him.
Hobday, José. *Stories of Awe and Abundance* (Sheed & Ward).
Jensen, Richard. *Lectionary Tales for the Pulpit* (CSS).
McKenna, Megan. *Parables: The Arrows of God* (Orbis Books) and any of her books and tapes.
Shea, John. *Stories of God* and anything he writes or tapes.
Wangerin, Walter. Jr. *Miz Lil* (Zondervan) and anything he writes.
Wharton, Paul. *Stories and Parables for Preachers and Teachers* (Paulist).
White, William. *Speaking in Stories, Stories for Telling, Stories for the Journey* (Augsburg).
Wilhelm, Robert. Lots and lots of grand tapes (Storyfest Publications) and storytelling techniques.
Williams, Michael. *Friends for Life: A Treasury of Stories for Worship and Other Gatherings* (Abingdon).
Best-Loved Stories. The annual collection from stories told at the annual National Storytelling Festival from the National Storytelling Press, P. O. Box 309, Jonesborough, TN 37659.

Helpful Books on Preaching, with Examples

Achtemeier, Elizabeth. *Creative Preaching: Finding the Words* (Abingdon).

Bakshian, Aram. *American Speaker: Your Guide to Successful Speaking* (Georgetown Publishing House).

Brueggemann, Walter. *Finally Comes the Poet* (Fortress).

Burghardt, Walter. Everything you can get your hands on.

Burke, John, O.P. and Thomas Doyle. *The Homilist's Guide to Scripture, Theology and Canon Law* (Pueblo Press).

Cox, James W. (ed.). *Best Sermons for the Year* 19__. A good yearly gathering of the best. Plus his annual *The Minister Manual,* 19__ (Harper & Row). The latter, full of sermons, is perhaps too Protestant in tone for Catholics.

Friedl, Francis and Edward Macauley. *Homilies Alive.* A good how-to (Twenty-Third Publications).

Hook, Dan. *Effective Preaching* (E J. Dwyer).

McNulty, Frank (ed.). *Preaching Better* (Paulist Press).

Papineau, Andre. *Let Your Light Shine: Scripture Stories for Self-Esteem* (Twenty-Third Publications).

Salmon, Bruce. *Storytelling in Preaching* (Broadman Press).

Wasznak, Robert, S.S. *Like Fresh Bread: Sunday Homilies in the Parish* (Paulist Press).

Willimon, William H. *Peculiar Speech: The Intrusive Word* (Eerdmans).

Audiotapes

Cassady, Marsh. *Creative Storytelling* (Resource Publications).

McKenna, Megan. *Eat This Bread: Stories to Feed Your Soul* (St. Anthony Messenger Press); *Hearing with the Heart: Stories to Nurture* (St. Anthony Messenger Press).

Morneau, Robert F. *The Power of Narrative: Poetic Stories and Stories of Poets* (Alba House).

Shea, John. *Gospel Spirituality* (ACTA Publications).

Wilhelm, Robert Bela. *Christmas Parables* and other tapes (from Storyfest Ministries, 18934 Rolling Road, Hagerstown, MD 21742).

Videotapes

Burghardt, Walter, S.J. *Preparing the Homily* and *Preaching the Just Word* (Liturgy Training Publications).

Pagliari, Robert, C.SS.R. *A Workshop on Homiletics: Preaching the Word* (Liguori).

"Father Bausch, master storyteller and excellent homilist, is at it again. He teaches the dynamics of effective preaching through the skillful use of narrative. And why not, for the Bible is a book of stories, not a theological treatise. Homilists who make use of the principles outlined in this book will see their congregations grow in understanding the Word and glow with appreciation of meaningful homilies."

Rev. Msgr. Francis P. Friedl
Co-author, *Homilies Alive: Creating Homilies That Hit Home*

"William J. Bausch is a pastor in love with the Lord and his people. His latest book, *Storytelling the Word: Homilies and How to Write Them*, is a treasure of preachers' gold. It is loaded with startling insights into the Sunday gospels that make the ancient stories new for one day. Furthermore, he tells emotion-packed stories that make the reader alternately laugh and cry as they reveal the truth about God's love. He knows the serious problems preachers face today, but he is able to hold out great hope because he offers so many practical suggestions on how to preach in a way that will change lives. He writes not only for priests, but for lay preachers as well. He fired me up once again with the power of preaching."

John Burke, O.P.
Director, The National Institute for the Word of God
Co-author, *The Homilist's Guide to Scripture, Theology and Canon Law*

"To be an effective homilist one must present material that is of interest to the congregation. Father Bausch's skillful use of storytelling is the most effective method of communicating directly with the people in the pews. His book explains how stories are used to gain interest and to make pertinent points to the congregation. This is a book the homilist will keep on his desk and probably refer to every weekend."

Deacon Edward C. Macauley
Co-author, *Homilies Alive: Creating Homilies That Hit Home*

Also by Rev. William Bausch

Telling Stories, Compelling Stories
35 Stories of People of Grace
Bausch illuminates the Gospels with these examples of people from the past and present and their living fully as Christians. The people described all translate grace into flesh and blood activity witnessing to the effects of being touched and transformed by God.
0-89622-456-2, 192 pp, $9.95

More Telling Stories, Compelling Stories
While capturing the essence of the lectionary readings, Bausch makes them relevant to the Christian assembly today. He tackles subjects such as anger, the failed parent, returning, love of self, and decision time, as well as specific occasions. This book contains an index referencing the content of *Telling Stories; Compelling Stories; More Telling Stories, Compelling Stories;* and *Timely Homilies* in lectionary context.
0-89622-534-8, 200 pp, $9.95

Timely Homilies
The Wit and Wisdom of an Ordinary Pastor
With a rare combination of warmth, insight and vitality, Bausch demonstrates his driving commitment to helping people live God's Word. These sermons use specific Gospel readings as springboards for pointed comments on current concerns.
0-89622-426-0, 176 pp, $9.95

Storytelling
Imagination and Faith
Bausch taps a treasured wellspring of stories from the masters of antiquity to authors of more recent days, and does so within religious and secular traditions. He celebrates the power of stories to capture and pass on the wisdom, imagination and faith of a people.
0-89622-199-7, 232 pp, $9.95

Of Related Interest

Homilies Alive
Creating Homilies that Hit Home
Msgr. Francis P. Friedl and Ed Macauley
Forewords by Joe Garagiola and Daniel W. Kucera, OSB
Francis P. Friedl, a priest with over 40 years of preaching and teaching experience, and "Easy Ed" Macauley, noted basketball star, sportscaster and public speaker, who is also an ordained deacon, team up to define, explain and exemplify 10 fundamentals that will make homilies come alive for congregations. 0-89622-574-7, 144 pp, $9.95

Available at religious bookstores or from

XXIII TWENTY-THIRD PUBLICATIONS
P.O. Box 180 • Mystic, CT 06355

To order or request a free catalog of other quality books and video call:
1-800-321-0411